NELSON
ENGLISH

Authors
Phil Davison
Michael Kunka

Instructional Writers
Kathy Evans
Nancy Fornasiero

First Nations, Métis, and Inuit Reviewer
Wilfred Burton

NELSON EDUCATION

Nelson English 10

Editorial Director
Linda Allison

Acting Publisher, Literacy and Reference
Lara Caplan

Managing Editor
Adam Rennie

Senior Editor
Diane Robitaille

Product Manager
Stephanie Gomez

Program Manager
Anita Reynolds MacArthur

Project Editor
Jennifer Stanicak

Developmental Editors
Jessica Pegis
Rena Sutton

Bias Reviewer
Nancy Christoffer

Researcher
Jennifer Delvecchio

Director, Content and Media Production
Carol Martin

Senior Content Production Editor
Jane High

Copyeditor
Linda Szostak

Proofreader
Elizabeth d'Anjou

Production Coordinator
Kathrine Pummell

Design Director
Ken Phipps

Managing Designer
Courtney Hellam

Interior Design
Jarrel Breckon
Courtney Hellam
Jennifer Laing
Jennifer Leung
Dennis Liwag
Cathy Mayer
Quarasan
Jan-John Rivera
Carianne Sherriff
Trinh Truong

Cover Design
Trinh Truong

Compositors
Courtney Hellam
Trinh Truong

Photo/Permissions Researcher
Natalie Russell

COPYRIGHT © 2013 by Nelson Education Ltd.

ISBN-13: 978-0-17-667874-6
ISBN-10: 0-17-667874-3

Printed and bound in Canada
1 2 3 4 16 15 14 13

For more information contact Nelson Education Ltd., 1120 Birchmount Road, Toronto, Ontario M1K 5G4. Or you can visit our website at www.nelson.com.

Excerpts from this publication may be reproduced under licence from Access Copyright, or with the express written permission of Nelson Education Ltd., or as permitted by law. Requests which fall outside of Access Copyright guidelines must be submitted online to www.cengage.com/permissions. Further questions about permissions can be emailed to permissionrequest@cengage.com.

ALL RIGHTS ARE OTHERWISE RESERVED. No part of this publication may be reproduced, stored in a retrieval system, or transmitted in any form or by any means, electronic, mechanic, photocopying, scanning, recording or otherwise, except as specifically authorized.

Every effort has been made to trace ownership of all copyrighted material and to secure permission from copyright holders. In the event of any question arising as to the use of any material, we will be pleased to make the necessary corrections in future printings.

Nelson English Advisers and Reviewers

Adriana Alvaro, Dufferin-Peel CDSB, ON

Cheryl Bashutski, Sun West SD (retired), SK

Christopher Clarke, Dufferin-Peel CDSB, ON

Jennifer Cronsberry, Avon Maitland DSB, ON

Amanda Gibson, Amos Comenius Memorial School, Hopedale, NL

Margaret Ingoldsby, Waterloo CDSB, ON

Natalie Jackson, Main River Academy, Pollard's Point, NL

Derek Johnson, Stephenville High School, Stephenville, NL

Lorne Kulak, Toronto DSB, ON

Kylie Lozon, Lambton-Kent DSB, ON

Ben Pare, Burnaby SD, BC

Sarah L. Patten, Peel DSB, ON

Susan Perry, Holy Trinity High School, Torbay, NL

Laura Schmaltz, Calgary SD, AB

Darrell Sneyd, Queen Elizabeth Regional High School, Conception Bay South, NL

Rick Stiles-Oldring, Edmonton Public Schools, AB

Nelson English Advisory Panel

Nadia Bearcroft, York Region DSB, ON

Melanie Clarke, Holy Spirit High School, Conception Bay South, NL

Tina Conlon, Niagara CDSB, ON

Lisa Dubé, SD 43, BC

James L. Falcone, Halifax Regional SB, NS

Iain Fisher, SD 36, BC

Bonnie Jones, Prince of Wales Collegiate, St. John's, NL

Leta Layton, Lethbridge SD 51, AB

Joanne Panas, District 38, BC

Anne Ratchford, York CDSB, ON

Keith Sled, Hastings and Prince Edward DSB, ON

Leonard Wong, SD 39, BC

Contents

Conflict

Unit Opener	1
Talk About It	2
Focus on Reading	**3**
Making Connections to Infer	

    The Trickster — 5
    Short Story by Jacqueline Pearce

    Gay Kids Need It to "Get Better" Now, Rick Mercer Rants — 12
    Blog Entry by Dakshana Bascaramurty
    No, Rick Mercer, Not All Gay Public Figures Need to Step Forward
    Editorial from the *Globe and Mail*

    Fish Cheeks — 16
    Personal Anecdote by Amy Tan

    What We Share — 18
    Memoir Excerpt by Richard Wagamese

Focus on Genre — **21**
Analyzing Narrative Writing and the Short Story

    Scars — 23
    Short Story by Don Aker

    Ashes — 30
    Short Story by Susan Beth Pfeffer
    Beyond Pastel
    Poem by Katherine Lawrence

    Accident — 36
    Short Story by Dave Eggers

    Tomorrow, Summer — 38
    Short Story by Naomi Shihab Nye

Up for Debate — 42

Focus on Media — **43**
Identifying Point of View and Bias

    You Will Not Stop Me from Learning — 45
    Newspaper Article by Rick Westhead

    Artists Respond to Conflict — 48
    Artwork by Gonçalo Mabunda, Sabina Zeba Haque, and Nora Heysen

Focus on Writing — **53**
Developing Ideas and Voice

    My Emergency Contact Information — 55
    Letter by Ryan Abbott

    Why People Can't Help Themselves — 58
    Opinion Piece by Andrew Potter

    Dulce et Decorum Est — 62
    Poem by Wilfred Owen
    And He Said, Fight On
    Poem by Pauline Johnson

    Teen on Strike — 64
    Newspaper Article by Tamie Dolny

    Remembering Joyce Atcheson — 66
    Letter of Remembrance by Jody Porter

What Do You Think Now? — 68

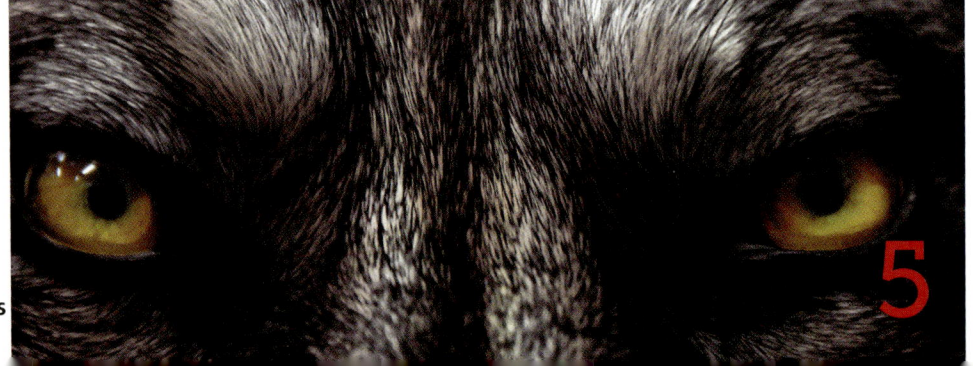

Innovation

Unit Opener	69
Talk About It	70
Focus on Reading	71
Responding Personally, Critically, and Creatively	
Earth (A Gift Shop)	73
Short Story by Charles Yu	
Mother of Invention	78
Poem by Celia Berrell	
Dreamer	
Poem by Langston Hughes	
Samantha Nutt: A Letter from 12 War Zones	80
Interview by Maura Kelly	
Preserving Knowledge, Empowering Communities	84
Article by Lisa Gregoire	
Top of the World	88
Biographical Article by Margaret Jetelina	
Focus on Genre	91
Analyzing Expository Writing and the Essay	
Design That Fits to a Tee	93
Article by Laura House	
Worldwide We	96
Expository Essay by Cheryl Gilbert	
The Pocket Camera Moment	100
Essay by Jonathon Keats	
The Mobile Photo Explosion	
Infographic by Over, Design by NowSourcing	
Up for Debate	104
Focus on Media	105
Analyzing Codes, Conventions, and Techniques	
The Canadian Oil Boom	107
Infographic by Visual Capitalist	
Saving the World through Game Design	110
Blog Entry by Jane McGonigal	
In Defense of Pinterest	114
Article by Clive Thompson	
Jeremy Gutsche: Mister Chaos	116
Newspaper Feature by Cathal Kelly	
Focus on Writing	119
Organizing Ideas	
Airbus: Plane of the Future	121
Photo Essay by Alex Davies	
Top 25 Innovations	126
Online Article posted on CNN	
The Kitchen at the End of the Universe	128
Essay by Scott Feschuk	
Giving Garments a Second Chance	130
Article by Patricia D'Cunha	
What Do You Think Now?	132

Humour

Unit Opener	133
Talk About It	134
Focus on Reading	135
Constructing and Extending Meaning	
Little Red Riding Hood	137
Fractured Fairy Tale by James Finn Garner	
Invasion of the Snotty Badgers	140
Flash Fiction by Karin Weber	
Really?!?	142
Blog Entry by Sabrina Jalees	
The Fault in Our Stars	144
Novel Excerpt by John Green	
Focus on Genre	149
Analyzing Narrative and Expository Writing in Scripts	
Form 17	151
Short Film Script by Seth Worley, Neil Hoppe, and Aharon Rabinowitz	
Yeti	160
The World Ends on Wednesday	
Skits by Tim Cooper	
I Am the Invisible Thing That Holds Together the Two Halves of a Compound Word	164
Monologue by Ben Greenman	
Up for Debate	166
Focus on Media	167
Analyzing Audience Responses	
Campaign Emails from the Donahue Family Pet Debate	169
Story by Johnny McNulty	
A Teenage Philospher Defends Missing Her Curfew	174
Rant by Haley Joelle Ott	
My Mom Is an English Teacher	
Song Lyrics by Alison Jutzi	
iPhone Left in Hot Car	178
News Parody posted on *The Onion*	
Focus on Writing	181
Improving Word Choice	
Sunken Oil Tanker Will Be Habitat for Marine Life	183
News Parody posted on *The Onion*	
How *Willy Wonka & the Chocolate Factory* Should Have Ended	186
Script by Danny Dillabough	
I See You Think I'm Not Very Interesting	188
Open Letter by Scott Feschuk	
Not Enough Horses	190
Short Story by Thomas King	
What Do You Think Now?	194

Perspective

Unit Opener	**195**
Talk About It	**196**
Focus on Reading Evaluating to Form Opinions	**197**
Anonymous Targets School for Suspending Student Who Refused a Tracking Chip Article by Liat Clark	199
Winston Novel Excerpt by Cory Doctorow	202
No Word for … Blog Entry by Sheila North Wilson	206
Heartbeat Flash Fiction by Dan Evon	208
Would You Like to Reconnect? Short Story by Joanne Harris	210
Focus on Genre Analyzing Persuasive Writing and the Opinion Piece	**215**
My Challenge to You: Only Speak Like a Human Opinion Piece by Daniel H. Pink Electronic Discrimination in the Skies Opinion Piece by Peter Nowak	217
Turning the Page Personal Essay by Robert Costanzo	222
Who Killed the Wooden Hockey Stick? Opinion Piece by Joe O'Connor	225
Maybe Zombies Can Save Us from Our Comforts Opinion Piece by Tisha McComb	228
Up for Debate	**230**

Focus on Media Evaluating Production Perspectives	**231**
Whose Art Is It, Anyway? Newspaper Article by René Adams	233
New Tool Provides Food for Thought Press Release by the Boston Public Health Commission	236
Don't Trust Hollywood to Teach You History Opinion Piece by And Palladino	238
Focus on Writing Creating Fluency	**241**
Who Are the Elders? Personal Essay by Daniel Crowfeather	243
On Unmaking Contact Poem by Deena Kara Shaffer Sifter Poem by Naomi Shihab Nye Life Poem by Charlotte Brontë Regeneration Poem by Glynnis Ritchie	246
Charity or Scam? Report by Norah Muldoon	250
World of Warcraft versus My Girlfriend Short Story by Tyler Curry	252
Facebook Controversy Newspaper Reports by Louise Brown	254
What Do You Think Now?	**258**
Index	**259**
Credits	**262**

WELCOME TO
NELSON ENGLISH

Nelson English offers a rich variety of selections—stories, poems, scripts, essays, opinion pieces, and media and visual texts. These selections contain the following features:

- sidebars that provide more information and suggestions for analyzing the texts
- personal notes from or about the authors and creators, which often include their thoughts on creating the text
- a Responding section with Discussion Questions and Tasks to further explore and creatively respond to the texts

In addition to these diverse selections, you will find the types of pages shown below in every unit.

Talk About It

These pages offer a collection of very short selections (such as quotes, headlines, visual art, infographics, and word clouds) to spark conversations about the unit themes.

Up for Debate

Partway through each unit, these pages present another collection of short texts that can serve as topics for debate and more serious discussion of the unit theme, while making connections to the selections already read and viewed.

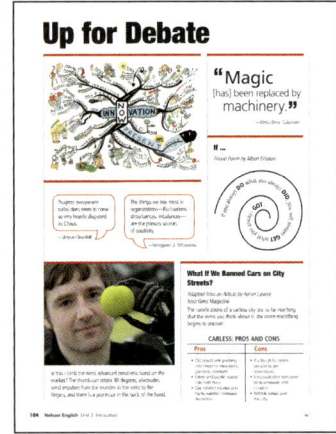

Focus Pages

These pages give information and practical suggestions on important reading, writing, genre, text form, and media analysis topics. They also help to establish a context for the series of selections that follow.

What Do You Think?

At the beginning of each unit, a question or statement related to the unit theme is presented for your consideration. Every selection starts with a "What Do You Think?" feature to generate critical inquiry and discussion before reading further. At the end of each unit, the "What Do You Think Now?" page asks you to reflect on the theme and apply the skills and strategies that were explored on the focus pages.

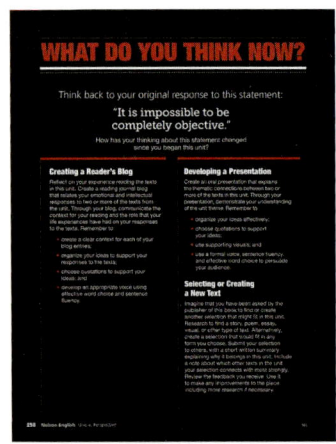

conflict

WHAT DO YOU THINK?
+ AGREE
— DISAGREE

When you avoid conflict, you avoid learning.

Unit Learning Goals
- making connections to infer
- analyzing narrative writing and the short story
- identifying point of view and bias
- developing ideas and voice

Talk About It

This painting of Harriet Tubman escorting escaped slaves into Canada is by Jerry Pinkney.

"You can't shake hands with a clenched fist."
—Indira Gandhi

"There's no story if there isn't some conflict. The memorable things are usually not how pulled together everybody is."
—Wes Anderson

What You Should Know About Interpersonal Conflict

1. Conflict is natural in any relationship because people are different.
2. There will always be at least two sides to every conflict.
3. Sometimes there is no right answer.
4. Sometimes the other person is right and you have to acknowledge it.

"An eye for an eye only leads to more blindness."
—Margaret Atwood

Common Types of Conflict in Literature

SELF — Internal Conflict
Examples: *The Catcher in the Rye* by J.D. Salinger; *The Shipping News* by E. Annie Proulx

SOCIETY — External Conflict
Examples: *The Handmaid's Tale* by Margaret Atwood; *Animal Farm* by George Orwell

HUMAN — External Conflict
Examples: *To Kill a Mockingbird* by Harper Lee; *Scott Pilgrim* series by Bryan Lee O'Malley

NATURE — External Conflict
Examples: *Life of Pi* by Yann Martel; *Lord of the Flies* by William Golding

human versus

FOCUS ON reading

> "You think your pain and your heartbreak are unprecedented in the history of the world, but then you read. It was books that taught me that the things that tormented me most were the very things that connected me with all the people who were alive, or who had ever been alive."
>
> —James Baldwin

MAKING CONNECTIONS TO INFER

Making connections and making inferences both require readers to participate in making meaning. Readers activate the appropriate prior knowledge to construct meaning and interpret a text.

MAKING CONNECTIONS

To make inferences, readers must make connections to their own personal experiences and knowledge, to other texts, and to real-world events. These connections enhance the quality of readers' inferences and conclusions. For example, if you've read or seen *Romeo and Juliet*, your response to movies with star-crossed lovers will be influenced by your understanding and response to that play.

In today's world, where one text so often plays upon another, analyzing the relationships between texts has become increasingly important. For example, think of a current TV show. How much of your understanding and appreciation of that show depends on the connections you make between it and other texts or shows you have read or viewed?

COMPARING TEXTS

Comparing one text to another helps readers make inferences. For example, after comparing "In Flanders Fields" and "Dulce et Decorum Est," two very different poems from World War I, you might make inferences about how each speaker feels about war.

//MAKE CONNECTIONS TO INFER
- Go beyond summarizing each text.
- Generate an analysis of the elements of each text, including characterization, plot, theme, and voice.
- Decide what details are interesting, important, and relevant.
- Ignore details that are unimportant or irrelevant.
- Reflect on the connections between the texts.

MAKING INFERENCES

Inferences are the conclusions that readers draw about what is unsaid in a text, based on a combination of their prior knowledge and what is actually said by a writer. To draw appropriate conclusions, readers must engage in a connection-making process that involves textual evidence and prior knowledge.

//GO DEEPER INTO A TEXT USING INFERENCES
- Make connections between ideas.
- Ask questions not answered by the writer.
- Recognize bias in a text.
- Identify perspective.
- Evaluate the relevancy of ideas or details.
- Evaluate the voice in a text.
- Determine the text's primary conflict, issue, or theme.
- Determine whose viewpoint was not included in the text.
- Speculate on what the writer wanted readers to infer.

Making an inference involves readers as much as it involves the writer, because the prior knowledge that readers bring to a text is as important as the written text itself. The inferences two readers make when reading the same text may not be similar, as each reader brings different background knowledge to the text. Readers can also go deeper into constructing meaning by thinking of how their inferences may differ from those of other readers, and by analyzing how their personal values or biases influence their inferences.

Successful and meaningful inferences are as dependent upon the readers and their prior knowledge as they are upon the writer and the text he or she has written.

WHAT DO YOU THINK?

"Cowards die many times before their deaths; the valiant never taste of death but once."

—William Shakespeare
(*Julius Caesar*, II.ii)

The Trickster

Short Story by Jacqueline Pearce

Josh eased into the last empty seat on the bus, trying not to jostle the cardboard box he carried. The top flaps wouldn't close properly, and he was afraid the smell might leak out. He wished he hadn't agreed to go to the university to pick the stuff up for his mom. Lately, he hated going anywhere on the bus or Skytrain—since those guys had jumped him to steal his leather jacket. The last thing he wanted to do was draw attention to himself. What if someone asked him about the box? He imagined the conversation.

"What's in the box?"
"A dead coyote."
"Huh?"
"I'm serious. A deceased …" What had that woman at the university called it? *Canis latrans*. You know, Latin for "barking dog."

Josh thought back to the meeting at the university. His mom had needed the coyote skull and pelt for a project she was doing with her Grade 6 class. She'd persuaded Josh to go for her. Finding the resource centre in the corridors of the science building was like trying to find a tiny piece of cheese in a maze. (Rats, mice, cats, roadrunners … that's what coyotes ate, wasn't it?) The room Josh finally entered was lined floor to ceiling with books. One wall was covered with shelves of stuffed dead animals. A raccoon. An owl. Lots of smaller birds. At the back of the room, a young woman was bent over a desk, writing.

"Excuse me. I'm here to pick up some coyote stuff."

"Oh, hi. Right. Just a minute." She stood up and disappeared into a back room. Whoa, she was good-looking. OK, she was at least five years older than he was, but that could work, couldn't it? Maybe this wouldn't be a wasted afternoon after all. Josh wondered if he could pass for a university student. Try and sound older, smarter. What was some of that stuff Mom had been babbling about coyotes? They were related to wolves, foxes, even dogs. They hunted in packs, usually—except for when they lived in the city. Yeah, that's right. City coyotes usually lived alone—or with a mate. He liked the sound of that last word.

"Here you go. One *Canis latrans*," she said, setting down a bundle of yellow-brown fur on the counter, along with a white skull.

"What?" Josh asked, stupidly.

"It's the Latin name," she explained. "It means 'barking dog.'"

Something small, grey-white, and pointed rolled across the counter. She picked it up.

"Oh, if any of the teeth fall out, just stick them back in."

She folded the skull and pelt together and wrapped them with tissue paper. Then she bent down behind the counter and came back up with the box.

Josh cleared his throat. OK, maybe he'd had a bad start, but things were still salvageable. Say something, you idiot.

"Ah, so do you get a lot of demand for dead coyotes?" Oh, that was brilliant. She smiled, carefully stuffing the bundle into the box.

"Not exactly," she said. "Though a lot of people seem to prefer them dead to alive."

He could tell by the way she said this that she was not one of those people.

"I guess they have a bit of a PR problem," he said, aiming for what he hoped was a kind of intellectual humour.

"You could say that." She seemed to appreciate his comment. "It's true they have lowered the city cat population a bit. But they've lowered the rat population a lot more."

// **Making Connections**

Accessing your prior knowledge, as well as making text-to-self, text-to-text, and text-to-world connections, can help you make inferences about the character and what he feels and experiences. Think about how you may have felt when you wanted to impress someone.

"Right," Josh nodded.

"It's ironic," she went on. "Coyotes are one of the few wild animals that have expanded their numbers and territory—despite people trying to get rid of them. It's because they're so good at adapting to things. That's why they can move into the city and do so well."

"Plus, they're not picky eaters," Josh put in. She laughed. Josh was beginning to feel that maybe things were going all right between them, after all. Adaptable, he thought. That's me. Fitting in with university students wasn't so tough. She handed him the box, still smiling. He pictured the hunting coyote, senses alert, ready to pounce.

"Do you want to go for a coffee?" he asked her straight out.

"I'd love to."

OK, so that last bit was how he rewrote the conversation afterward, sitting on the bus. In actual fact, he'd taken the box from her and sputtered something like, "See you around." As he'd left, he imagined the coyote again. Ahead of the coyote, a rat ran down the alley and scuttled under a fence. Once out of the building, Josh realized he'd been wearing his Fraser High School jacket the whole time. What an idiot.

Josh squirmed mentally in the bus seat. Of course he was wearing the dumb high-school jacket instead of his leather one. Even when he managed to put getting mugged the other night out of his mind, it still came back to stalk him.

He'd been on his way to Nick's house around nine o'clock, got off at the Skytrain stop, and there they were. Four guys about his age, leaning against the railing by the steps to the street.

"Hey, nice jacket," one of the guys said. He had a dark, narrow face and wore a blue bandana tied around the top of his head. Two other guys stepped toward him.

"Why don't you give us your jacket?" At first, Josh thought maybe they were joking. He laughed. OK, well, he tried to laugh. It sounded more like a squeaky door imitation.

"You laughing at us?" All four pressed in on him. There was something tight and coiled up about them. As if they could let go and do anything. Josh glanced around. The Skytrain stop and the surrounding street looked deserted.

> **// Bullying**
>
> Recent statistics from the World Health Organization suggest that bullying is on the rise even though school violence, on the whole, has decreased. It is estimated that 41% of Canadian students are involved in bullying, either as a victim, bully, or both.

The guy with the bandana shoved him. He fell against a big guy who felt kind of soft.

"You looking for a fight?"

"Just a minute." Josh took off his leather jacket—not to give it to them, just to free up his arms. He dropped the coat and sprang into Kung Fu readiness. OK, so that's where the replay deviated a bit from what actually happened that night. In actual fact, he'd dropped the jacket and run.

On the bus, Josh wondered what the woman at the university would have thought of him if she'd known what happened that night—how shaken up he'd been. He still felt unnerved, off balance. He couldn't even go out of the house without looking over his shoulder. He felt uncomfortable around people in a way he hadn't before. All because of some jerks. His stomach twisted with frustration and anger. Part of him wished he could have fought them and hurt them. He felt like a coward for giving up his jacket so easily and running. But then, on the other hand, running was not so stupid. He was still in one piece, wasn't he? So what if he had lost an expensive piece of clothing? He'd done what he needed to do to survive—like the coyote.

Josh tried to concentrate his thoughts on the woman in the biology museum and forget about the other stuff. It was a much better memory. Maybe she had known he was in high school, but he'd still had a good conversation with a great-looking older woman who hadn't even cared that he was younger. Maybe he could feel good about the whole thing after all.

As he looked out the bus window, something caught Josh's eye. Had he seen a flash of yellow-brown tail as some animal trotted around the back corner of a 7-Eleven store? He shifted the box on his lap, remembering the dead coyote. Had that coyote lived around here when it was alive? It was hard to imagine such a large wild animal living in the city. They were smart, elusive—tricky, even. He smiled to himself, remembering how coyotes in legends could change shape. Coyote shape one minute, human shape the next. Sometimes the legend Coyote gave things to people, sometimes he tricked them out of things. You never knew what to expect. Pretty cool, really.

// **The Trickster Mythology**

Jacqueline Pearce has carefully selected the title of her short story. The mythology of the trickster has a very long and significant tradition among Canada's First Nations people. The trickster is a clever, mischievous creature (sometimes a coyote) that tries to survive the dangers and challenges of the world using trickery and deceit. Often, the trickster uses its trickery to triumph over those who are in the wrong or who are behaving unfairly. One of its greatest tricks is the ability to change shapes. As we are told in the story, "Coyote shape one minute, human shape the next."

Josh looked up. At the front of the bus, a group of girls was getting on. Across the street from the bus, Josh could see a bunch of kids spilling out of a pizza/video-game place. Three guys were leaning against a shiny black Mazda parked in front. Suddenly, with a sick feeling, Josh recognized them. One wore a blue bandana just like the other night. One was wearing a leather jacket just like the one Josh had lost. Josh's first instinct was to duck, melt into the seat. His heart pounded.

Cautiously, he looked again. There was the fourth guy, talking to a girl with long brown hair. She was holding on to his arm as if she wanted to keep him with her, but he was shaking his head and pulling away. The other three guys got into the car. The fourth guy tried to kiss the girl, but she didn't seem to want to kiss him back. He hesitated, then shrugged and turned to join the others. The bus started to move then. Josh could still see the girl standing on the sidewalk, arms crossed, watching the black car pull away. She didn't look happy.

Josh realized he was sweating. He'd been afraid of seeing them again and now he had—he'd seen them, and nothing had happened. It was weird how ordinary they seemed. It almost gave him a feeling of power to know that he'd watched part of their lives—perhaps even knew something about them—and they hadn't even seen him.

A screech of tires drew Josh's attention to the window again. The black car had made a U-turn and was now picking up speed and passing the bus. He wondered where they were going, what they were planning to do.

It was almost dark out now, and the bus's progress was painfully slow. Finally, the bus pulled up next to the Skytrain station where Josh got off. From here, he could transfer to another bus for a five-minute trip home or walk the rest of the way. It was a twenty-minute wait until the next bus. Might as well walk. Josh stepped out of the lighted area onto the dark sidewalk.

It was then that he saw them. They were leaning on the black Mazda, parked where they could watch people come and go from the Skytrain and buses. Josh's heart jumped, and his hands on the box grew immediately sweaty. What were they doing here? Had they followed him? No, they couldn't have. Cruising Skytrain stops was their thing, wasn't it? Seeing them now was just a coincidence, right? They were just here waiting for some poor victim to walk off into the dark alone—like he'd just done. Maybe he could get around the corner before they even noticed. Too late. They were coming.

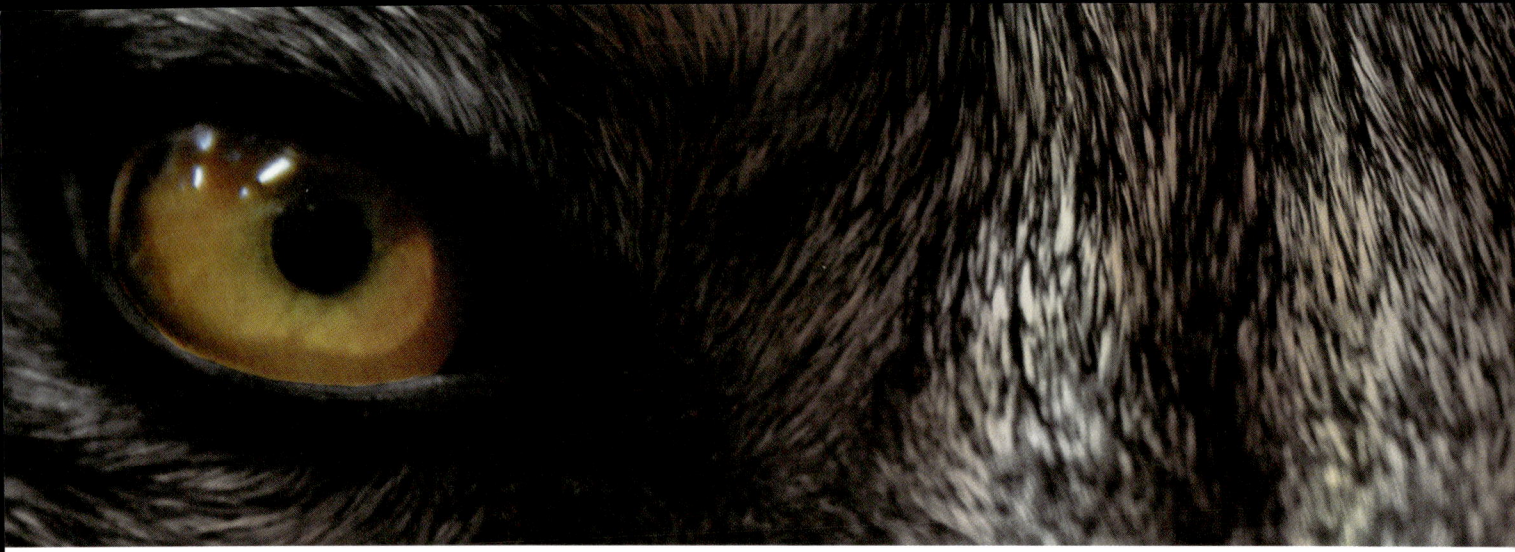

> **//Fight or Flight Response**
>
> The fight or flight response is our body's automatic response to prepare us to either fight or flee from perceived attack, harm, or threat. Many call it a survival instinct. When Josh confronts the gang for the second time, this survival instinct emerges: he can either fight or flee.

Josh kept walking, forcing himself to stay calm. Maybe they wouldn't bother him. Maybe they were just going somewhere in this direction. Maybe cows could fly. Who was he kidding?

Images flashed in his mind. The coyote, the rat, himself holding the box, the coyote again—one image transforming into another.

"What's in the box?" The guy with the bandana had come up on one side of Josh. They pressed closer. It was like in the nightmares he'd been having. Someone shoved him.

"We asked you, what's in the box?"

Josh turned to look at the guy who'd spoken. It was the one with the girlfriend. Josh remembered how he'd looked on the street with her—pleading, apologetic. Now, he was changed—swaggering, confident. The others, too, had an edge to them that hadn't been there before. They'd seemed like ordinary individual guys then. Now they were something else—tied together, fuelling each other.

Josh felt like a cornered animal. He thought of the fragile skull being pulled out, smashed on the ground. He thought of himself running again—running and running, always looking over his shoulder. Anger flared in his gut, then was gone. He realized he no longer felt afraid. Instead, he felt sort of numb and strangely detached.

Hands grabbed for the box. Josh felt a small click inside himself—like something moved, shifted, and snapped into a new place. With one easy movement, he opened the box flaps and reached his right hand inside. Carefully, he placed his fingers on the furred nose of the pelt head and the skull beneath it. For a moment, the bodies around him drew back, giving space. Swiftly Josh drew out his hand, gripping fur and bone. He thrust the grinning coyote head in one guy's face and growled. It was a deep, menacing animal sound—not human at all.

"I am Coyote," a gravelly voice rose out of the dark, authoritative and mocking. It finished the statement with a sharp yipping howl. What the …? Had he actually just howled?

"I have other names, too," the voice continued.

"You don't know me, but I know you. I know everything about you—where you live, what school you go to … Livingston High School," the coyote voice hissed. Josh heard several sharp intakes of breath. Someone laughed, but it sounded nervous. Josh wondered why they didn't do something. The whole thing was crazy. He was crazy.

The pelt moved again, the tips of the hairs shining for a moment in the dark. Josh felt himself take two steps. They were no longer pressing in on him.

"I know a brown-haired girl who wants you to play," the coyote teeth flashed in front of the fourth guy. "You keep leaving her, you're going to lose her…."

"Hey, how does he …?"

Josh turned again, facing the guy with the leather jacket. The guy glanced toward the car, as if he'd rather be getting in it than standing so close to Josh.

"You shouldn't wear things that aren't yours," the coyote voice chided. "Someone might not like it."

"Come on." The guy with the bandana said. His voice sounded deflated. "Let's go … this guy's nuts."

"Yeah, this is getting boring." The guy with the leather jacket turned away, started walking in the direction of the waiting car. Josh could hardly believe they were actually walking away.

The coyote pelt continued to jerk and move, the voice yipping softly, as the four guys climbed into the black car. The engine revved, and the car pulled away from the curb with a squeal.

Josh dropped his arm and let out a long breath. He bent down to set the cardboard box on the sidewalk so he could fold the coyote pelt back inside. His knees felt suddenly weak, and his hands were shaking. He looked at the pale skull in his hands. A moment before it had seemed so full of power—so alive.

Something small and whitish *tinked* onto the sidewalk and rolled in a short arc. A tooth. Josh laughed, feeling close to normal again. He picked up the tooth and placed it back in the coyote's jaw. Ahead of him the street was dark, but he didn't mind. He began walking, feeling a prickle of elation rise up his neck. He tilted his head back and howled—a laughing, yowling, animal-human sound. ◆

RESPONDING

DISCUSSION QUESTIONS

MAKING INFERENCES
Identify the points in the story where Josh either misleads the reader about the outcome of events or doubts his own actions. What can you infer about Josh's character as a result of these repeated behaviours?

ANALYZING LITERARY DEVICES
Identify the two flashbacks in this short story and summarize the main events in each. What purpose do these flashbacks serve?

EVALUATING
From beginning to end, how does Josh change? Is this just a change in mood or a change in his character? Support your answer.

TASKS

CREATING A NEWS REPORT
Write a news report on the events that unfold on the night of the second encounter between Josh and the gang of boys. Consider how your report can accurately reflect the personalities of the characters, without showing any bias.

PREPARING A PRESENTATION
Identify the characteristics and motivations behind bullying. To what extent does the behaviour of the boys who mugged Josh fit your criteria for bullying? Prepare a short presentation with your observations and conclusions.

ABOUT THE AUTHOR
Jacqueline Pearce couldn't imagine being anything but a writer. "I think most writers, like most artists, feel a compulsion to create. It's who we are, and we have to do it."

Pearce has spent most of her life in Vancouver, British Columbia, where "The Trickster" is set. Pearce primarily writes young adult fiction, poetry, and historical fiction.

Gay Kids Need It to "Get Better" Now, Rick Mercer Rants

WHAT DO YOU THINK? + AGREE   − DISAGREE
You have to be patient to change society.

Blog Entry by Dakshana Bascaramurty, posted on the *Globe and Mail*, October 27, 2011

"It gets better"—the reassuring message for gay teens that has passed through the lips of everyone from Glee *star Chris Colfer to Conservative cabinet minister John Baird—just doesn't cut it.*

That's what CBC funny-man Rick Mercer has said in his latest signature rant, which has gone viral since it was posted online yesterday. The rant, a big departure from the absurd, light-hearted approach he usually takes to issues, was inspired by the suicide of 15-year-old Jamie Hubley from Ottawa, Ontario, a boy who was bullied by classmates for being gay.

Mr. Mercer says simply telling young people that the bullying will eventually end when they reach adulthood isn't enough—they need things to be easier when they're getting through the tough years of junior high or high school. He ends his rant by calling on gay public figures to be more open about their sexual orientation and serve as role models to gay youth.

"If you're gay and you're in public life, I'm sorry, you don't have to run around with a Pride flag and bore everyone, but you can't be invisible, not anymore," he said.

Though the message was powerful, Mr. Mercer caught flak from some viewers for not ending his rant with a declaration about his own sexual orientation (he's been openly gay for much of his career).

This morning on CBC's *The Current*, with host Anna Maria Tremonti, he was much more upfront about being gay.

While he says he knew he was gay in high school, he didn't tell anyone and never endured any bullying. He didn't come out until his 20s. "The idea of kids out in high school is so foreign to me," he said.

If you're a public figure, being out of the closet goes beyond telling your family, friends, and colleagues, he said. For the sake of gay teens, but perhaps even more importantly their close-minded bullies, it's important to know there are plenty of successful adults out there who are gay. "It would be nice if there were more role models so people could say, 'What about Rick Mercer? He's gay. He went to this school.' 'What about Sergeant so-and-so?'"

But do soldiers, media personalities, politicians, judges, and all others in the public sphere have a responsibility to be "out" to people they don't even know? Or are they entitled to keeping their private life—which has nothing to do with their job—private? ◆

MAKING CONNECTIONS

Jamie Hubley's suicide spurred many provincial governments into action. In 2012, the Ontario government passed the Accepting Schools Act, which treats bullying as seriously as physical assault. Making text-to-world connections like this one can help you understand the impact of events.

Rick's Rant

"Every year in this country, 300 kids take their own lives. It is a mind-boggling number. And this past week, one of those kids was Jamie Hubley. He was 15, he was depressed, and he happened to be gay....

It's no longer good enough for us to tell kids who are different that it's gonna get better. We have to make it better now. That's every single one of us. Every teacher, every student, every adult has to step up to the plate. And that's gay adults, too. Because I know gay cops, soldiers, athletes, cabinet ministers, a lot of us do, but the problem is, adults, we don't need role models. Kids do.

So if you're gay and you're in public life, I'm sorry, you don't have to run around with a Pride flag and bore the hell out of everyone, but you can't be invisible. Not anymore; 300 kids is 300 too many."

Mercer's rant went viral around the world.

No, Rick Mercer, Not All Gay Public Figures Need to Step Forward

Editorial published in the *Globe and Mail*, October 28, 2011

Rick Mercer, the comedian, is wrong, terribly wrong, about the moral obligation he would put on gay people in the public eye.

"I know gay cops, soldiers, athletes, cabinet ministers," the 42-year-old Mr. Mercer, who is gay, said on his CBC TV show this week. Gay teenagers need them as role models, he said, because gay teens are being bullied, and some take their own lives—Jamie Hubley, just 15, of Ottawa, did so this month. "… if you're gay and you're in public life … you can't be invisible. Not anymore."

With the best of intentions, Mr. Mercer would impose a burden on gay people that is on no one else in our society. And anyone who did not bear up under that burden would be, by implication, a moral failure—a coward. That is a very big burden, indeed.

How different (and yet not so different) it is from the burden of recent times in which gay people felt they had to keep their orientation secret, even from family members. One of the signal victories of the past few decades has been to free gay people from the burden of secrecy. Should they now be placed under an obligation of openness?

> There are many reasons why some gay cops, soldiers, athletes, and politicians might wish not to be open about their orientation. They may consider it a private matter.

That would not be fair. There are many reasons why some gay cops, soldiers, athletes, and politicians might wish not to be open about their orientation. They may consider it a private matter. They have entered these professions for the same reason anyone else has, and wish to pursue them in the same way, without differentiating themselves in a way that may feel, to them, irrelevant. They may even be "out" to the people who know them well. Would every gay person now need to hold a news conference?

And yet Mr. Mercer may be right that if all gay athletes, soldiers, etc., were somehow able to make their orientation known far and wide, it would reduce the power of stereotype and spread tolerance.

It might weaken the position of the bullies, or at least give comfort to vulnerable gay teens.

What Mr. Mercer is saying amounts to this: it falls to successful gay adults to protect vulnerable gay teens from the problems associated with being different. He's wrong. The job of protecting gay teens, or anyone else, from bullying falls to everyone. ◆

ANOTHER PERSPECTIVE ON PRIVACY

"Privacy and security are those things you give up when you show the world what makes you extraordinary."
—Margaret Cho

RESPONDING

DISCUSSION QUESTIONS

COMPARING TEXTS
Compare and contrast the views expressed in the blog entry and the editorial. Start by identifying the thesis for each text. Which of the texts more clearly expresses the writer's opinion? Which more closely reflects your views on the topic? Explain.

METACOGNITION
What strategies did you use to compare the texts in this selection? Of the strategies that you used, which were the most effective and why?

DIGITAL LITERACY
Are online public forums the best vehicles to explore complex issues, or do they only express personal opinions without addressing serious social issues such as bullying? Explain your response.

TASKS

CREATING AND DELIVERING A RANT
Conduct research on the topic of bullying and on the rant form. Create a rant to deliver to classmates to express your opinion on any aspect of teen bullying. Use evidence from your research to support your views. Be sure to use language appropriate for your audience and purpose.

WRITING TO RESPOND
What type of conflict is reflected in these texts: human versus human, human versus self, or human versus society? Write a short response explaining the type of conflict that is primarily focused on in this selection.

WHAT DO YOU THINK?
Life's not about fitting in, it's about standing out.

Fish Cheeks

Personal Anecdote by Amy Tan

MAKING INFERENCES

In the third paragraph, Amy Tan gives a detailed description of the food her mother is preparing. She uses precise adjectives and comparisons to describe the food. Readers can use this description to make inferences about how she feels.

I fell in love with the minister's son the winter I turned fourteen. He was not Chinese, but as white as Mary in the manger. For Christmas I prayed for this blond-haired boy, Robert, and a slim new American nose.

When I found out that my parents had invited the minister's family over for Christmas Eve dinner, I cried. What would Robert think of our shabby *Chinese* Christmas? What would he think of our noisy *Chinese* relatives who lacked proper American manners? What terrible disappointment would he feel upon seeing not a roasted turkey and sweet potatoes but *Chinese* food?

On Christmas Eve I saw that my mother had outdone herself in creating a strange menu. She was pulling black veins out of the backs of fleshy prawns. The kitchen was littered with appalling mounds of raw food: A slimy rock cod with bulging fish eyes that pleaded not to be thrown into a pan of hot oil. Tofu, which looked like stacked wedges of rubbery white sponges. A bowl soaking dried fungus back to life. A plate of squid, their backs crisscrossed with knife markings so they resembled bicycle tires.

And then they arrived—the minister's family and all my relatives in a clamour of doorbells and rumpled Christmas packages. Robert grunted hello, and I pretended he was not worthy of existence.

Dinner threw me deeper into despair. My relatives licked the ends of their chopsticks and reached across the table dipping them into the dozen or so plates of food. Robert and his family waited patiently for platters to be passed to them. My relatives murmured with pleasure when my mother brought out the whole steamed fish. Robert grimaced. Then my father poked his chopsticks just below the fish eye and plucked out the soft meat. "Amy, your favourite," he said, offering me the tender fish cheek. I wanted to disappear.

At the end of the meal my father leaned back and belched loudly, thanking my mother for her fine cooking. "It's a polite Chinese custom to show you are satisfied," explained my father to our astonished guests. Robert was looking down at his plate with a reddened face. The minister managed to muster up a quiet burp. I was stunned into silence for the rest of the night.

After everyone had gone, my mother said to me, "You want to be the same as American girls on the outside." She handed me an early gift. It was a miniskirt in beige tweed. "But inside you must always be Chinese. You must be proud you are different. Your only shame is to have shame."

And even though I didn't agree with her then, I knew that she understood how much I had suffered during the evening's dinner. It wasn't until many years later—long after I had gotten over my crush on Robert—that I was able to fully appreciate her lesson and the true purpose behind one particular menu. For Christmas Eve that year, she had chosen all my favourite foods. ◆

RESPONDING

DISCUSSION QUESTIONS

EVALUATING
Using a graphic organizer, identify Amy Tan's attitude toward Chinese culture and American culture, looking particularly at her attitude before the end of the dinner. Support your response with specific textual evidence. What does this analysis reveal about Tan?

CRITICAL LITERACY
If this anecdote were retold from the perspective of Amy's mother, Robert's father, or Robert, what lesson would that person have learned by the end of the evening? Would their lessons be similar or different? Explain.

METACOGNITION
What types of connections helped you make inferences about the characters?

TASKS

DEVELOPING DIALOGUE
Create the dialogue that might occur between Amy and Robert 10 years later in which they talk about how they felt that evening, why they felt that way, and how their viewpoints or values have changed over the years. Rehearse the dialogue and be prepared to present it to your class.

WRITING TO RESPOND
Write a poem, paragraph, story, or other type of text to explore your thoughts on the words of Amy's mother, "You must be proud you are different. Your only shame is to have shame."

ABOUT THE AUTHOR
Amy Tan was born in Oakland, California. Tan believed her childhood was duller than most people's, until she began writing at the age of 33. Tan took up writing in an attempt to find meaning in her life. She lists "discarding all her beliefs and starting over again, the American Dream and her Chinese family's interpretation of that, and luck," as among the biggest influences in her writing.

WHAT DO YOU THINK?

"There are no simple answers in matters of the soul."

What We Share

Memoir Excerpt from
One Story, One Song
by Richard Wagamese

There's an airy sort of confidence in knowing that you've seen your share of ups and downs. Staying on your feet, answering the bell for the next round, is what we mean by maturity. But, for many years, I found it difficult to see my life as anything but a series of injustices and slights. Being a Native person seemed a prescription for agony. I wrestled with a need to square the deal.

For a long time, my main motivation was payback. Every success, every forward step, was an opportunity for showmanship, for sneering in the face of society. I had a "look what I can do despite you" sort of swagger. Anger creates barriers. Resentment builds distance. But I didn't know that then. All I knew was that indifference relayed back to the source was what life asked of me, and I was hell-bent on delivering.

It made things difficult, that constant measuring up. Some good people are no longer in my life because of my relentless cultural and political one-upmanship. I broke hearts and relationships because I couldn't see any other way of easing the churning in my belly. Then I met Jack Kakakaway.

Jack was an Ojibway man who'd fought in a war, beat the bottle, found his cultural centre, and reclaimed a ceremonial, traditional life for himself. He was a teacher, and a good one. I think he saw a lot of himself in me. He recognized the angst, the feeling of being lost that was masked as protest. Jack understood my heart and spirit far better than I did. When he began to guide me, I think that was his own form of payback, a thanks for the gift of grace in his life. He led me to ritual and the stories of my people. He helped me to see who I was and led me to a vision of who I might become.

Jack and I were talking one day about the challenges I saw to my burgeoning sense of identity. I spouted off about the Canadian mosaic and the displacement I felt as a First Nations person. I felt threatened by the new Multiculturalism Act. I believed it was an assimilationist document that would cause us to lose our identities and our rights as First Peoples.

Jack listened as he always did, with an expression I couldn't quite read and a half smile at the corner of his lips. Then he said something I'll never forget: "All tribal people are the same." He took his time answering when I asked what he meant. Elders do that a lot. They force you to sit with your question so that you understand there are no simple answers in matters of the soul. By making you wait, they help you to develop patience. They guide you to mindfulness and a sharpened ability to listen.

VALUE AND DIGNITY FOR ALL

The 1971 Multiculturalism Policy of Canada (also known as the Multiculturalism Act) affirmed the value and dignity of all Canadian citizens, regardless of ethnic origins, language, or religious affiliation.

VISUAL LITERACY

The designer of this selection wanted to visually reflect how Richard Wagamese's thinking changed. Consider how the designer has symbolically represented the message in this selection.

"There are no pure cultures anymore," Jack said finally. He meant that everyone else has to let go of something in order to get something else. As First Nations people, he said, we had to let go of snowshoes and toboggans to get snowmobiles and pickup trucks. We had to let go of smoke signals to get telephones. Ultimately, we had to let go of our languages to speak English. It was the same for everyone everywhere, he said. The world asks us to sacrifice something in order to be included.

What we need to look for in this world, Jack told me, are the things we share. There are as many things that make us the same as there are those that make us different. The difficulty is seeing them. The things that join us are as basic as breathing, as small as a tear. We all began as people huddled in a band around a fire in the night. We all longed for the comfort of a voice in the darkness. We've all sacrificed part of our identity to become part of the whole. What we've lost is what binds us, what makes us the same.

Old Jack has been gone more than 16 years now, but I've always remembered his teaching. It changed my life. I moved away from my us-and-them mentality and started looking for what makes people alike. That's what life really asks of us, and it's the most humble, yet profound, gift we can offer one another. ◆

RESPONDING

DISCUSSION QUESTIONS

COMPARING TEXTS
Compare "Fish Cheeks," on page 16, to "What We Share." Organize your observations and insights.

CRITICAL THINKING
How does Richard Wagamese view the relationship between First Nations peoples and others living in Canada? Have his views remained the same or have they changed? Explain.

MAKING INFERENCES
Why does Wagamese consider Jack Kakakaway to be a great teacher and guide? What qualities does Kakakaway possess, and why does Wagamese value them? Support your response.

TASKS

RESEARCH AND INQUIRY
Research recent news events involving First Nations communities. What function did the Elders play? Be prepared to present your findings and conclusions.

COMMUNICATING IDEAS
Identify and discuss Wagamese's purpose in this memoir excerpt. How effectively has Wagamese achieved his purpose? Record your conclusions, indicating how the discussion may have changed your thinking.

AUTHOR NOTE

"All that we are is story. From the moment we are born to the time we continue on our spirit journey, we are involved in the creation of the story of our time here. It is what we arrive with. It is all we leave behind. We are not the things we accumulate. We are not the things we deem important. We are story. All of us. What comes to matter, then, is the creation of the best possible story we can create while we're here; you, me, us, together. When we can do that and we take the time to share those stories with each other, we get bigger inside, we see each other, we recognize our kinship—we change the world, one story at a time...."

—Richard Wagamese, *Indian Horse*

FOCUS ON genre

Legend has it that Ernest Hemingway was once challenged to compose a complete story in just six words.
He wrote:

For sale: baby shoes, never used.

He is said to have considered it his best work.

ANALYZING NARRATIVE WRITING AND THE SHORT STORY

Narrative writing comes in a variety of forms, including blog entries, biographies, stories, and novels. While all narratives tell a story, the narrative form that a writer chooses depends on his or her primary purpose: to entertain, to inform, or to persuade. Understanding the writer's purpose allows readers to activate the appropriate prior knowledge, engage in making meaning, and more readily determine theme.

NARRATIVE STRUCTURES	CHARACTERISTICS	SAMPLE FORMS
Personal Narrative	• tells about a real experience that happened to the writer	• autobiographies, memoirs, blogs, and anecdotes
Biographical Narrative	• tells about a real event that happened to a person other than the writer	• biographies and profiles
Fictional Narrative	• tells a made-up story	• short stories, tall tales, and novels

ANALYZING THE SHORT STORY

Several elements work together to make a short story appealing to its audience: plot, conflict, setting, characterization, style, and theme. Through a careful analysis of each of these elements, a writer's message can be interpreted and evaluated. Note that these elements appear in other narrative forms, and similar questions can be asked about those forms.

WHEN ANALYZING ...	CONSIDER ...
Plot, Conflict, and Setting	• How do conflict and plot work together? How does the narrator reveal information about internal or external conflicts?
	• What critical literacy questions arise as a result of the conflict?
	• How does setting affect conflict or plot? How would a different setting change the conflict?
Characterization	• How do a character's words, actions, and thoughts reveal personality, motives, and values? How do those words, actions, and thoughts connect with the observations of other characters?
	• What motivates the character? Do motives change over the course of the story?
	• What new understanding does the character have by the end of the story?
Style	• How are stylistic devices (e.g., word choice, sentence fluency, and literary devices) used to develop the story?
Theme	• How does the writer's purpose complement what he or she wants readers to believe or understand?
	• What is the writer saying about the human condition, society, or life?
	• How do conflict, plot, characterization, and style reinforce the writer's message?

SCARS

WHAT DO YOU THINK?
Family conflict can only be resolved through discussion.

 STRONGLY AGREE   STRONGLY DISAGREE

Short Story by Don Aker

The axe was double-bitted. Maybe that was a warning—double-bitted: biting twice. First the metal of the old Volkswagen van and then the flesh and bone between my eyes.

My father bought old vehicles and bullied them back to life, transplanting parts from one to the other, then chopping up the derelicts with his axe and hauling them to the dump on the back of his old Fargo. I had none of his mechanical skill. Sometimes I got tools for him, always having to ask if the Robertson screwdriver was the one with the square or the cross. Sometimes I held trouble lights or steadied the block and tackle. Sometimes I turned the ignition while he coaxed, manipulated, or threatened tired parts back into operation. I often wondered why he asked me to help. Even loading the large metal pieces on the back of the truck was something I couldn't do alone, although my father could lift them with ease.

On this particular day, he was dismantling an ancient VW Kombi van in the field behind our house. The August air lay on us like a quilt, and I watched my father's green work shirt grow black with sweat as the axe pistoned up and down. I longed to slip away to the river for a swim, but I knew my father. We would stop when the job was finished.

I looked at the growing pile of scrap metal and felt resentment work its way up my neck in hot waves. I hated being there. Not just because it was a Saturday and it was August, but because the work was a constant reminder of my brother's absence.

My brother, who could make kites out of bread bags, who could build a raft out of poplar saplings and twine, who could fix the radio my father had given him, and who could die in four months from a disease I still couldn't spell.

I hated being there.

"Daniel!"

I turned to see my father staring at me. "What?"

"I need the pinch bar."

I reached toward the tools spread on the grass.

"Not the cat's paw. The pinch bar!"

My hands darted from one meaningless implement to another until my father strode over and picked up an iron bar inches from my fingertips. My ears burned as I waited for the look and the silence. My father had a habit of staring at me for a moment when he was angry, saying nothing, as if he couldn't quite believe that I and all my ineptness had sprung from his loins. Then he'd turn away, back to the work he'd been doing, that he was always doing. And we would go on.

He used the pinch bar to pry off a door whose hinge had stubbornly resisted the pounding of the axe, and I moved closer to watch as he worked the metal bar back and forth. This was the only part I enjoyed, watching steel give way to steel, bending and groaning as it rippled and then tore apart in ragged smiles. And then, like all things, it was over and the axe again rose and clanged in the mid-morning heat.

My thoughts returned to the river that ran along the western edge of my father's property. Fed by mountain springs, even the slower water of August was so deep and cold that the only way to bear it was to dive straight in. I thought of my brother, his slim body a white blade slicing the water.

Then the axe struck me.

//Analyzing Literary Devices

Don Aker describes the brother's body as a "white blade" and says "the axe pistoned up and down." Aker uses imagery throughout this story that reflects machinery or machines.

I would learn later that the force of the final upward swing pulled the axe from my father's tired, greasy hands; that the metal-reinforced frame of the thick glasses I wore and hated saved my sight and quite possibly my life. But I knew none of this now. I was somehow in that river, floating beneath a crimson sky. Oddly, there was no pain, only a strident jangling inside my head, and I felt myself beginning to sink before I was jerked into awareness by my father.

Shouting my mother's name, he ran to the house with me in his arms. Moments later, all three of us were in our old Cutlass, my mother holding a dishtowel over my face. My father said nothing as he drove, of course. What needed to be said? I'd been standing too close. It was my fault.

When the car skidded to a stop in front of the hospital, I thought about my glasses lying somewhere in the field behind our house. Broken again, no doubt. My father had already paid for a new pair this year. I told him I'd smashed them in gym class and he hadn't discovered my lie, that I'd broken them myself, enjoying the sound the plastic frames made as I twisted them between my hands.

My mother opened her door even before the car stopped moving and, keeping the towel pressed against my forehead, she got out, guiding me behind her.

"I'll park the car," said my father.

My mother hesitated for only a moment. Then, her arm around me, she turned and steered me up the steps and through the large doors. Behind me, I could hear my father's Cutlass driving away.

Emergencies in the county hospital were handled at the outpatients' department. My mother spoke to the woman at the admitting desk. Standing beside her now, I remembered the last time I was there. My brother had been sick for days, and at first we thought it was the flu. My mother could do nothing but wipe his face with a cold cloth as he knelt over the toilet retching and heaving. I remembered lying in bed listening to the strangled coughing followed by the inevitable splash, my own stomach churning. Incredibly, my father slept—until my mother woke him to tell him about the blood. Then we brought him here.

I heard footsteps approach. "Well, that's quite a mess you've got there," came a young woman's voice. Crusted with dried blood, the dishtowel clung to my forehead until she gently eased it away. Everything was a blur and again I thought of my glasses lying in the field behind our house. "How did this happen?" the nurse asked.

"An axe," said my mother. "It was an accident."

//Who Is Most at Risk of Injury?

From 2009 to 2010, an estimated 4.27 million Canadians aged 12 or older suffered an injury severe enough to limit their usual activities. Overall, young people (aged 12 to 19) had the highest likelihood of injury (27%)—twice as high as all other age groups (13%).

(Statistics Canada)

"I'll make sure the doctor sees you next. Have a seat in the waiting room." Three other people were already there, but my nearsighted eyes could make out only their forms. No one spoke as my mother and I sat. Voices echoed everywhere, crying and conversation knitted together by nurses bustling importantly back and forth. A speaker hummed and quietly asked for a maintenance worker to report to the mechanical room, and I thought of my father, who still had not appeared.

"How does it feel?" my mother asked.

"Doesn't hurt. How's it look?"

My mother brushed my hair off my forehead. "Swollen quite a bit." Taking something from her purse, she got up and walked down the hall and, in a moment, I could hear the *shir* of a water fountain. She returned carrying a wet handkerchief, which she rubbed gently over my face.

The wetness brought things into clearer focus. My mother's face suddenly looked old, lines like the branches of bare trees on her forehead and under her eyes. But it was the fear in them that surprised me. I had seen that fear the night we brought my brother here. That was the first time I'd realized my mother could be afraid.

The nurse returned. "The doctor can see you," she said. I saw my mother glance toward the entrance. "You can wait here," I told her.

"No." Her voice was firm. "I'll come with you."

The examining room was blue with two high beds separated by a drawn curtain. From the second came voices, the doctor with another patient speaking in low tones, but I had no desire to listen. My legs were trembling and my face was beginning to wake up, nerve endings whispering about the pain I would feel. My mother stood at the door.

The night we brought my brother here, the on-call doctor immediately admitted him for tests, so my father went to fill out the necessary papers while my mother and I followed a nurse who pushed my brother in a wheelchair to the men's ward. At first I thought it would be better than the children's ward, but most of the patients were old. Someone's grandfather lay in the bed nearest my brother. He was perfectly still from the waist up, his wrists strapped to the bed's metal side-rails, but his legs were in constant motion, hilling and troughing the blankets. I couldn't stop staring at that old man, forever walking with his mouth open and eyes closed, and it was then that I knew my brother was going to die.

Four months later he did.

//Perspectives on Life

"Time is too slow for those who wait, too swift for those who fear, too long for those who grieve, too short for those who rejoice, but for those who love, time is eternity."
—Henry Van Dyke

"Nothing in life is to be feared, it is only to be understood. Now is the time to understand more, so that we may fear less."
—Marie Curie

I must have slept because one moment the doctor and his low tones were behind the curtain and then he was bending over me. When he spoke, it was with the same low voice. "Your mother tells me you had a run-in with an axe."

I turned my head and saw that my mother was sitting near the doorway. My father wasn't there.

"You need stitches, but I have to disinfect it first. Keep your eyes closed," he said as he swabbed the area, then added, "This will sting a bit."

My face slowly bloomed with pain as the wound took root between my eyes and grew, unfolded, blocked out everything else with bright red buds of fire. I squeezed my eyes tight and clung to the bed.

Finally it was over. "Now I'm going to freeze you," he said.

This time the pain was immediate, yellow sunlight wrung to a white point under a magnifying glass, and my hands lost the sheets they'd been gripping, pawed the air until I forced them down again. And then, slowly, there was nothing.

"We'll wait a few minutes to make sure it's completely frozen," he said. Then, "What were you doing with the axe?"

The question surprised me, made me feel I'd been doing something wrong. "Helping my father junk a van. We were cutting it up to take to the dump."

He raised his eyebrows. "You must be pretty strong."

"My father is."

"Where's your father now?"

I had no answer to this question. It made me think of Jimmie MacBurnie and his red yarn. Jimmie was the only mentally challenged person I'd ever seen. Thirty-something, he lived with his parents near Taylor Lake where my brother and I used to fish. Often we found pieces of bright red yarn tied to trees a few feet apart around the lake, and we asked my mother about them. "Jimmie puts them there so he can find his way in the woods," she'd said, then warned us not to touch them. A few years earlier, some kids had hidden several pieces as a prank and Jimmie had gotten lost. It had taken a search team all night and the following morning to find him curled up on the ground crying. I thought of Jimmie wandering about looking for that red yarn, knowing it had to be there but not being able to find it—like the answer to the question the doctor was asking me now.

My mother spoke for me. "He went to park the car."

Yes. Except that by now he probably had the hood up and was cleaning the spark plugs or tightening the fan belt. Important things that needed doing. I thought about how my father hadn't come up from the admitting office the night we brought my brother here, although my mother and I stayed in the men's ward over an hour. I thought about when we'd gotten home from my brother's funeral, listening to my mother crying in the next room while my father went outside to change the oil.

I thought about my mother sitting near the doorway of the examining room now, watching the corridor when she wasn't watching me.

And before I could stop myself, I was crying. Long, uncontrolled sobs that seemed to come from somewhere else, someone else. Ashamed, I tried to bury them in the pillow but, muffled, they resembled the sounds my mother still made at night sometimes when she thought everyone was asleep. I cried even harder. Then my mother was bending over me, her hands stroking my hair.

"It's shock," I heard the doctor say.

My mother said nothing, just kept stroking my hair. I cried for what seemed a long time. And then I couldn't cry anymore.

"The freezing should be ready now," the doctor said finally. "He won't feel anything." I thought he was probably right.

The stitching didn't take long. This time I kept my eyes open, watching the doctor's smooth hands move deftly over my face. They were nothing like my father's hands, thick and scarred, the nails always dark with grease or oil. These hands were soft and white against the room's blue walls, snowbirds in an October sky. They were like my hands, yet capable and sure. I wondered what my father would think of these hands.

"The stitches should come out in a week," the doctor said to my mother, perhaps afraid I'd burst into tears again. I didn't care. I just wanted it to be over.

And then it was. Ten minutes later, we were outside shielding our eyes against the sudden sun, scanning the parking lot for the car.

"There it is." My mother pointed.

Without my glasses, I knew which car was ours—the hood was up. As we made our way down the steps and over the loose gravel, I stumbled and silently cursed the stones under my feet. Then I cursed the car. And then my father.

As we approached the Cutlass, I could see his blurred form leaning in under the hood and I wondered what he could possibly have found to fix this time. As we came closer, though, I didn't hear the familiar tap and creak of tools in the act of resurrection and repair. Instead came the crack and snap of something breaking.

I had never seen my father break anything, my father who only ever put together or took apart. Even the dismantling of the vehicles in the field behind our house was purposeful and controlled. The sounds I heard as we walked toward the car were anything but that. I'd heard these sounds before, but their meaning was unclear, blurred like my vision.

His back to us, my father was staring at something in his hands, but he straightened when he heard us coming. Stepping back, he pushed the hood shut, the sound heavy and final. Without turning, he shoved something in his pocket, but the flash of sun off its polished surface told me what he'd been holding, what he'd been breaking.

I was sitting in English class, everyone reciting the parts of speech ("A *noun* is the name of a person, place, or thing"), when the principal had come across the PA telling Mrs. Wheaton that my mother was in the office.

"You may go, Daniel," the teacher said.

But I didn't want to *go*, didn't want to hear what my mother had to tell me. Instead, I sat there looking at the board, wanting only to crawl inside the safety of those rules that made people and things the same.

"I said you may go," she repeated, and there was nothing else I could do. But I didn't go to the office. I ran for the exit, flying out the door and toward the woods behind the school. Branches lashed my face and arms as I crashed through the trees but I kept running, ploughing through jack pine and cat spruce until I fell headlong into spongy, dark soil.

When I got up, I wasn't wearing my glasses. I had to scratch and paw through leaves and pine needles to find them, unaware I was crying. When my hands finally closed on them, I didn't put them on my face. Instead, I bent back one of the bows like a wishbone and listened to it *crack*, the brown plastic snapping cleanly in two.

My brother had stopped dying.

My brother was dead.

I bent the other bow—this time more slowly—and watched the plastic cloud before it broke. This time the *crack* and *snap* were almost simultaneous. It somehow seemed important that I could do this, that I could make this happen.

It made it easier to be angry and afraid and alone.

These were the sounds my father had made under the hood of the Cutlass, made with the glasses he'd gone back and found but would never give me.

I'd expected to go on feeling hurt, expected to feel the fury swell in me like our river during spring melt, but my anger evaporated. I climbed into the back seat while my mother slipped into the front beside my father. He started the car and backed it out of the shade into bright sunlight and we headed home. ◆

RESPONDING

DISCUSSION QUESTIONS

ANALYZING CONFLICT
Identify the conflicts Daniel experiences. Which conflict is the main conflict of the story? Why?

ANALYZING LITERARY DEVICES
Identify examples of flashback, foreshadowing, and symbolism in the story. Why are these literary devices used? How do these devices support your understanding of the story?

METACOGNITION
Did you find this story difficult to understand? If so, what strategies did you use?

TASKS

WRITING TO RESPOND
At the end of this story, what has Daniel learned? How does it relate to the theme of the story? Explain your response in at least one paragraph. Read the Author Note below and write a second paragraph to explore any new understanding the note gives you.

RESPONDING CREATIVELY
Imagine you are Daniel's brother and that you have created something (e.g., a song, piece of art, or photo collage) to help your family deal with their grief when you're gone. Create that memorial work and share it with others, explaining how it represents the family in this story.

AUTHOR NOTE
"Scars" began as an autobiographical piece. Like his character Daniel, Aker was struck accidentally in the head with an axe, and he had a brother who died. As Aker was writing the piece, he saw that it had more potential as a fictional story, that he could use the accident as an "inciting incident" that would illuminate an uncomfortable dynamic between a son and his father.

Of the story, Aker says, "Although there are elements of 'Scars' that are true, the story itself is fiction. I wrote it early in my career when I had a lot to learn about writing anything, but it remains my favourite of all my short fiction."

WHAT DO YOU THINK? + AGREE — DISAGREE
It is better to be a dreamer than a realist.

Ashes

Short Story by Susan Beth Pfeffer

That winter, it felt like every time I saw my father, the sun cast off just a little more warmth than it had the day before. I'd been seeing him Tuesdays for almost two years at that point. Mom, who was still working on completing her degree, took Tuesday and Thursday evening classes, so I'd go straight to Dad's from school, wait for him to show, and then we'd have supper together and talk.

Dad drove me home Tuesday nights, and the moon always shone as brightly as the sun had and the winter stars looked joyful and beckoning. When I was little, Dad used to promise me the stars for a necklace, but like most of his promises, that one never quite happened.

"I'm a dreamer," he said to me more than once, which really wasn't all that different from what Mom said. "He's an irresponsible bum" was her way of wording it. I knew he was both, but I also knew that winter that the sun and the moon dreamed with him.

Sometimes when I haven't seen Dad for a few days, on a Saturday or a Sunday, I'll try to figure out why Mom ever married him. She's the most practical person I know, always putting aside for a rainy day. With Mom, there are a lot of rainy days and she takes a grim sort of pleasure in being ready for them. The flashlight with working batteries for a blackout. The extra quarters when the laundry isn't quite dry.

Dad gets by on a grin and a willingness to help. He's always there if you need him. Well, not always.

He's unexpectedly there, like a warm day in January. He's a rescuer. "I saw a woman stranded on the road," he'd say. "So I changed her tire for her." Or he found a wallet with the ID intact, and returned it in person to its owner (and, of course, turned down a reward).

He told me once, "If I've done one thing, no matter how small, that made the world a better place, I'm satisfied. All I can give you is dreams, Ashes. But one good dream is worth a thousand flashlight batteries."

Ashes. I can still hear the fight. It was just a couple of months before the breakup. I was in bed when they went at it.

"Her name is Ashleigh!" Mom shouted. "A name you insisted on. So why do you call her 'Ashes'?"

"That's just my nickname for her," Dad replied. He was always harder to hear when they fought.

"But ashes are cold, grey, dead things," Mom yelled.

"It's just a nickname," Dad repeated, a little quieter.

"You call her that just to annoy me!" Mom yelled, but Dad's reply was so soft, I could no longer hear him.

A couple of days later, when Dad forgot to pick me up at school, or didn't have the money for the class trip, or got all his favourite kinds of Chinese and none of Mom's and mine, I thought maybe Mom was right, and Dad did call me Ashes just to annoy her. I made a list that evening of all the words that rhymed with *ashes*—*smashes* and *crashes*, *trashes* and *bashes*, *clashes* and *mashes*—and it didn't seem quite so nice anymore, having a special nickname. But then Dad gave me roses or sang a song he'd written for me. Or maybe he moved two buses away. And I realized he still called me Ashes, where Mom couldn't hear him to be annoyed. And that made me feel special all over again. Mom might never be caught without batteries or tissues, but she just called me Ashleigh—a name she didn't even like—and never promised me anything.

What could Dad have promised her to get her to love him? And what could Mom have offered to make Dad love her back? Whatever it was, it was dying by the time I was born, and dead before I turned six. Dad could make everyone in the world smile, except Mom. And Mom was always prepared, except for what Dad did to her.

> Mom might never be caught without batteries or tissues, but she just called me Ashleigh—a name she didn't even like—and never promised me anything.

It was toward the end of February that winter, and the sun was shining and the air was crisp and clean. I sat waiting for Dad, who I knew would show up eventually.

When he got in, he was full of smiles and kisses. "Ashes!" he cried, as though it had been years since we'd last seen each other. "Have you ever seen such a day?"

I had, seven days before. But I smiled at Dad, who always seemed to discover the weather each time we visited.

"You look radiant," he said. "You get more and more beautiful." I was wearing jeans and a bulky brown sweater that Mom had given me for Christmas.

"You have flair, Ashes. Style. You're sure to make your mark."

Last week he'd told me to be an astronaut. The week before that, the CEO of a Fortune 500 corporation. And the week before that he'd been stunned by my spirituality.

"Oh, Ashes," he said, taking off his winter coat and dropping it on the sofa bed. "I wish I deserved you."

"I wouldn't have any other dad," I told him. "My friends' fathers, they just tell my friends to study more. They never tell them they have flair or style."

"Maybe they don't," Dad said. "You're the special one, Ashes. You're the one-in-a-million girl."

"Am I really?" I asked, not needing the reassurance. I knew I wasn't a one-in-a-million girl, no matter how often Dad told me I was. I still loved hearing him say it.

ANALYZING SENTENCE STRUCTURE

The use of specific phrases and sentence structures can tell readers a lot about a character's mental or emotional state. If a character suddenly uses atypical phrases or sentence structures, readers can infer that a change of some type has occurred.

VISUAL LITERACY

Readers' reactions to a text can be affected by the visuals as much as by the written words. Visuals can help establish the mood or tone of the story, as well as the setting.

"One in a million," he said. "And don't let anyone ever tell you otherwise, Ashes. They will, you know. They'll try to tear you down. They'll laugh at your dreams. Even your mother—and she's a saint to have put up with me all those years—even she will discourage you from being all you can be. I hate to speak against her, but she's not a dreamer, Ashes. She's the most level-headed woman I know. As straight as a yardstick. But I was the only dream she ever believed in and once I failed her, she never let herself dream again."

We were both silent as we pondered Mom. Then Dad laughed. "She'd never let you go hungry," he said. "What do you want for supper, Ashes? I can offer you pizza, Chinese, or fast." He clapped his hands. "There's a new diner, opened right around the block. Let's treat ourselves, Ashes, and go out on the town."

"Can you afford it?" I asked.

"For a special date with my daughter?" he replied. "Of course I can afford it. Besides, I have something to celebrate."

"What?" I asked.

"I have a chance at something really big," he said. "All I need to do is put together a little financing, and I'll be set for life."

"For life?" I said, and I must have sounded like Mom because he stopped smiling.

"All right, not for life," he said. "But it'll be the start of something really big, Ashes. I can feel it. Just a couple hundred bucks and then all the pieces will fall into place."

I had no idea where Dad thought he could get two hundred dollars. But he looked so happy I had to smile, too.

"Then diner it is," I said.

"Rice pudding for dessert," he said as we walked out the door. "You can always tell the quality of a diner by its rice pudding."

The diner might have been brand new; but already it had a shabby, run-down quality that made it fit right in with the neighbourhood. Dad took a booth that faced the door, and sat in the seat where he could check who was coming in. He hadn't done that with me in a long time, and my stomach was hurting in an old familiar way.

"Waiting for someone?" I asked him.

"Of course not," he said. "Not when I'm with you. Take your pick, Ashes. Hamburger, triple-decker, chicken-salad platter. Whatever you want."

I ordered the burger and fries, hoping that by the time it came I'd feel like eating. Dad ordered coffee.

"You'll share my fries," I said to him.

"I'll even eat your pickle," he said. But then he looked back at the door.

"What is it?" I asked him.

"It's nothing," he said. "Oh well, Ashes, you can always see right through me." He was the one who'd been looking right through me toward the door, but I didn't say anything.

"That money," he said. "The two hundred dollars?"

I nodded.

"Well, it isn't so much for a deal as to help pay off one I already made," Dad said. "But I've got to tell you, honey, once that money is paid, I'm on my way to easy street. Just a little setback. But you know how those guys are. They get itchy when you owe them money. And it's not always comfortable to be where they can scratch you."

"You owe them two hundred dollars?" I asked, trying to keep the panic out of my voice.

"Give or take," Dad said. "But don't worry about it, honey. I'll work it out. I always do."

My burger and fries came then. Dad took a long sip of his coffee, while I poured ketchup on my plate and twirled a fry in it. "Can I help?" I asked.

Dad smiled like I'd offered him the key to the mint. "I love you so much," he said. "You're ten thousand times better than I deserve, Ashes."

"Have a fry," I said, pushing my plate toward him. Dad took one. He seemed to have more of an appetite than I did.

"I had a thought," he said as he reached for my pickle. "Your mother keeps a couple hundred cash at her place."

I didn't think either of us was supposed to know that.

"In that pretty teapot her mother gave her," Dad said. "Unless she's changed her hiding place. I know she changed the locks, so maybe she changed her hiding place as well."

Sometimes, when Mom wasn't home, I'd take the lid off the teapot and stare into it, imagining what I could do with two hundred dollars. I looked at Dad and realized he'd had those same fantasies. Well, why not. I was his daughter, after all.

> "Your mother would never know the difference. Unless there's an earthquake or the Martians invade."

"The money's still in the teapot," I said. "What do you want to do, Dad?" I asked. "Come into the apartment with me and take the money?"

"Oh no," he said, and he looked really shocked. "I would never steal from your mother. I've caused her pain enough."

He added casually, "No, I just thought maybe you could borrow the money. Just for a day or two, until I straighten out all my finances. Your mother would never know the difference. Unless there's an earthquake or the Martians invade. I think we can gamble neither of those things will happen before Friday."

"You'll be able to pay her back by Friday?" I asked.

"You," Dad said. "I'd be borrowing the money from you. And I swear to you, Ashes, I'd have the money in your hands by Friday at the latest." He wiped his hand on the napkin and offered it to me as though to shake on the deal.

"That's a lot of money. What if Mom finds out?"

"It's me she'd be angry at," Dad said. "Which is why she'll never find out. I wouldn't jeopardize our time together, honey. You let me have the money tonight, I'll straighten out my little difficulty, and Thursday night, when your mom is out, I'll give you back what I owe you. No earthquakes, no Martians, no problem."

"Mom'll be home soon," I said.

"You all through?" he asked. I nodded. "Let's go, then," he said, the rice-pudding test long forgotten. We went back to his place so I could pick up my books. Then we walked down to his car.

"Why don't you sell your car?" I asked him.

INTERNAL CONFLICT

Many short stories explore a protagonist's internal conflict. Such conflicts are often difficult to resolve because a choice must be made between two or more equally unattractive solutions. The resolution of an internal conflict gives readers great insight into the complex mental and ethical traits of a protagonist.

ANALYZING SENTENCE STRUCTURE

Notice that the author has used many sentence fragments within the dialogue of this story (e.g., "Good head on your shoulders."). These fragments affect the pacing and mood of the dialogue. They also reveal personality.

"You're your mother's daughter," he said. "Good head on your shoulders. Problem is, I'd never be able to find another car this cheap to replace it. No, Ashes, the teapot's the way to go."

We drove back to Mom's in silence. For a moment, a cloud drifted past the moon and the sky turned greenish grey.

"Snow tomorrow," Dad said. "Maybe you'll get a snow day."

"Maybe," I said.

Dad parked the car a block away from Mom's. "Just in case she gets home early," he said. "I don't want her to see me waiting. You go up to the apartment," he said. "Take the money, and come right down. Then I'll drop you off in front of her place, like always, and she'll never know the difference."

"What do I do if Mom's already there?" I asked.

"Just stay where you are," he said. "If you're not back here in ten minutes, I'll go home."

"All right," I said, and reached to unlock the door.

"You're one in a million," he said to me.

I got out of the car and ran over to the apartment. I took the elevator to the tenth floor and unlocked the door. I walked into the kitchen and turned on the light. The teapot was right where it belonged. I lifted its lid and stared at her emergency money. Her earthquake money. Her Martian money. What should I do?

I looked out the window and saw only ash-grey sky. In the cold stillness of the night, I could hear my father's car keening in the distance. "You're one in a million," it cried. ◆

Beyond Pastel

Poem by Katherine Lawrence

They're getting divorced but tell us nothing
will change though I don't know how moving
from a bungalow to a row house & seeing
Dad once a month doesn't add up to change.
So I go along for the ride because Dad's
supposed to pick us up after we've shopped
for bedroom stuff & I've got nothing
better to do anyway.

Mom smiles sweet as cold cash at each salesman
in the carpet & drapery store where they offer
my sister & me white mints fat as mushrooms
while we walk up & down the aisles trying to make
earth match the sky.

My sister stays forever loyal to her soft pink world,
not me, I've moved beyond
pastel. Mom suggests a white twist
carpet, purple drapes with a bedspread to match,
a timeless combination, she says. But I know
just because something matches doesn't mean
it will stay that way & I leave her sitting on a roll end
sucking a mint.

Outside I find Dad in his car waiting to take us back
To a rental house he's furnished with second-hand
couches & chairs, a set of grandma's cottage dishes.
Two single cots on wheels fold up like praying hands
he stores in a bedroom closet between our sleepover visits.
Nothing matches except by accident.

I open the passenger door, slide over beside him.
Not even the radio is playing. He puts his arm around
me, hugs me hard as the glare of the sun bouncing off
the hood of our old blue Chevy.

Mom brings my sister over to the car, tells me I'm impossible,
that I'm just like my father. Says here she is ready to decorate
my new bedroom in whatever colour a teenage girl might like
& all I do is stomp out of the store to pout in a hot car.

Black, I tell her. It matches everything.

RESPONDING

DISCUSSION QUESTIONS

COMPARING TEXTS
Compare "Ashes" and "Beyond Pastel." Consider the theme and mood of both texts and how both authors created strong characters and sympathy for those characters.

ANALYZING CONFLICT
With what internal and external conflicts does the protagonist, Ashes, struggle? Why does Susan Beth Pfeffer leave these conflicts unresolved?

ANALYZING VOICE
Identify the words and sentence structures used to develop each character in "Ashes." How would you describe the voice of Ashes? Her father?

TASKS

WRITING IN CHARACTER
Imagine you are the character Ashes. Decide whether you're going to take the money for your father or not. As Ashes, write a final paragraph for this story explaining what you plan to do and why. Try to use the same voice as Pfeffer.

DEVELOPING DIALOGUE
Develop and perform dialogue for the conversation Ashes might have with the narrator of "Beyond Pastel." Focus on creating resolutions to the problems the characters face.

ABOUT THE AUTHORS

Susan Beth Pfeffer is an award-winning young adult author from New York City. To date, she has written over 60 novels. She explains her reason for writing this way: "For better or worse (and it can go either way), I write for myself."

The poem "Beyond Pastel" is from *Ring Finger, Left Hand*. Katherine Lawrence explains, "The poem is written in the voice of a young teen who seethes with anger as she tries to go along with the pretense that nothing has changed in her life. I was that teenager.... I was expected to cooperate but it was too late for me to pretend that I cared about something as trivial as home décor; the circumstances of my life had shifted. I was no longer a young girl living in a pastel world." Lawrence lives in Regina, Saskatchewan.

WHAT DO YOU THINK? + AGREE — DISAGREE
Conflict brings us together.

Accident

Short Story by Dave Eggers

You all get out of your cars. You are alone in yours, and there are three teenagers in theirs. The accident was your fault, and you walk over to tell them this. Making your way to their car, an old and restored Camaro, which you have ruined, it occurs to you that if the three teenagers are angry teenagers, this encounter could be very unpleasant. You pulled into an intersection, obstructing them, and their car hit yours. They have every right to be upset, or livid, or even violent. As you approach, you see that their driver's side door won't open.

The driver pushes against it, and you are reminded of scenes where drivers are stuck in submerged cars pushing against the weight of a lake, an ocean. The door won't open, so soon he and his passengers exit through the passenger side door and walk around the Camaro, inspecting the damage. "Just bought this today," the driver says. He is 18, blond, average in all ways. "Today?" you ask. You are a bad person, you think. You also think: what an odd car for a teenager to buy in the twenty-first century. "Yeah, today," he says, then sighs. You tell him that you are sorry. That you are so, so sorry. That it was your fault and that you will cover all costs. You exchange insurance information, and you find yourself, minute by minute, ever more thankful that none of these teenagers has punched you, or even made a remark about your being drunk, which you are not. You become more friendly with all of them, and you realize that you are much more connected to them, particularly to the driver, than possible in perhaps any other way. You have done him and his friends some psychic harm and you jeopardized their health, and now you are so close to them, to the driver in particular, you feel like you share a heart. He knows your name and you know his, and you almost killed him and, because you got so close to doing so but didn't, you want to fall on him, weeping, because you are so lonely, so lonely always, and all contact is contact, and all contact makes us so grateful we want to cry and dance and cry and cry. In a moment of clarity, you finally understand why boxers, who want so badly to hurt each other, can rest their heads on the shoulders of their opponents, can lean against one another like tired lovers, so thankful for a moment of rest. ◆

ANALYZING PARAGRAPH STRUCTURE

Dave Eggers wrote this story as one long paragraph. As you read, consider the effect this has on readers.

RESPONDING

DISCUSSION QUESTIONS

ANALYZING SHORT STORIES
Why does Dave Eggers tell his story from the second-person point of view? Was this point of view the best choice? Explain.

ANALYZING LITERARY DEVICES
"Accident" ends with an analogy. How does the analogy affect your understanding of the story's message or theme?

ANALYZING LANGUAGE CONVENTIONS
There are several compound-complex sentences toward the end of "Accident." What does this sentence structure reveal about the narrator? What mood does this create?

TASKS

DIGITAL LITERACY
One way we can use technology to look at the printed word in a new way is to copy and paste text from a source into a word cloud creator (like Wordle or Tagxedo). This allows you to see patterns and key words. Choose a passage from "Accident," remove unimportant words (such as *the*, *and*, *that*, and *to*), and create a word cloud. Write an analysis of what the word cloud reveals about Eggers's writing style.

DEVELOPING DIALOGUE
Develop a dialogue the teen driver might have with a parent or guardian about the accident. The dialogue should reflect the driver's age and should use an appropriate tone of voice.

AUTHOR NOTE
Of this story, Dave Eggers says: "Some years ago, I used to do a weekly short-short piece of fiction for the *Guardian*. 'Accident' was one of the earlier pieces, and it's still one of my favourite ones. In 'Accident,' I was trying to get at the weirdly profound connection you can have, in seconds, with someone with whom you share some traumatic experience. And because a run-in like the one in the story is so brief, the short-short form seemed appropriate."

> **WHAT DO YOU THINK?**
> Sometimes pangs of guilt never disappear.

Tomorrow, Summer

Short Story by Naomi Shihab Nye

"We were stooges. We were freshmen." Manny wished he had not brought it up. Especially today, when they were excited about graduating—he'd thrown a shadow into the room.

Mirage said, "Please tell me it is not true. I can't stand it."

Four years ago, they'd been loitering outside the cafeteria when, for whatever reason (she and Manny liked to linger and flirt), she'd impersonated their horrible biology teacher. Mirage rarely mocked people—even the girls painstakingly repairing their black nail polish in the bathroom. But the biology teacher had made fun of her name—"Do some people call you Illusion?"—and he was the dullest person on Earth.

Mirage had mastered his low, crackly drawl. "Stooooooo-dents, re-moooove all your excess beLONGings from the TOPS of your desks. No cellphones, all SYStems OFF. Prepare for classssssssss. ToDAY! We will analyze the compoNENTS of … DUMB DUMB DUMB AND BORING THINGS!" Then she gargled and coughed, raising her right hand to half-cover her mouth, as he always did, to the consternation of people sitting in the front row. Why did he emphasize certain syllables so strangely? Was he translating from nematode language even as he spoke?

There was almost no way to escape having Mr. Ray, unless you had an allergy to frogs. Tall and bald, with one of those protruding stomachs on an otherwise beanpole frame, he had by the fourth day of class succeeded in hypnotizing even the most avid academics into a biological stupor. Mirage said his first name was Ambien. Ambien Ray. Sounded like a fish.

Manny had laughed and said, "I think he has acid reflux. That hacking dry cough thing. Do you think he goes on automatic pilot the minute the bell rings?"

ANALYZING STORY STRUCTURE

Many stories use flashbacks to develop character or provide background information. As you read, pay close attention to words that might signal either a flashback or a return to the present.

Manny said, "Ouch." Mirage covered her face with her hands.

Mirage had once, in class, answered Mr. Ray in his own cadence unconsciously. He asked, "Do I detect an insult?" which made everyone titter.

Amal helped her out that day. She interjected, "Mr. Ray, we were discussing the possibility of a visit to the botanical gardens, since they have that new frog pond and we could perhaps get a group tour…. Would you like me to check on it?" Mirage and Amal chatted more often after that. At the botanical gardens, they watched together as a Venus flytrap ate a fly.

But Amal was nowhere nearby the day Mirage impersonated Mr. Ray and he came around the corner and stopped right in front of her and Manny. He stared into her eyes. He said, "Am I that bad?"

Mirage froze. A sadness shaded his gaze. He said, "I know, I'm not the most animated guy on Earth." He looked down, and up again. "Sorry about that," he said. Then he walked away. Manny said, "Ouch." Mirage covered her face with her hands.

The year rolled on. Mirage wrote an apology note to Mr. Ray and left it on his desk, but he never mentioned it. She worked hard on biology but felt awkward answering questions in class or even meeting his eyes. At the end of the year, her grade was a B. The next year, when she and Manny were sophomores, Mr. Ray retired at Christmas, surprising the new crop of hypnotized biologists.

"We all make mistakes. C'mon, forget about it! Geez, I should have never said anything."

ANALYZING CHARACTERS

Characters' personalities can be revealed to readers by what they say or do, by what others say about them, and by how they react to what is done or said to them.

Then Manny had run into him at a grocery store a few months later. He was looking thinner and paler than usual.

"Mr. Ray!" Manny said. "How are you doing?" and Mr. Ray said, "Not so good, actually, I've had some challenges." After a long pause, he added, "They tell me I have about a month or two."

Manny said, "That's terrible!" He struggled for something else to say. Then, "Mr. Ray, we—miss you at school. You were—a really good teacher."

"No, I wasn't," he said. "I'll never forget your little friend—how well she played me. I guess I didn't have that stand-up gene that would have made me interesting. I just loved my—topic."

His obituary would say he had a brother in Rockport. That was it. There wasn't even a memorial mentioned.

RESPONDING

DISCUSSION QUESTIONS

ANALYZING CHARACTERS
What can you infer about the personalities of both Mirage and Mr. Ray? Support your response with examples from the text.

RESPONDING PERSONALLY
Recall a time when you unintentionally upset someone or when someone unintentionally upset you. Why were feelings hurt? Were apologies made? How do you feel about the event today?

TASKS

WRITING A NOTE
Imagine you are Mirage. Write her note of apology to Mr. Ray. What tone of voice will you use? How will you make your apology believable and sincere?

WRITING A CONCLUSION
What will Mirage do to overcome her guilt? Write a plausible ending that explains how Mirage deals with her feelings about Mr. Ray's death.

RESPONDING CREATIVELY
Create a portrait representing Mirage or Mr. Ray. Place words and images that describe how the world perceives that character outside the head. On the inside, place words and images that best describe the character's inner thoughts and feelings. Present the portrait to your class.

And Manny had made the mistake of repeating the whole grocery store conversation to Mirage, right now, today, because they were graduating and might not see each other again and he'd never brought it up before.

She looked as if he'd punched her. Her eyes filled with tears and spilled right over. "I hate myself."

"No, you don't. We all make mistakes. C'mon, forget about it! Geez, I should have never said anything."

She said, "He told you that, and then he died."

"Well, trust me, you had nothing to do with his death. Change the subject. Think of summer! I am truly ready for summer, aren't you? I am looking forward to returning to my old apron and being charming to nasty people again."

Manny was a waiter at Joe's Crab Shack. He had the patter down. ◆

ABOUT THE AUTHOR
Naomi Shihab Nye was raised in San Antonio, Texas. She started writing stories and poetry as soon as she learned to write. Her love of reading and writing stems from a longing to feel less lonely. As she explains, "It is really hard to be lonely very long in a world of words. Even if you don't have friends somewhere, you still have language, and it will find you and wrap its little syllables around you and suddenly there will be a story to live in."

Up for Debate

Anger is an emotion, **aggression** is a behaviour, and **hostility** is a behavioural style.

The Stages of Conflict

1. discomfort
2. incident
3. misunderstanding
4. tension
5. crisis

Stay alert!

Did you know?

- Both bullying and harassment are criminal.
- Harassment is a human rights issue.
- When youths stand up and speak out against bullying, they are successful in stopping the bullying behaviour in about 10 seconds 57% of the time.
- About 75% of the time, peers don't intervene when they witness bullying.
- Those who stand by and watch bullying are part of the problem.

> **"Understanding** the nature of conflict **leads to peace."**
>
> —Lester B. Pearson

> **"** Never doubt that a small group of thoughtful, committed **citizens can change the world.** Indeed, it's the only thing that ever has. **"**
>
> —Margaret Mead

your days are numbered by Nidal El-Khairy

From weapon to fashion statement

From War to Peace is a jewellery and accessories company that wants you to wear your dedication to peace around your neck. They recycle disarmed nuclear weapons into an alloy they call *Peace Bronze*, which is then turned into accessories. The company's mission is to see a demilitarized world.

FOCUS ON media

When people create media products, they cannot turn off their biases.

IDENTIFYING POINT OF VIEW AND BIAS

Everyone has biases. From the moment you were born, you have experienced the world from your point of view. Your gender, the places you've lived, the experiences you've had, the way people have treated you—everything in your life contributes to the biases through which you see the world.

WHY DO POINT OF VIEW AND BIAS MATTER?

Imagine that a website devoted to luxury cars reports the launch of a new, super-expensive sports car. How might a website devoted to social justice report the launch of that same car? If you only ever heard one point of view, you wouldn't know that there were any others. Challenge yourself to be aware of the point of view in media texts.

In some cases, a media producer intentionally creates biased texts to promote a point of view or product. For example, a corporation with plans to build a power plant will produce media texts that support building it. Individuals (more often than groups or corporations) may unintentionally produce biased texts as a result of stereotypes or misinformation.

HOW CAN YOU ANALYZE POINT OF VIEW AND BIAS?

WHAT DO I ANALYZE?	QUESTIONS THAT HELP ME ANALYZE	EXAMPLES
Intended Purpose The perspective from which a media text is presented may be exclusionary or insensitive to an opposing viewpoint.	• Who constructed the text and why? • What do the creators value? What do they want the audience to believe?	A controversial event that is sponsored by a corporation is given positive news coverage because the news outlet that is covering the event is owned by the same corporation. All opposing viewpoints are excluded from the coverage.
Selection and Omission Choosing which parts of a story to tell and which parts to leave out contributes to bias.	• Do the arguments and evidence support only one side of an issue? • Whose viewpoint is not included? Why?	A liberal journalist's obituary for a conservative politician mentions her union-busting legacy, but neglects to mention the economic boost her time in office brought to the country.
Word Choice The words chosen for use in a media text can have either positive or negative connotations, and they can influence a message.	• Does the language favour one person or group over another? • How does the language indicate bias?	A group of protestors is referred to as an angry mob on a news program with conservative political views.

When your beliefs are challenged by a media text, you can either disprove and discount the point of view presented in the text, or reflect on the media text as a new experience that leads you to modify your point of view.

You Will Not Stop Me from Learning

Newspaper Article by Rick Westhead, from the *Toronto Star*

WHAT DO YOU THINK?
Education is a privilege, not a right.

Malala Yousafzai knew her courage might kill her.

Only 14, the Pakistani schoolgirl and women's rights activist is a rare bright light in a country hobbled by violence and extremism.

A prediction she made to me a year ago was realized on October 9, 2012, when a Taliban gunman boarded a bus transporting children home from school in Pakistan's volatile Swat district and demanded to know which one of the passengers was Yousafzai.

Another girl on the bus pointed to Yousafzai. When she denied her identity, the gunman shot both girls. Yousafzai was shot in the head and the neck.

After complicated surgery at a military base, doctors removed a bullet from Yousafzai's neck.

I often cite Yousafzai in conversation with friends and readers, saying that so long as there are young Pakistanis like her, the battered country has cause for optimism.

Even amid the tragedy of her shooting, there was a glimmer of hope. As news of the incident spread through Mingora, Yousafzai's hometown, several hundred residents went to the local hospital, offering to donate blood—a reminder that Pakistan remains a country with a population of moderates and liberals.

The Taliban claimed responsibility for the attack on Yousafzai, calling her work "obscenity."

For more than two years, in 2007 and 2008, Mingora, which is located in Swat, was a base for Islamic militants. They routinely rounded up people they perceived to be enemies, dragged them to a local traffic circle near crowded bazaars and butcher shops, and killed them.

Malala's Recovery

On January 4, 2013, less than three months after she was shot, Malala Yousafzai was released from the Queen Elizabeth Hospital in Birmingham, England. Upon her release, doctors described the 15-year-old as "a strong woman [who has made] a remarkable recovery." Doctors and supporters were amazed by her resilience and strength.

People from all over the world show their support for Yousafzai at vigils and demonstrations.

> //Analyzing
> Paragraph Structure
>
> Why do journalists, like Rick Westhead, write articles with lots of short paragraphs, some with just one sentence? Analyze the article and its paragraphs to see what is achieved by this convention.

Against this backdrop of terror, Yousafzai spoke out.

In September 2008, she travelled with her father, Zia, to Peshawar to speak to a press club.

"How dare the Taliban take away my basic right to education," Yousafzai said in front of a packed room of journalists, some of them broadcasting live.

I met with Yousafzai for the first time in October 2009 in the courtyard of the private school her father ran. She said she would never bow to the Taliban's demands and explained how she hid her textbooks under her clothes while walking to school.

In January 2011, we sat down for another interview.

"Education is not a gift for children, it should be their right," Yousafzai said, "and, hopefully, our country's leaders will give us the rights we deserve. This is their responsibility."

The then-13-year-old girl's words sent chills up my spine. I was struck by how mature and fearless she was in a country where the promise of violence has prompted a culture of silence.

Yousafzai walked past a large government billboard that proclaimed a pledge to Swat: "You don't have to worry about suicide bombing attacks…. These bad days are not forever. Every night has a morning."

I asked Yousafzai and her father whether they felt Pakistan's bad days had, indeed, passed.

She looked at the ground, shaking her head.

Her father was slightly more optimistic. "*Insha'Allah*," he said. "God willing."

Zia Yousafzai told me how the Taliban took control of Mingora.

"They didn't show up one day with a Jeep with rocket launchers and machine guns," he said.

Before the Taliban took over, tourists flocked to Swat, nicknamed "Little Switzerland," to ski and fish. But gradually, Swat began to change.

In 2004, a local religious leader named Mullah Fazlullah began broadcasting sermons from his own radio station, "Radio Mullah." Initially, Fazlullah merely discussed the tenets of Islam.

But it wasn't long before Fazlullah's message became more hardline.

Fazlullah, a former ski lift operator, demanded that Mingora's movie theatre close. He called music and art secular evils. Polio vaccinations, he said, were a Western conspiracy, and he preached that women did not belong in schools or public markets.

Throughout Pakistan, women's education has become a battleground with extremist Islamists pitted against Western governments that inject billions of dollars in aid money.

In a blog she kept for the BBC, Yousafzai wrote of life in Mingora under the Taliban. Under a pen name, she highlighted the rights abuses that were occurring in her hometown.

"I had a terrible dream yesterday with military helicopters and the Taliban," she wrote on January 3, 2009. "My mother made me breakfast and I went off to school. I was afraid of going to school because the Taliban had issued an edict banning all girls from attending schools. Only 11 students attended the class out of 27.

"On my way from school to home, I heard a man saying, 'I will kill you.' I hastened my pace and after a while I looked back [to see] if the man was still coming behind me. But, to my utter relief, he was talking on his mobile and must have been threatening someone else over the phone."

I asked Yousafzai about that blog entry and whether her fear had subsided.

"Well," she said. "The Taliban are gone from the police station and main bazaar, but you know they are still here. They are in shadows. They are waiting. I am not afraid. They may hate me and want me dead, but I know my family supports me. And so do countries like yours." ◆

RESPONDING

DISCUSSION QUESTIONS

MEDIA LITERACY
What bias does Rick Westhead show in this newspaper article? Support your response with specific evidence from the text.

CRITICAL LITERACY
Is it necessary for people in different parts of the world to help address injustices that occur in other countries? For example, should Canadians help Malala Yousafzai fight for gender equality in her home country? Support your response.

TASKS

ROLE-PLAYING AN INTERVIEW
Develop an interview between a reporter and Yousafzai. Questions and answers can be based on the article, on information discovered through research, and on reasonable inferences. Practise performing the interview before sharing it with others.

WRITING A LETTER
Write a letter to the editor of a major Canadian newspaper expressing concern about the suppression of women's rights in different parts of the world (you may need to research the issue). In your letter, express your point of view, provide supporting information, and persuade others to help advance the rights of women.

DIGITAL LITERACY
Using online media outlets, research Yousafzai's fight for women's rights, or another issue involving women's rights. Consult at least one online newspaper and its comments section and one blog or forum. Determine the impact the issue has had on these digital communities. Are these digital communities helping or hindering the cause? Explain.

Artists Respond to CONFLICT

WHAT DO YOU THINK?
Artistic expression can help heal the wounds created by conflict.
+ AGREE
− DISAGREE

Artwork by Gonçalo Mabunda, Sabina Zeba Haque, and Nora Heysen

Conflict is a grim reality that every country faces at some time—whether it's rioting, civil unrest, or all-out war. Sometimes artistic inspiration can come from unlikely subjects. Artists responding to conflict can capture its harsh realities and send a message—a plea for change.

Gonçalo Mabunda

Gonçalo Mabunda poses with several of his sculptures. All the pieces, including the chairs and saxophone, are created from instruments of war.

AK-47s, land mines, rocket launchers, tank parts, and the boots of soldiers are all just art supplies for sculptor Gonçalo Mabunda.

Mabunda was born in Mozambique in 1975. Two years later, a civil war that would last until 1992 broke out in the country. Though Mozambique has spent the last two decades in relative peace, the land is still littered with hidden weapons, unexploded land mines, and other instruments of war. Mabunda takes these instruments and turns them into works of art. "If we destroy the weapons, the same weapon's not going to kill anymore," he explains.

Mabunda began sculpting shortly after the civil war ended. He describes his early works as coming from a place of insecurity; his art reflected his fear that the peace in his country would not last. He hopes that his art will serve as a reminder of Mozambique's history and ensure peace for future generations.

Mabunda finds inspiration in traditional African art and modern artists like Picasso.

Objects of destruction take on anthropomorphic forms in Mabunda's art.

Mabunda is best known for his throne sculptures, which comment on power in Mozambique during the civil war.

THE MOZAMBIQUE CIVIL WAR

The Mozambique civil war began in 1977, only two years after the country gained independence from Portugal. Before peace was declared in 1992, about 1 million people died in the conflict or from starvation; another 5 million civilians were displaced.

VISUAL LITERACY

As you examine the artwork, consider the choices the artists have made. Ask yourself the following questions: What materials have they used? Have they used materials in new ways? What choices have they made that express their points of view?

Sabina Zeba Haque

Sabina Zeba Haque created her *Nishana* series to personalize and ground these "dangerous places" from video games in emotion and history.

Artist Sabina Zeba Haque's *Nishana* series, made up of mixed-media paintings, started with a simple idea. "We need to question the world that the media creates for us. We need to create our own maps," says Haque.

Haque was born in the United States, but was raised in Karachi, Pakistan, by her American mother and Pakistani father. Haque turned to art to express her experiences of living between two cultures. Her work often combines photography, collage, and painting, but her *Nishana* series blends scenes from video games and Google Maps.

She was driven to create this series by the images of Pakistan that she saw in video games, where her beloved country is a place of violence and conflict. Haque wanted to create a virtual space that could challenge the negative images. Armed with her oil paints, Haque changes the Karachi maps in Modern Warfare 2 into the beautiful city that she grew up in.

MAKING CONNECTIONS

The war depicted in Modern Warfare 2 is not actually happening. Consider how players would respond if they played a game that portrayed their community in a negative way.

The bleak landscapes of Modern Warfare 2 are transformed in this painting, *Crater*.

Haque blends aspects of classic Indo-Persian art with images from video games as seen in *Day Watchman*.

The negative portrayal of Karachi in Modern Warfare 2 is reinterpreted with Haque's use of bright colours in *No Man's Land*.

Karachi comes to life in *Pandora's Box*.

Nora Heysen

Nora Heysen was a formally trained Australian artist whose talent was evident from early on. As a student at the School of Fine Arts in Adelaide, she was able to sell her paintings to art galleries across Australia. After graduation, she began winning awards, and in 1943 she was bestowed the great honour of becoming Australia's official War Artist. She was the first female to be appointed to the role.

Heysen was responsible for portraying the women supporting the war effort. "... I was lent around to all the services, the air force, the navy and the army, to depict the women working at everything they did during the war," said Heysen. Her 170 portraits and still-life paintings from the war exposed Australians to realistic depictions of women hard at work.

Nora Heysen, in 1945, completes paintings she began while stationed in New Guinea as Australia's War Artist.

Heysen's *Transport Driver* depicts 21-year-old Ethel Miles driving a large military bus.

RESPONDING

DISCUSSION QUESTIONS

ANALYZING POINT OF VIEW AND BIAS
Describe how each artist featured in this selection uses art to convey different views of conflict. What does each artist value? What does each artist want the audience to think or believe?

METACOGNITION
With which work of art was it hardest to make a connection? Why was it difficult?

CRITICAL LITERACY
When you think of war, what images come to mind? Is what you visualize depicted by any of the artists? If so, how is it the same? If not, why do you think that is?

TASKS

WRITING AN ART REVIEW
Imagine you are a writer for an art magazine. You have been commissioned to write a review for an art show displaying the works presented in this selection. What will you tell your audience about the art and the artists at the exhibit? Write your review.

DELIVERING A MONOLOGUE
Imagine you are one of the works of art included in this selection. Give voice to the piece by telling your story in a monologue. Consider your origin and your purpose. Share your monologue with others.

FOCUS ON Writing

Voice is how a writer's personality and individuality are translated onto the written page. The ideas and voice that emerge from your writing are as unique as you are. Since every writer has a unique style, every writer has a unique voice.

DEVELOPING IDEAS AND VOICE

When writers begin a task, they consider how idea development and voice influence one another. These are two distinct aspects of writing, but both are influenced and connected by purpose and audience.

DEVELOPING IDEAS

Whether writing fiction or nonfiction, experienced writers begin the writing process by asking themselves two important questions:

1. Who is the audience?
By keeping the audience in mind, writers can purposefully generate ideas, conduct research, and organize their thoughts. They can also more readily distinguish between information that is and is not of interest to the audience.

2. What is the purpose for writing?
Similarly, by understanding the purpose for writing, writers are better able to determine what form of writing to choose, how to focus their writing, and whether to use formal or informal style.

DEVELOPING VOICE AS A WRITER

The intended purpose and intended audience influence the ideas that writers include, as well as the form and voice that they choose. Whether writers choose a voice that is academic, humorous, serious, or sarcastic will ultimately depend on the audience, purpose, and form of their texts.

> **// 10 PURPOSES FOR WRITING**
> 1. to express
> 2. to describe
> 3. to explore
> 4. to entertain
> 5. to inform
> 6. to explain
> 7. to argue
> 8. to persuade
> 9. to evaluate
> 10. to problem solve

Audience	Purpose and Form	Word Choice	Sentence Patterns	Paragraph Structure
Who is the target audience? What are their ages, interests, and professions?	What is the intended purpose and form (e.g., short story, poem, or obituary)? How will form influence voice?	What specific words will create the desired voice (e.g., active or passive verbs, slang or formal language)?	What sentence patterns will best create the desired voice (e.g., long or short sentences, simple or complex sentences)?	What types of paragraphs will best create the desired voice (e.g., short and simple or long and complicated)?

SAMPLE TEXTS	
excerpt from young adult dystopian fiction	After, Eva thought, after all. After all that we've lost, what is there left to dream about … to hope for … to love … to reach for?
excerpt from politician's speech at a fundraising event for her campaign	WE will be the leaders of the next generation! WE are the ones whom our children will follow! WE are the answer, not the question! Rise up and say "NO" to those who oppose peace in our time!
excerpt from sportscast based in Toronto	The score is tied here tonight with the crowd going wild! Thirty seconds to go in the last period—who will win the Stanley Cup, folks? Will the Leafs finally bring 'er back home? Or will the Habs pour maple syrup all over those dreams?

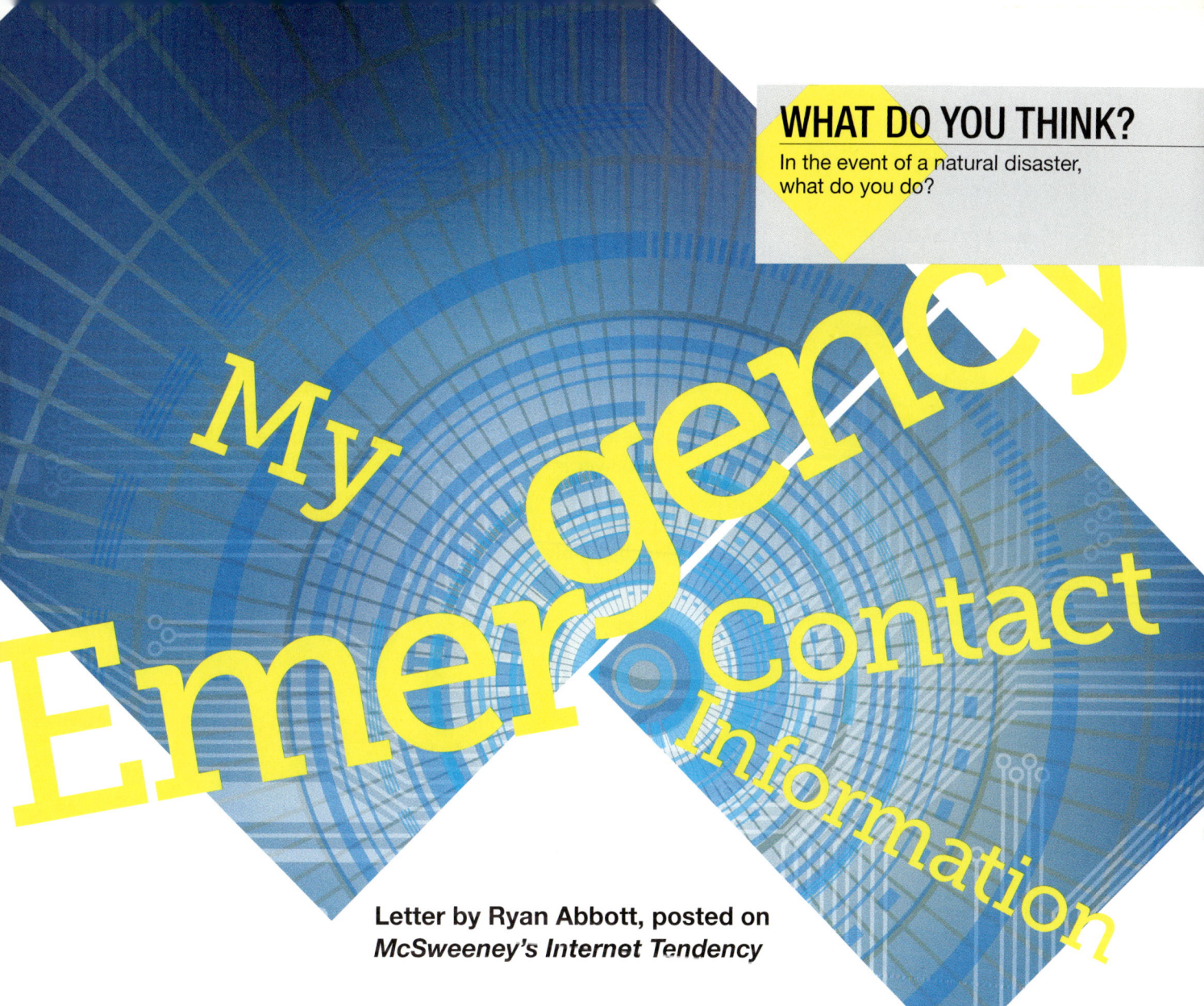

My Emergency Contact Information

Letter by Ryan Abbott, posted on *McSweeney's Internet Tendency*

WHAT DO YOU THINK?
In the event of a natural disaster, what do you do?

Hello family, friends, and selected co-workers,

In light of recent events in Somalia, Thailand, Zanzibar, Libya, Yemen, Norway, Syria, Vancouver, and Japan, I thought it would be a good idea to provide you with my current emergency contact information, in the unfortunate, though increasingly likely, event of an emergency.

First, if possible, try me on my cellphone. You should all have the number. I'd really prefer an emergency text message instead of a phone call, especially if the incident occurs before 8:00 p.m. on a weekday. Also, I don't have a data plan, so please do not text images, regardless of the scale of devastation. Instead, Tweet or post pictures to your Flickr or Instagram photo streams and I will download or view them later, when I pass through a hotspot. Don't forget to geo-tag them so I can determine your location.

If my cell doesn't work, try me at my landline, which is the same number as my cell, but with a 604 area code. I don't use the landline often, but I keep it active to save $5 a month as a "bundling benefit" on my digital TV package.

If I don't respond to either phone number, send a Skype voice call, or text to my handle at "hypochondriac78."

//Analyzing Conflict

Almost all texts involve conflict, whether it is human versus human, human versus self, human versus nature, or human versus society. As you read, consider what type of conflict is central to this letter.

//Hyperbole

People exaggerate for many different reasons: to create emphasis because they have strong feelings about a subject, to draw attention to an issue, or to create humour. When a writer uses exaggeration, it is called *hyperbole*. Writers can either extend hyperbole throughout a text or use it sporadically for effect.

If the buses are no longer running here in Vancouver due to a flash flood, tsunami, or post-game riot, I won't be able to get to the office to work, since I no longer drive after the bridge-shaking incident. The best way to reach me is to email my Gmail account. Assuming the power is still on, I will be working from my laptop at Kafka's Cafe on Main Street, near my condo. The cafe itself does not offer free WiFi, but I borrow from the nearby network PEGGYALLEN. I figured out Peggy and Allen's password. It's "password."

If there is a power outage in my neighbourhood, I will be using my parents in Ontario as out-of-province contacts. Call them to leave a message if you are trying to reach me. I will call them when the power is back on. Do not be alarmed if my father pretends he does not know me; he is just kidding. Also, please do not laugh at his jokes. He has been reusing the same ones for years, and your laughter only discourages him from generating new material.

In the event of a nationwide snowstorm that makes the entire country unreachable for an extended period of time (may also be caused by an emergency hockey game), my out-of-country contacts are Dmitri and Mitanka Dimov. I selected them because they live in Estonia, which, according to a recent Yahoo! News article, is the safest place to live in the world for avoiding natural disasters. The Dimovs can be reached at 011 372 58 723. Dmitri and Mitanka live above a laundromat, and it's a little noisy when all the dryers are on, so please speak loudly. The laundromat has been torched twice in the past month by the owner of a rival laundromat (allegedly), who is also an arms dealer with known connections to the Gaddafi regime in Libya. If no one picks up after 10 or so rings, don't bother leaving a voicemail.

In the event of an earthquake, if the phone networks and Internet connections are all disabled, the best way to reach me is to write a note on a piece of paper, seal it in an empty Jameson Irish Whiskey bottle, and throw it in the Pacific Ocean. Be sure to get the bottle into the waters of the Alaska Current, a warm-water current that flows mainly north along British Columbia. I will take frequent walks along the ravaged shoreline to scour for messages. Don't forget to use a Jameson bottle; its distinctive shape and emerald green colour make it highly noticeable, which will enable me to ignore other notes in different bottles, to respect the privacy of others. I hope to respond to all letters within 30 years.

In the event of a sudden surge in the effects of climate change, my wife Sheena and I will be moving to our cabin in Yukon. We haven't built the cabin yet, but we bought the property, on spec, over the Internet. Ten stunning acres of pristine tundra, with plenty of natural light several days a year. We're not sure what we'll do up there, maybe grow potatoes or start a vineyard. We've talked about opening a gelato place that also serves waffles, so everyone's happy. When the time comes, you can drop us a line at 122 Arctic Circle Drive, Yukon, Canada. Visitors welcome!

If an asteroid is found to be on a collision course with Earth, Sheena and I will be aboard our spaceship. Program your satellite to Ku-band 12.21 GHz to communicate with us. I will be responding to the name Buzz Lifeson.

If you wish to share your updated emergency contact information, that would be great!

Love,
Ryan

RESPONDING

DISCUSSION QUESTIONS

ANALYZING LITERARY DEVICES
Identify specific examples of hyperbole and explain why they have been used. How does hyperbole contribute to the voice of the narrator?

ANALYZING PURPOSE AND AUDIENCE
Consider both the original context for this letter and Ryan Abbott's message. What is its purpose? Who is the target audience?

ANALYZING CONFLICT
What conflict is central to Abbott's letter? How is his message connected to that conflict?

TASKS

DIGITAL LITERACY
Write at least one paragraph in response to this letter explaining why you value (or don't value) how easily others can contact you using social media.

WRITING A STORY
Respond to the conflict in this letter by writing a story. You can use a satirical voice, as Abbott has, or another voice of your choice.

WHAT DO YOU THINK? + AGREE − DISAGREE
Protests are a symptom of an unhealthy society.

Why People Can't Help Themselves

Opinion Piece by Andrew Potter, posted on *Maclean's*, August 19, 2011

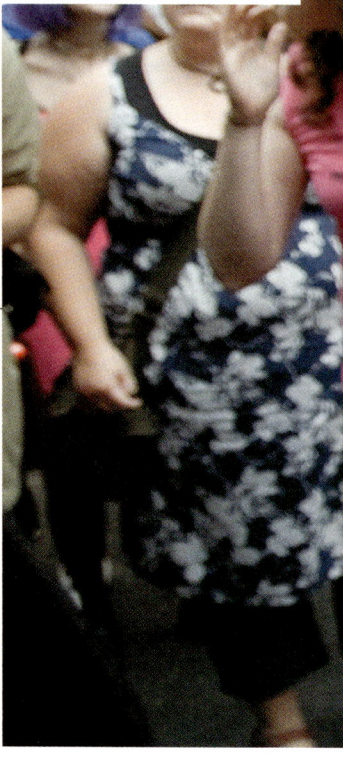

2011 ENGLAND RIOTS

On August 6, 2011, protests broke out in Tottenham, England, after 29-year-old Mark Duggan was shot by police. The protests escalated into riots after protestors clashed with police. Some sociologists have hypothesized that idleness was behind the riots (a result of many youth centres in Britain losing funding after government cuts).

Anyone who has ever taken part in a riot, or even just hovered on the periphery of one, knows how exhilarating it can be. Windows smashed, cars torched, stores looted—it's like being in the middle of a video game. Yet there is a tendency to try to psychoanalyze society and interpret the mob's behaviour as a symptom of some great underlying malaise: hockey's culture of macho violence in the case of the Stanley Cup riot in Vancouver, racism or poverty or the welfare state in the case of the looting that hopscotched across England in August 2011.

People are over-thinking things way too much. Any proper discussion of a riot and why it happens has to start with the recognition that rioting, especially for young men, is a huge amount of fun. At any given moment, there are far more people willing to riot and loot than we like to admit. The only reason there isn't more of it is that if you do it by yourself or in a small group, you'll almost certainly get caught. But if you can get enough people to riot, you can all get away with it, which is why when it comes to getting one started, what the participants are faced with is essentially a coordination problem. The trick is getting a critical mass of people willing to do it, in the same place, and at the same time.

Certain events, like Game 7 of the Stanley Cup Final, have become reliable opportunities to riot—a bunch of people show up precisely because they know that a lot of other people will also be showing up to riot. Another reliable opportunity is any sort of anti-authority protest, such as a meeting of the G20 or—what sparked the events in Tottenham before they spread all over England—a demonstration against police violence. No matter how peaceful the initial gathering is meant to be, it is easily overwhelmed by those who are there just to smash stuff.

... delinquents have discovered the flash mob, using social networking tools like Twitter and BlackBerry Messenger to organize riots with unprecedented speed and efficiency.

All that has happened in the past year or so is that delinquents have discovered the flash mob, using social networking tools like Twitter and BlackBerry Messenger to organize riots with unprecedented speed and efficiency. Hipsters have been organizing flash mobs for years now, flooding into subways and financial districts to have impromptu dance parties or pillow fights. In China, consumers have been using social networking to organize group shopping expeditions, where they descend upon a retailer and use the pressure of 50 or 60 people to extract deep discounts from the shop owners. It is not a big step from there to arranging for a few hundred people to show up to loot an electronics shop or a shoe store, or having a few thousand people get together to torch a department store.

ANALYZING WORD CHOICE

Reread the last two sentences on this page. Andrew Potter is suggesting that the distance between shopping in large groups and looting is really just a small step. You can make inferences about a writer's attitudes, values, fears, and so on, by analyzing word choice.

SOCIAL NETWORKS AND THE ARAB SPRING

In the spring of 2011, protestors in the Middle East and North Africa used social networking sites to organize anti-government protests. These uprisings have collectively been called the *Arab Spring*—using a metaphor to suggest the blossoming of democracy and freedom.

This is a genuine challenge to law enforcement. Organized crime has always been structured along the lines of the family or the state because, for much of human existence, the family and the state have been the most effective mechanisms for solving coordination problems among self-interested individuals. The police have traditionally responded by infiltrating the crime families and other trust networks, using undercover agents, wiretaps, and other staples of police procedurals.

Social media have the obvious capacity to increase the amount of rioting—that's why the Tottenham riot spread so quickly across England, and why the protests of the Arab Spring popped up in so many places at once. On the other hand, technology can also work against the rioters by reducing the impunity that comes with the anonymity of crowds. The most important thing the Toronto police did with the G20 riots was not all the head cracking and the random detentions, but crowdsourcing the identities of people who were photographed committing crimes. The Vancouver police have been busy gathering videos and images of the rioters, and Scotland Yard is now doing likewise.

They won't catch everyone, but they might identify enough people that it will serve as a significant deterrent to future riots. But to really put an end to flash mob rioting, police are going to have to do the social networking equivalent of going undercover. They will have to infiltrate the groups of wannabe rioters, find out their codes and coordination mechanisms, and turn the technology against them.

Protestors confront riot police on June 26, 2010, in Toronto, Ontario, at the G20 Summit.

In the meantime, we need to stop assuming that these occasional flare-ups of mass social unrest are signs of profound social dysfunction. You certainly can't discount the role of unemployment, since being unemployed sharply reduces the risks associated with rioting. If I get caught smashing a shop, I'm probably going to lose my job and my reputation. If a chap on welfare in Tottenham gets caught, what does he have to lose? If anything, a spell in prison will only increase his status.

> Those horrible people writing those nasty things aren't drooling troglodytes sitting in their parents' basements; they are your husbands and wives, your colleagues, your doctor and your lawyer, and everyone else you know.

Yet if you don't believe that almost anyone can take genuine pleasure in the antisocial behaviour that anonymity enables, then you haven't been reading the comment boards on the Internet, or you've never scanned the graffiti in the typical public bathroom stall. Those horrible people writing those nasty things aren't drooling troglodytes sitting in their parents' basements; they are your husbands and wives, your colleagues, your doctor and your lawyer, and everyone else you know.

Do you want to know what sort of person joins in a riot and trashes their city and loots their neighbour's shop? Just look around you. Or better, look in the mirror. Rioting is fun, and we'd all do it if we could. ◆

RESPONDING

DISCUSSION QUESTIONS

ANALYZING PERSPECTIVE
What attitude does Andrew Potter express toward riots in the opening paragraphs of this opinion piece? What specific evidence suggests this? Compare his attitude to your own or to the attitudes of those you know.

ANALYZING IDEAS
Identify how Potter organizes and supports his ideas. Consider whether his organization supports or detracts from the clarity and effectiveness of his message. What is his strongest point? How effectively is it delivered?

CRITICAL LITERACY
Discuss Potter's statement that "rioting, especially for young men, is a huge amount of fun." Why might some find his statement to be insensitive, offensive, or even flawed? Look through the text for other statements that might spark debate or cause offence. Discuss why Potter might have chosen to make these statements.

TASKS

DEVELOPING A COMPARISON
Potter compares organized crime in the past to crimes organized today via social media. Using a graphic organizer, illustrate how the two are similar and different.

PREPARING AN ORAL PRESENTATION
Prepare an oral presentation in response to this opinion piece. Which points from the opinion piece do you agree with? Which points do you disagree with? Create an outline to organize your ideas and opinions. Research these riots to help form your response. Be prepared to deliver your presentation to your class.

ABOUT THE AUTHOR
Andrew Potter is a journalist by trade but a philosopher by training. He is the author of two books about popular culture, including the recent *The Authenticity Hoax: How we get lost finding ourselves*.

> **WHAT DO YOU THINK?** + AGREE — DISAGREE
> "Poetry is nearer to vital truth than history."
> — Plato

DULCE ET DECORUM EST

Poem by Wilfred Owen

Bent double, like old beggars under sacks,
Knock-kneed, coughing like hags, we cursed through sludge,
Till on the haunting flares we turned our backs,
And towards our distant rest began to trudge.
Men marched asleep. Many had lost their boots,
But limped on, blood-shod. All went lame, all blind;
Drunk with fatigue; deaf even to the hoots
Of gas-shells dropping softly behind.

Gas! Gas! Quick, boys!—An ecstasy of fumbling
Fitting the clumsy helmets just in time,
But someone still was yelling out and stumbling
And flound'ring like a man in fire or lime.—
Dim through the misty panes and thick green light,
As under a green sea, I saw him drowning.

In all my dreams before my helpless sight
He plunges at me, guttering, choking, drowning.

If in some smothering dreams, you too could pace
Behind the wagon that we flung him in,
And watch the white eyes writhing in his face,
His hanging face, like a devil's sick of sin,
If you could hear, at every jolt, the blood
Come gargling from the froth-corrupted lungs
Bitter as the cud
Of vile, incurable sores on innocent tongues,—
My friend, you would not tell with such high zest
To children ardent for some desperate glory,
The old Lie: Dulce et decorum est
Pro patria mori.

LATIN TRANSLATION

Dulce et decorum est is Latin for "it is a sweet and fitting thing," the first part of a statement that is completed in the last line of the poem, *"pro patria mori,"* which means "to die for your country." The lines are originally from a poem by Horace, a Roman poet from the first century BCE.

And He Said, Fight On

Poem by Pauline Johnson

Time and its ally, Dark Disarmament,
Have compassed me about,
Have massed their armies, and on battle bent
My forces put to rout;
But though I fight alone, and fall, and die,
Talk terms of Peace? Not I.

They war upon my fortress, and their guns
Are shattering its walls;
My army plays the cowards' part, and runs,
Pierced by a thousand balls;
They call for my surrender. I reply,
"Give quarter now? Not I."

They've shot my flag to ribbons, but in rents
It floats above the height;
Their ensign shall not crown my battlements
While I can stand and fight.
I fling defiance at them as I cry,
"Capitulate? Not I."

ANALYZING CONTEXT

Reread this poem and consider the following information: Pauline Johnson wrote this poem shortly after doctors told her she was dying. She took her title from the poem "The Revenge: A Ballad of the Fleet" by Lord Alfred Tennyson.

RESPONDING

DISCUSSION QUESTIONS

ANALYZING VOICE
Read one of these poems aloud and describe the speaker's voice. Support your response.

COMPARING TEXTS
Compare and contrast the poems, examining their ideas, themes, values, and use of language, as well as how they connect to the theme of conflict.

METACOGNITION
What strategies and skills help you interpret poetry?

TASKS

DEVELOPING TWEETS
Choose one of the poems and imagine you are its speaker. Create a series of tweets for that person that captures the poem's message or theme.

PRESENTING THE POEM
Choose one of these poems to present to your class. Prepare for the presentation by experimenting with volume, tone, pacing, emphasis, pauses, expression, and gestures. Before you begin, listen to some recordings of the poem.

RESEARCH AND INQUIRY
Research the life and work of one of these poets. Prepare a presentation, including poems or other writings, a brief biography, and a conclusion about how the poet influenced others.

ABOUT THE AUTHORS

Wilfred Owen (1893–1918) was one of the leading British poets of World War I. His realistic poetry about the horrors of war was very different from what other poets were writing about at the time. Owen was killed one week before World War I ended.

Pauline Johnson (1861–1913), also known as Tekahionwake, was a popular Canadian poet and performer. She travelled all over Canada, the United States, and the United Kingdom reciting her poetry. Her performances often celebrated her First Nations heritage and incorporated artifacts she inherited from her father, a Mohawk chief.

Teen on Strike

Newspaper Article by Tamie Dolny, from the *Toronto Star*, July 15, 2009

> **WHAT DO YOU THINK?**
> During any sort of conflict, respect is essential.
> + AGREE
> − DISAGREE

I'm supposed to be working as a lifeguard and swimming instructor this summer at Etobicoke's Memorial Pool. Instead, as a member of CUPE Local 79, I'm on strike. And on Canada Day, I picketed at the Ingram Transfer Station.

I've never really spent time with a group of men. Boys, certainly, but not honest-to-goodness men. And to tell you the truth, they're not that different—just bigger, smellier, hairier, taller, and wider. During a strike, they're also incredibly interesting.

How could Canada Day be boring when your mother drives you to a dump site in the middle of nowhere, smiles and waves at you, and then drives away, screeching her tires?

Just 16, I was left to fend for myself in the testosterone jungle of picketing members of CUPE Locals 79 and 416.

Ingram Transfer Station, I learned, is code for a dump-and-run garbage zone where peeved-off unemployed workers stand around and burn stuff. It was the most potentially dangerous situation I'd ever been in at seven in the morning. Tall, ferocious-looking unionized garbage workers and office staff stood around amid piles of rotting trash. There was nobody, aside from me, under the age of 25. So I set myself down on a curb, rested my head in my hands, and glared at everyone in that I-am-a-spoiled-teenager-and-I-don't-want-to-be-here fashion.

Little did I know how much I would learn.

I'm not your typical city worker. As a teenager, I fervently practise three activities: staying up too late, talking back to my parents, and giggling about boys. Going on strike was not part of my summer plans.

I started off not caring at all about the actual meaning of the dispute: I was there for the strike pay, not to support my fellow workers. If I worked for just four hours a day, five days a week, CUPE 79 would pay me $200. For a student like me, that seems like decent enough money. I soon got a reality check.

I am currently scheduled at the York Civic Centre, where I picket in the back parking lot. On my first day, a woman brought along her two-year-old toddler, for whom she couldn't find daycare. The second day, I overheard another woman talking about being behind on her phone bill.

We've been striking for nearly four weeks now: $200 times four equals $800, right?

In an expensive city like Toronto, $800 barely manages to cover rent, if you're lucky. On top of that are food, clothes, utility bills, and miscellaneous needs and desires. Some people live from paycheque to paycheque. A strike could cost them their home and credit rating.

You might wonder, "Why are you on strike? And why should I care?" Well, first, when your parents tell you to go on picket duty instead of sitting around watching TV, as a dependent child, you tend to do what you're told. It's particularly ironic because my father is a manager for the City of Toronto. Imagine our dinner conversations.

ANALYZING VOICE

The use of first person in a newspaper article is unusual and gives this selection a distinctive voice; the article is more personal and informal. As you read, consider how the article would have sounded if the third person had been used.

And why should you care? Because it's so incredibly, mindbogglingly unfair. The public isn't on our side. Most of the summer workers like me aren't even on our side.

I know that, and all unionized workers know that. But stay with me.

Under their current contract, which expires in 2010, Toronto police get a pay raise of at least 3 percent each year, and had to make no concessions. Toronto firefighters, public transit workers, and Toronto Housing workers also get an increase of 3 percent annually with no concessions. Even city councillors got a pay raise of 2.4 percent while arguing that the city cannot afford any more union pay raises.

When initially discussing our contract with Mayor David Miller, Local 79 president Ann Dembinski reported back to the union that the city was offering something along the lines of a 0 percent raise in the first year and a 1 percent raise in the second year. As workers, we could lose money that first year because of inflation. That's pretty vile.

Back at Ingram Transfer Station, I was soon forgotten in the maze of litter and trash bags and overwhelming stench of garbage. So I continued sitting, nearly getting my feet squished by cars, the drivers eager to drop off their stinky secrets.

Lying low turned out to be a good idea, since by that point two fights had nearly broken out between garbage dumpers and strikers, due to the overpowering scent of maleness and that crazy, I-am-tougher-and-more-macho-than-you emotion in the air.

Even so, in most of the cases when verbal fights did break out, they were started by people impatient about waiting an extra 15 minutes to dump their trash because of the picket. When one guy hissed in the face of a striker, the striker hurled insults back at him. But, if certain media had been present, the striker's behaviour would probably have been described as "unprovoked," right?

I can barely claim to understand the complexities of the labour dispute. However, I can say that it's mean and hurtful when a man parks his car and grinds his wheels against the pavement, releasing pungent fumes and causing the pregnant woman who was picketing with me to start coughing.

I can say that it's insulting and degrading when a patron decides to drive through the crowd of strikers, nearly bowling us all over. I can especially say that it's so, so painfully wrong to be malicious, rude, and spiteful to a group of people who just want to make a point for 15 minutes of your day.

I'm just pleading for a bit of respect, really. You don't need to agree with what the unions are fighting for. All you need to do is grant us the basic dignity any human being deserves. Don't get angry. You'll get to where you need to go … just a couple of minutes later, that's all. ◆

RESPONDING

DISCUSSION QUESTIONS

ANALYZING PURPOSE AND AUDIENCE
What was Tamie Dolny's purpose in writing this article? What did she want the audience to believe? Support your responses.

MAKING INFERENCES
Based on her language, what inferences can you make about Dolny and how she views those with whom she is picketing? How do her views change as the strike lingers?

ANALYZING CONTEXT
Read the About the Author below and then reread the newspaper article. Look for evidence in the article that Dolny wrote it in direct response to public anger about the strike. What did the newspaper achieve or hope to achieve by having a teenaged, part-time worker write the article?

TASKS

CONDUCTING A SURVEY
Prepare and conduct a survey to explore generational perceptions of strikes. Subjects for the survey should include people from your generation and an older generation. When finished, prepare an oral report on your findings.

RESEARCH AND INQUIRY
Using the Internet and other resources, learn more about labour strikes and other forms of protest. What do these types of protests have in common? Are they effective? Present your findings in an expository report. Use an appropriate citation method.

ABOUT THE AUTHOR
This article was written as a worker response to public anger against the union Local 79 during the Toronto City Workers' strike in the summer of 2009. At the time of publication, Dolny was a 16-year-old lifeguard working for the City of Toronto. Her article captures her experiences on the picket line.

WHAT DO YOU THINK? + AGREE — DISAGREE
It takes guts to tell the truth.

Remembering Joyce Atcheson

Letter of Remembrance by Jody Porter, from *Wawatay News*, December 6, 2012

I could fill a whole newspaper with the teachings I received from Joyce Atcheson.

But the one I feel compelled to share on Joyce's passing seems even more relevant today than it was a decade ago when we worked together at *Wawatay News*.

It was late, as it often was in the newspaper office, and we were pushing the deadline to get an important story out: an employee from a big company that operated in Nishnawbe Aski Nation (NAN) territory had made racist comments toward a family from Kitchenuhmaykoosib.

It's never easy for someone to talk about being the target of something so demeaning, and it was almost unheard of back then for racism to become news.

But Joyce had tracked down the people the comment was directed at and earned their trust.

As the editor, it was my job to decide whether to print the story. As the reporter, it was Joyce's name and reputation that would stand beside it.

It felt like we were staring over the edge of a cliff ... both exhilarating and terrifying.

We were about to take a run at a company that seemed to "own" NAN.

Think of every journalistic cliché you want: we were slaying a giant; we were exposing the nakedness of the proverbial emperor; we were uncovering the TRUTH.

The opportunities to do such things in the media are not as common as you might think. It takes guts and there is often little glory in it.

You rip off a bandage, and people start blaming you for making them stare at an exposed wound.

Still, Joyce and I were giddy with the thought of doing justice to the experience of the people who had been hurt by the remarks.

That's when the phone rang.

The head of the corporation was returning Joyce's call ... finally. He yelled at her and threatened her and told her not to run the story.

He reminded her of his clout, of what a good "corporate citizen" he was, of all the charities he supported, of all the fine things he did for the people of the North.

"Just because you take someone out for dinner, it doesn't give you the right to slap them in the face," Joyce said.

He hung up on her, angrier than ever.

ANALYZING LITERARY DEVICES

Jody Porter highlights some of the clichés that came to mind when she and Joyce Atcheson considered running the story ("slaying a giant," "over the edge of a cliff," "you rip off a bandage"). Consider how these very evocative expressions help you understand the events and the issues Porter is sharing with readers.

And Joyce laughed.

She laughed and laughed, that great resounding chuckle of hers that could erase all the tension in a room in an instant.

She stood up from her desk and mimed the act of stirring an enormous vat of soup with a giant spoon. She so loved to "stir the pot." And then she laughed some more.

We ran the story.

And in the rarest of journalistic experiences, it resulted in change.

Joyce's story prompted other people to speak out about their experiences of racism with the company. We ran their stories, too.

There was more anger from the owner, and a few uneasy weeks wondering if the paper would survive it all. The company was a major advertiser and had ties to powerful people within NAN.

But, eventually, there was an apology from the company and an acknowledgment that First Nations people deserved more than charity given with one hand, while the other slapped them in the face.

Of all the things I learned from Joyce, this is what sticks with me the most: Never be afraid to stand up for what you believe in, even if it means you have to go hungry for a while.

I will miss my great friend, her wisdom, her courage, her incredible generosity of spirit, the way she greeted every single person she met with a smile.

An Elder tells me these things are not lost to me; I need only access them in a different way.

If we share Joyce's stories with each other, and have a good laugh the next time we meet, I'll know that's true. ◆

RESPONDING

DISCUSSION QUESTIONS

EVALUATING
Do you agree or disagree with Jody Porter's character assessment of Joyce Atcheson? Explain.

MAKING INFERENCES
If a letter of remembrance about Atcheson were written by the head of the corporation mentioned in this selection, how might he characterize Atcheson?

ANALYZING LITERARY DEVICES
Analyze the evocative expressions Porter uses. Which expression do you find most effective? How does it add to the voice of the text?

TASKS

RESPONDING PERSONALLY
Imagine that you have read this letter online. Write the comment you would post in response.

SHARING STORIES
Recall a time when you or someone you know had to stand up for a cause. Share the circumstances surrounding the event. Listen as others share their stories. Choose one of the stories to use as the basis for a skit that clearly presents your conclusions about standing up for a cause.

ABOUT THE AUTHOR
Jody Porter is a CBC journalist who reports on social justice issues in northwestern Ontario. She is based in Thunder Bay, Ontario. She worked at *Wawatay News* with Joyce Atcheson from 1998 to 2002.

WHAT DO YOU THINK NOW?

Think back to your original response to this statement:

"When you avoid conflict, you avoid learning."

How has your thinking about this statement changed since you began this unit?

Preparing a Presentation

Choose a selection from this unit that demonstrates how ineffective listening and/or speaking strategies have led to conflict. Discuss what specifically broke down in the communication process. What role do you think effective listening and/or speaking strategies have in bringing about a resolution to the conflict?

Be prepared to present your ideas and analysis to the class using a digital format that includes audio and visuals. While preparing your presentation, be mindful of the oral and visual strategies you will need to effectively communicate to your audience.

Comparing Texts

Choose two selections from this unit that best demonstrate your response to the unit statement: "When you avoid conflict, you avoid learning." Demonstrate your response to the statement and an understanding of the texts through an essay that includes visuals.

Writing a Short Story

Review the nonfiction selections in this unit. Choose one as inspiration for developing a short story. Begin by brainstorming ideas for the story's theme, characters, problem, and solution. Write your story, using voice effectively to develop your characters. Ask your peers for feedback.

Creating a Media Text

Choose the selection in this unit that best connects with your feelings about the unit statement: "When you avoid conflict, you avoid learning." Create one of the following media products to demonstrate your understanding of the text and your feelings about the conflict within it:

- a digital presentation with audio and visuals
- a video interview that has the characters discussing their conflict
- a storyboard for a movie trailer based on the conflict

innovation

WHAT DO YOU THINK?

What drives innovation?

Unit Learning Goals

- responding personally, critically, and creatively
- analyzing expository writing and the essay
- analyzing codes, conventions, and techniques
- organizing ideas

Talk About It

Grow your own tissue with nano-scaffolding
Frank Ko, at University of British Columbia, researches human tissue regeneration

Sounds of hope
Inspired by her family, Kayla Cornale develops teaching system that allows autistic children to learn through music

Poll Results

What is the impact of innovation?

95% Competition
feel innovation can drive a more competitive economy

91% Go Green
feel innovation can create a greener economy

88% Jobs
feel innovation is the best way to create jobs

86% Partnership
feel partnership is more important than stand-alone success

87% Society
feel we should bring value to society as a whole not only to individuals

Improve Lives
can successfully change citizens' lives in the next 10 years in:

90%	87%	84%	84%
Communications	Health Quality	Job Market	Environmental Quality

Hadfield Tweets with Starfleet

On January 3, 2013, William Shatner, a Canadian actor best known for his role as Captain Kirk in the original *Star Trek* series, opened up a hailing frequency to Canadian astronaut Chris Hadfield.

> **William Shatner** @WilliamShatner — 3 Jan
> @Cmdr_Hadfield Are you tweeting from space? MBB
> Expand

> **Chris Hadfield** @Cmdr_Hadfield — 3 Jan
> @WilliamShatner Yes, Standard Orbit, Captain. And we're detecting signs of life on the surface.
> View conversation

> "At first people refuse to believe that a strange new thing can be done, then they see it can be done—then it is done and all the world wonders why it was not done centuries ago."
>
> —Frances Hodgson Burnett

FOCUS ON reading

> "'Isn't it odd how much fatter a book gets when you've read it several times?' Mo had said ... 'As if something were left between the pages every time you read it. Feelings, thoughts, sounds, smells ... and then, when you look at the book again many years later, you find yourself there, too, a slightly younger self, slightly different, as if the book had preserved you like a pressed flower ... both strange and familiar.'"
> —Cornelia Funke, *Inkspell*

RESPONDING PERSONALLY, CRITICALLY, AND CREATIVELY

Whether the text is a story, essay, poster, speech, or play, readers participate in making meaning. Although the ideas that a writer presents are important, prior knowledge is also important when responding personally, critically, and creatively.

> **// WHAT TO DO WHEN YOU CAN'T MAKE PERSONAL CONNECTIONS**
>
> At times, responding personally might require you to go beyond your own experiences and to consider the experiences of family or friends.

RESPONDING PERSONALLY

When you respond personally, you are connecting your own experiences and prior knowledge to the new experience(s) in the text. Consider the following:

- What thoughts or feelings do you have about the text? Why?
- How does the text connect to your life? How does this connection help you interpret the text?
- How did the writer expect you to respond? Why did you or didn't you respond as expected?

RESPONDING CRITICALLY

When you respond critically to a text, you are examining, analyzing, and judging its ideas, purpose, point of view, and organizational structure. A critical response moves beyond reading for information (or facts) to reading with the intention of critically analyzing ideas and the way these ideas are developed. Consider the following:

- What assumptions does the writer bring to the text? What argument or perspective does the writer present? Do you agree?
- What evidence supports the writer's point of view? Is the evidence biased or exclusionary?
- When was the text written? How does it reflect the time period in which it was written? Does it support or challenge what is now acceptable?
- How has your personal response influenced your critical response?

> **// CONTEXT AND CRITICAL RESPONSE**
>
> The quality of critical response is heightened when you understand the context in which a work is created. Having knowledge of the writer's world can help you develop the fullest meaning of a text.

RESPONDING CREATIVELY

When you respond creatively, you are transferring your understanding of the ideas in a text into a creative world beyond that text. The most effective creative responses are related in very direct ways to the arguments, assumptions, themes, and characters found in the original text. Consider the following:

- When will the events in your response occur? (Before, during, or after the original text?)
- What voice or point of view will you use? (The same as the original, or a new voice or point of view?)
- Where will you focus your creative response? (On the whole text, or on a particular part of the text?) Consider what motivates that choice.
- What form will your response take? (Paper, live, or digital?)

Earth
(A Gift Shop)

Short Story by Charles Yu

Come to Earth! Yes, that Earth. A lot of people think we're closed during construction, but we are not! We're still open for business.

Admittedly, it's a little confusing.

First, we were Earth: The Planet. Then life formed, and that was a great and good time.

Then, for a little while, we were Earth: A Bunch of Civilizations!

Until the fossil fuels ran out and all of the nation states collapsed, and a lucky few escaped Earth and went out in search of new worlds to colonize.

Then, for what seemed like forever, we were Earth: Not Much Going on Here Anymore.

And that lasted for a long time. Followed by another pretty long time. Which was then followed by a really long time.

// **Making Inferences**

Readers can analyze voice, sentence structure, and word choice to help them make inferences about who is speaking, when the story is set, and what has happened prior to the story starting (the back story).

Then, after a while, humans, having semi-successfully established colonies on other planets, started to come back to Earth on vacation. Parents brought their kids, teachers brought their classes on field trips, retirees came in groups of twenty or thirty. They wanted to see where their ancestors had come from. But there was nothing here. Kids and parents and teachers left disappointed. That's it? they would ask, or some would even say, It was OK, I guess, but I thought there would be more.

So, being an enterprising species and all, some of us got together and reinvented ourselves as Earth: The Museum, which we thought was a great idea.

We pooled our resources and assembled what we could find. To be sure, there was not a whole lot of good stuff left after the collapse of Earth: A Bunch of Civilizations! The main attraction of the museum was the painting we had by some guy of some flowers. No one could remember the name of the guy or the painting, or even the flowers, but we were all pretty sure it was an important painting at some point in the history of paintings and also the history of people, so we put that in the biggest room in the centre of everything.

But parents and teachers, being humans (and especially being descendants of the same humans who messed everything up in the first place), thought the whole museum was quite boring, or even very boring, and they would say as much, even while we

were still within earshot, and we could hear them saying that to each other, about how bored they were. That hurt to hear, but more than that, what was hurtful was that no one was coming to Earth anymore, now that it was a small and somewhat eclectic museum. And who could blame them? After the collapse of civilization, school just has never been the same. By the time kids are done their five years of mandatory schooling, they are eight or even nine years old and more than ready to join the leisure force as full-time professional consumers. Humans who went elsewhere have carried on that tradition from their days on Earth. They are ready to have their credit accounts opened, for their spending to be tracked, to get started in their lifelong loyalty rewards programs—especially those humans who are rich enough to be tourists coming back here to Earth.

Eventually, one of us realized that the most popular part of the museum was the escalator ride. Although you would think interstellar travel would have sort of raised the bar on what was needed to impress people, there was just something about moving diagonally that seemed to amuse the tourists, both kids and adults. And then one of us finally woke up and said, well, why not give them what they want?

So, we did some research, in the few books we had left and on the computer, and the research confirmed our hypothesis: Humans love rides.

> //Making Connections
>
> Responding personally, critically, or creatively to "Earth (A Gift Shop)" requires the reader to make connections. Understanding human behaviour is critical to understanding the satire in this story.

Earth (A Gift Shop)

So Earth: The Museum was shuttered for several years while we reinvented ourselves and developed merchandise and attractions—all of the things we were naturally good at—and after another good long while, we finally were able to reopen as Earth: The Theme Park and Gift Shop, which did OK, but it was not too long before we realized the theme park part of it was expensive to operate and kind of a hassle, really, as our engineering was not so good and we kept making people sick or, in a few cases, really misjudging G-forces, and word got out among the travel agencies that Earth: The Theme Park and Gift Shop was not so fun and actually quite dangerous, so we really had no choice but to drop the theme park part, and that is how we became Earth: The Gift Shop.

Which was all anyone ever wanted anyway. To get a souvenir to take home.

We do have some great souvenirs.

Our top-selling items for the month of October:

1. History: The Poster! From the Age before Tools, through the short-lived but exciting Age of Tools, to the (yawn) Age of Learning, and into our current age, the Age after the Age of Learning.
2. War: The Soundtrack. A three-minute musical interpretation of the experience of war, with solos for guitar and drums.
3. Art: The Poster! Beautiful paintings of a nature scene. Very realistic looking, almost like a photograph.
4. Science: The Video Game. All the science you ever need to bother with! Almost nothing to learn.
5. Summer in a Bottle. Now comes in two odours: "Mist of Nostalgia" and "Lemony Fresh."

All of the items above also come in ring tones, T-shirts, cups, and key chains.

And coming for the holidays, get ready for the latest installment of Earth's greatest artistic work of the last century: Hero Story: A Hero's Redemption (and Sweet Revenge), a computer-generated script based on all the key points of the archetypal story arc that we humans are.

Which brings us back to our original point. What was our original point? Oh yeah, Earth: The Gift Shop is still here. Not just here, but doing great! OK, maybe not great, but OK, we're OK. We would be better if you came by and shopped here. Which is why we sent you this audio catalogue, which we hope you are reading (otherwise, we are talking to ourselves). Earth: The Gift Shop: The Brochure. Some people have said the name, Earth: The Gift Shop, is a bit confusing because it makes it seem like this is the official gift shop of some other attraction here on Earth, when really the attraction is the gift shop itself. So, we are considering changing our name to Earth (A Gift Shop), which sounds less official but is probably more accurate.

//Epic Stories

Charles Yu refers to the "archetypal story arc that we humans are." An *archetype* is a theme or character that recurs across stories, myths, popular culture, and so on. The *archetypal story arc* is an extended storyline that weaves people and events together across a series (novels, TV shows, or movies—such as *Star Wars* or *Lord of the Rings*). With his allusion, Yu suggests that human history is really just one long story with recurring themes, issues, people, and ideas.

RESPONDING

DISCUSSION QUESTIONS

RESPONDING PERSONALLY
How are the humans described in this story similar to humans today? Is the depiction of humans favourable? Explain.

ANALYZING VOICE
Describe the narrator's voice in this story. How do word choice and sentence structure help to create that voice? Why has Charles Yu given the narrator this voice?

METACOGNITION
What helped you respond personally or critically to this short story? How could you respond creatively to it? Why would you respond that way?

TASKS

WRITING TO RESPOND
What is Yu saying about society both today and in the future? Explain in at least one complete paragraph. Support your ideas with details from the story.

PERFORMING THE STORY
With a partner, take turns reading aloud parts of this story using a tone of voice that you believe accurately reflects the narrator's voice. Experiment with pacing, pauses, and the volume and pitch of your voice. Describe to your partner how reading the story aloud affects your understanding and response to it.

So, again, we say, come to Earth! We get millions of visitors a year, from near and far. Maybe you are coming because you just want to look, or to say you were here. Maybe you are coming to have a story to tell when you get back. Maybe you just want to be able to say, I went home. Even if it isn't home, was never your home, is not anyone's home anymore, maybe you just want to say, I touched the ground there, breathed the air, looked at the moon the way people must have done nine or ten or a hundred thousand years ago. So you can say to your friends, if only for a moment or two, I was a human on Earth. Even if all I did was shop there. ◆

ABOUT THE AUTHOR

Charles Yu is the author of one novel (*How to Live Safely in a Science Fictional Universe*) and two short-story collections (*Sorry Please Thank You* and *Third Class Superhero*). Yu's science fiction and fantasy stories have been published in several magazines and literary journals.

WHAT DO YOU THINK?

We are nothing without our dreams.

+ AGREE
− DISAGREE

Mother of Invention

Poem by Celia Berrell

Neotenic humankind
is ceaseless of inquiring mind.
With science and technology,
the stopper's out, dynamically!

From fire to furnaced energy;
from steam to electricity.
We modify genetically,
and glean the stars effectively.

We can't slow down this gain in pace.
The fascination's well in place.
Much to learn—with good intention,
drives this mother of invention.

ANALYZING LITERARY DEVICES

Poets can play with language in many different ways. For example, one of these poets uses rhyme and rhythm with very structured stanzas, while the other uses a free-verse poem without rhymes.

Dreamer

Poem by Langston Hughes

I take my dreams
And make of them a bronze vase,
And a wide round fountain
With a beautiful statue in its center,
And a song with a broken heart,
And I ask you:
Do you understand my dreams?
Sometimes you say you do
And sometimes you say you don't.
Either way
It doesn't matter.
I continue to dream.

RESPONDING

DISCUSSION QUESTIONS

COMPARING TEXTS
Compare the language, literary devices, and messages in these two poems. How does comparing the poems affect your understanding of each?

RESPONDING PERSONALLY
Which poem do you connect with more? Why? Read the About the Authors information below. How does that information affect your response to each poem?

VISUAL LITERACY
Evaluate how effectively the image for each poem captures its mood and message, and whether the images work well together.

TASKS

RESPONDING CREATIVELY
Choose two or three lines from one of these poems. Decide how you will respond creatively to those lines (e.g., create a digital photo essay, write your own poem, or choreograph a dance). Share your work to see if you have captured what you wanted to in your response.

RESEARCH AND INQUIRY
Choose one of these poems. Research a new poem that presents a different perspective. Develop a compare–contrast essay.

ABOUT THE AUTHORS
Australian poet Celia Berrell became inspired to create poetry for science students after writing poems in response to a friend's nature-inspired artwork. Berrell successfully combines her two passions—science and rhymes—as a way of helping students learn about science.

James Langston Hughes (1902–1967) was a highly acclaimed American author who wrote poetry, novels, short stories, and plays. Much of his work was inspired by his passion for language and music, but he also wrote to shed light on the hardships African Americans in the United States faced during his lifetime.

> **WHAT DO YOU THINK?**
> Innovation is more than just new technology.

Samantha Nutt: A Letter from 12 WAR ZONES

Interview by Maura Kelly

Through her organization, War Child, Samantha Nutt empowers children and families in areas of conflict. Nutt was appointed to the Order of Canada in 2011.

From Samantha Nutt's website: Dr. Samantha Nutt is a medical doctor and the Founder/Executive Director of War Child in North America. For 15 years, she has been at the front line of many of the world's major crises—from Iraq to Afghanistan, Somalia to the Congo, and Sierra Leone to Darfur. With her uncompromising and powerful advocacy for justice and peace, she has inspired thousands of people across the continent to see global conflict as a problem that can and must be solved.

Nutt was recently named one of Canada's 25 most influential figures by the Globe and Mail, *the latest in a long list of awards and tributes.* Time Magazine *named her one of Canada's Five Leading Activists, while the* World Economic Forum *recognized her as one of 200 young global leaders. In 2010, she was awarded the Order of Ontario and, in 2011, she was appointed to the Order of Canada.*

Nutt meets with local children to assess their needs in the Afar region of Ethiopia.

Q: What was your first experience as a humanitarian doctor?

A: I'd always been interested in human rights issues, and women's health in particular, and the relationship between the two. So when I was 25, after graduating from medical school, I went to Baidoa—Somalia's "City of Death"—to do UNICEF research on how war affects women's health. This was the mid-nineties; 300 000 people there had died of disease and starvation. Somalia was the black eye of the world, a humanitarian effort that had unravelled. The lawlessness was shocking. You couldn't go anywhere without armed security guards. At every turn, every good deed I thought I might do was thwarted by the anarchy and the rampant proliferation of small arms in that country.

Q: What did you learn from your experience?

A: I went into Somalia thinking the solutions were easy, and came out realizing how incredibly complex the situation was (and 20 years later, it's still the same). But once I was exposed to the horror of war and saw the courage of the women and kids there, the adversity they live with every day, I couldn't ignore it.

Q: What event in your learning curve prompted you to start War Child?

A: I was in Liberia [in 1997, when the country was under the control of warlord Charles Taylor] to do UNICEF research. A physician's assistant, a Liberian who was running a UN clinic there, was suspected of selling medical supplies to a local market, and I'd been asked to confront him.

I show up in this big UN car, and here is this guy who is treating hundreds of people a week, through a food-for-work program. He was selling surplus supplies he hadn't been able to use so that he could feed himself and his family. And he was swapping medications—if he had a surplus of one kind of medication, he'd use it to buy another he needed. He was probably making $5 a week. He hadn't been given the food he'd been promised [as compensation], and I was the first UN worker he'd seen in three months. The man's actions were, morally, wholly justifiable, and I thought, *We can't keep chasing our tails. We need to allow people on the ground to be involved in their own reconstruction.*

War Child does exactly that, working with local partners, like government ministries and community groups, in countries wrestling with war. Most of our overseas staff is recruited locally, and the end goal is always that our partners will take full ownership and our presence will no longer be necessary.

THE SOMALI CIVIL WAR

The Somali Civil War began in 1991. In the years following, attempts to bring stability to the region failed. Over 100 000 Somalis have been killed, over 2 million have fled the country, and millions more have been displaced within the country. Today, the civil war rages on and lives continue to be lost.

The Afghanistan Women's Council (some members shown here) and War Child work together to provide microloans to help women start businesses.

Q: Tell us about your two friends who were killed in Iraq.

A: Aquila al-Hashimi was a multilingual Iraqi politician and internationalist from a prominent family. I was able to work in Iraq because she personally vouched for me, which was a huge risk for her. Once [former dictator] Saddam Hussein fell, she was one of three women who were appointed to the interim government. We were having tea in her home, and she said she felt as if Saddam and war had stolen the last 30 years of her life. She said, "I hope it's over, because I'm ready to live my life." I thought she'd be prime minister someday. Instead, in 2003, she was shot and killed.

Margaret Hassan was a British national married to an Iraqi. She'd lived in Iraq since 1972, working for the British Consulate in Baghdad, and she became the head of CARE's program there in 1991. She was on her way to the office one morning in 2004 when armed men kidnapped her. Hundreds of Iraqis marched to demand her release; she'd spent half her life helping wounded and malnourished Iraqi children. And yet she was killed—to protest the British presence in Iraq, it seems. This is still very difficult to talk about. It's so clear how deathly afraid she was, and she was not a person who backed away from difficulty.

HARROWING STATISTICS

As a result of armed conflict, more than 2 million children have died in the last 10 years. In that same time period, more than 20 million children have had to flee their homes because of conflict.

SAMANTHA NUTT ON LEADERSHIP

"A leader has to provide inspiration; to be steadfast in their commitment.... Sometimes I'm told 'no' 50 times.... Leadership involves perseverance and the willingness to go further than others. It's a commitment to integrity, and a refusal to acquiesce when you know it's the right thing."

("Doctor Samantha Nutt Creates Global Change," interview by Barbara Goodman in *Canadian Health & Lifestyle*)

SYNTHESIZING

Use all of the information (interview, photos, captions, etc.) to help you respond critically to the selection and understand what Samantha Nutt has accomplished.

Q: Did the deaths of these women change you?

A: I was angry. I really questioned what we were doing; in my mind, there was no one more emblematic of the humanitarian experience than Margaret. I thought if you had local support and clear objectives, you would be protected. But all those things that we cling to as humanitarian workers no longer counted. What pulled me back was hearing from my partners around the world and from kids in the programs who want to become doctors and lawyers. But we now operate very differently. We try to be as quiet as possible, especially in places like Afghanistan and Iraq. You want to have a very low profile. In some places, I've had to travel around under a carpet in an unmarked car.

Q: In your years of doing this work, is there one survivor who stands out as a symbol of hope?

A: There was a young woman at a camp for displaced people in West Darfur, where she was attending a literacy program we'd been supporting for three months. She'd lived through so much atrocity, and I thought, "What are we doing here? This is never going to be enough [to help her]." She was a new mother; when they heard the militia coming, her family told her to grab her baby boy and go hide. Her mother and father and husband and housemates were gunned down in front of her, and then her house was torched. She arrived at the camp traumatized. She couldn't barter for food at the town market—she couldn't add or subtract—which is why she wanted to be in the literacy program. I asked her, "Has this program helped you?" She leaned forward and proudly wrote her name in the sand and said, "Now that I can write my own name, I will learn how to write my son's." I realized you don't have to have all the answers. But we want to invest in hopefulness. We don't know exactly what will result, but we want to invest in a better and more secure world. ◆

RESPONDING

DISCUSSION QUESTIONS

DRAWING CONCLUSIONS
What does Nutt mean when she says, "You want to have a very low profile"? Why is keeping a low profile important?

CRITICAL THINKING
Why does Nutt, and War Child, support the idea of allowing local "people on the ground to be involved in their own reconstruction"? Why might it be considered the most effective way to aid those in areas of conflict?

TASKS

WRITING EXPOSITORY PARAGRAPHS
In one to three paragraphs, explain why Nutt is or is not a true innovator. Use the interview as a starting point, but also develop a critical inquiry question and research this topic.

DELIVERING A MONOLOGUE
Create a list of words that would be associated with one of the following people in an area of conflict: a child, a parent, a humanitarian worker, or a rebel soldier. Using your list, write a short monologue that the person might give to a news reporter.

DIGITAL LITERACY
Conduct an online search for musical artists who support War Child. Who are these artists and how do they show their support for this organization? Why would War Child consider their support important? Create a digital presentation for your conclusions.

> **WHAT DO YOU THINK?** + AGREE — DISAGREE
> Preserving the past is as important as preparing for the future.

Preserving Knowledge, Empowering Communities

Mapping software brings Inuit oral culture to life

Article by Lisa Gregoire

For decades, cartographers have made maps of Northern Canada, portraying it as a big, empty space with European place names so that people around the world, most of whom would never visit the Arctic, could imagine cold, exotic locations.

But if Northerners made their own maps, what would they look like? What would Inuit put on them? Inuktitut place names, for one, and traditional trails. They would map sea ice and play the voices of Elders talking about animal migrations. Inuit come from an oral tradition: They'd want their maps to talk and to move.

For Fraser Taylor, who coined the term *cybercartography* to describe a "new form of multi-sensory, multimedia, interactive atlas," this was the perfect challenge.

An award-winning and world-renowned geographer at Carleton University's Geomatics and Cartographic Research Centre in Ottawa, Taylor has been working with colleagues since 2005 to help Inuit map their land their way.

"Our multimedia cybercartographic techniques fit so well with their oral culture," says Taylor. "Print is totally inadequate to capture the Inuit storytelling traditions."

MAPS IN THIS CENTURY

Often referred to as *geomatics*, modern maps use digital technology to gather, store, process, and deliver geographic information.

Cybercartography takes geomatics one step further by using digital technologies to gather, organize, analyze, and communicate information in interactive and multi-sensory formats.

Taylor recently received funding from the Canada Foundation for Innovation (CFI) to support much-needed hardware replacement and upgrades to his open-source map-making software he calls *Nunaliit* (*settlement*, *community*, or *habitat* in Inuktitut). Nunaliit has been used to map everything from the risk of urban homelessness in southern cities to snowmobile trails.

For his Northern work, Taylor teamed up with Claudio Aporta, an associate professor in Carleton's department of sociology and anthropology, who specializes in Northern indigenous knowledge. With Aporta's connections and a host of Northern partners, they helped Inuit create several online atlases that allow users to experience Nunavut from the inside out.

Taylor says it is crucial to record that perspective now, since language and local knowledge—of the land, the weather, the animals, and more—are disappearing due to rapid social, climatic, and economic changes.

"In an oral tradition, knowledge dies with the holder of the knowledge," says Taylor. "We need to escape from our silos of specialization into more holistic views of realities, not just in Northern communities but in all communities and all science."

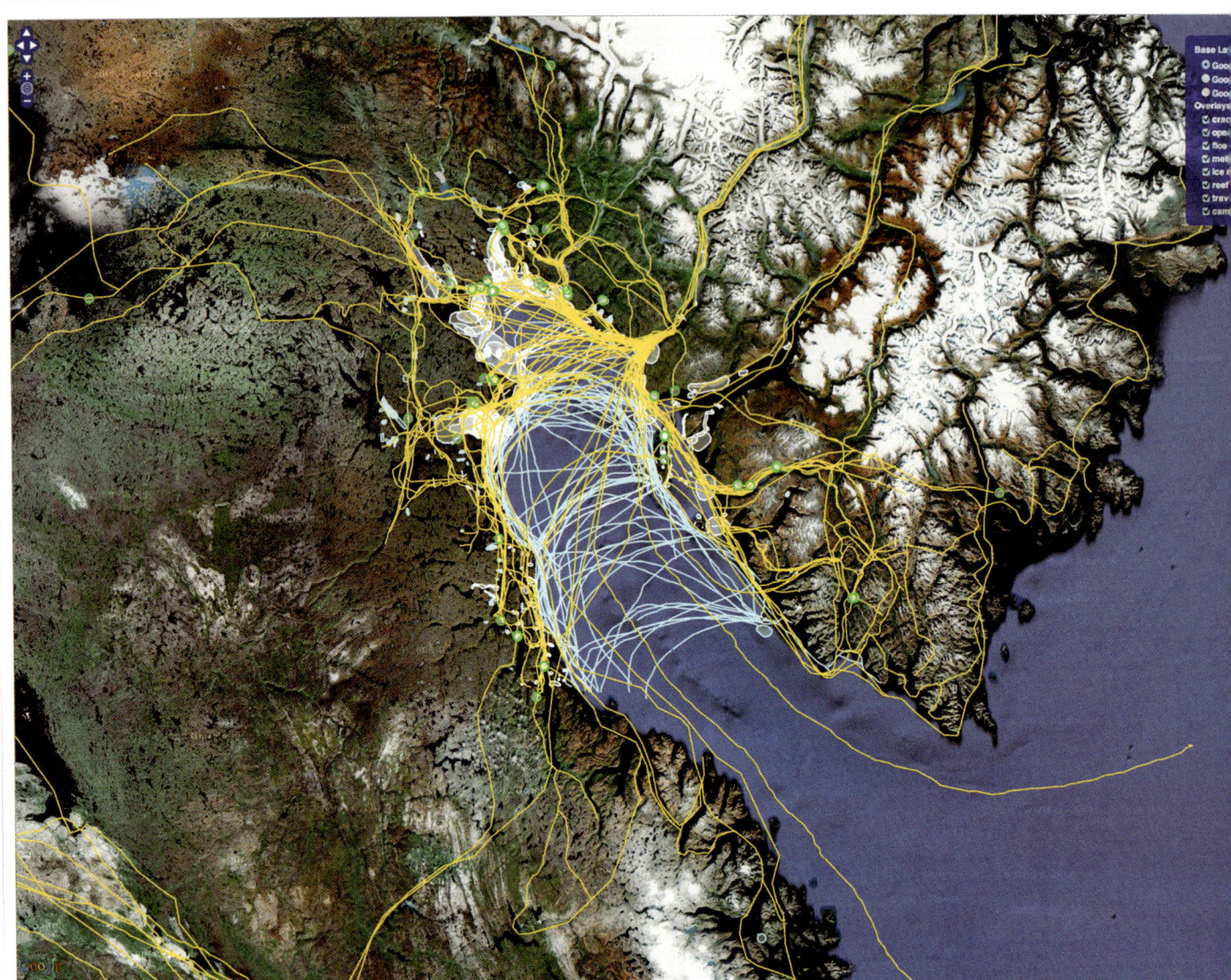

VISUAL LITERACY

Consider traditional maps and the codes, conventions, and techniques you expect them to use. Reflect on how a map of your community would change with cybercartography. What new codes, conventions, and techniques could be used?

It is Nunaliit's flexibility that makes it so special. It can handle multiple forms of data, including video, audio, office documents, and mapping documents. In this way, users can map whatever, and however, they want.

The Inuit *siku* (sea ice) Atlas, for example, contains a wide range of information about the ice around Baffin Island, including translated interviews with hunters on the importance of sea ice and travelling, and their observations on how the ice is changing and why.

Sea ice data is critical not only for Inuit, says Taylor. Localized observations are valuable to researchers around the globe who study Earth's cryosphere.

Some of the CFI funding will go to building local servers—the "distributed data" portion of the project—so that residents can store and retain control over their content. This concept of indigenous empowerment is key to Taylor's work. He wouldn't do it otherwise.

Carleton researcher Fraser Taylor has developed mapping software that enables Inuit to make their own online maps to help preserve their oral culture and traditions. This map documents a variety of things, from ice cracks to trails and camp locations.

> "To my mind, it's a profound tool for reversing discrimination. Whose knowledge is privileged? Whose worldview is privileged?"

Cindy Cowan, Director of Community & Distance Learning programs at Nunavut Arctic College in Iqaluit, met Taylor through the Arctic Bay Atlas project. The college now uses Taylor's cyber atlases to teach students and adults how to participate in external research and conduct their own research using Taylor's software to collate their data.

The atlases also help demystify science for adult learners, says Cowan, many of whom live in small communities, speak Inuktitut as a first language, and may not have had the opportunity to graduate from high school. Inuit discover how they can pursue topics they find relevant and useful.

And the atlas projects also create a profound power shift, since they allow Inuit to switch roles from specimen to scientist. "To my mind, it's a profound tool for reversing discrimination," says Cowan. "Whose knowledge is privileged? Whose worldview is privileged? There have been colonizing relations between Canada and Inuit, between researchers from the South and those who have been researched, and I think we need to decolonize that process. Fraser's work, Nunaliit software, and his vision for how it might be used, is a decolonizing methodology."

As an added bonus, says Cowan, the atlases appeal to youth who yearn for a connection to their Elders and the past but who live in a digital world. In building atlases of their communities, they are building bridges between the two worlds. ◆

RESPONDING

DISCUSSION QUESTIONS

ANALYZING ORGANIZATION
What organizational pattern does Lisa Gregoire use in her article? Explain your response with specific reference to the text.

CRITICAL LITERACY
Discuss the role of cybercartography in empowerment. How does this article change the way you think about the power of maps?

CRITICAL THINKING
The reader is told that Fraser Taylor believes "it is crucial to record that [Inuit] perspective now." Why does he believe there is such urgency? Do you agree with him? Explain.

TASKS

CREATING AN ANNOTATED MAP
Create a map of your neighbourhood, city, or region, identifying 10 to 15 specific locations where different events have occurred. For each of those locations, create at least one annotation (e.g., an explanation, an image with a caption, or an anecdote) that documents the event in some way.

RESEARCH AND INQUIRY
Develop a critical inquiry question to explore one of the ideas raised in this article. Conduct research to answer your question. Develop a digital or oral presentation to share your conclusions.

ABOUT THE AUTHOR
Lisa Gregoire is a writer based in Ottawa, Ontario. She is a regular contributor to *Canadian Geographic*, *The Walrus*, and *Ottawa Magazine*. A self-described "wanderer," Gregoire has covered stories all over the world.

Top of the World

WHAT DO YOU THINK?

"Success is liking yourself, liking what you do, and liking how you do it."
—Maya Angelou

Biographical Article by Margaret Jetelina

Bruce Poon Tip created an ecotourism company that makes over $100 million a year. He uses a portion of its profits to help others around the world.

TYPES OF SUSTAINABLE TOURISM

Ecotourism stresses low-impact adventure in a natural setting and learning about and preserving wilderness.

Wilderness tourism involves travelling into isolated areas and includes activities such as hiking, camping, and portaging.

Adventure tourism takes place in extreme environments and includes activities such as mountain climbing, whitewater rafting, and skiing.

Bruce Poon Tip calls himself an open book. If that's the case, then his story is a pretty good read—from his struggles as a young immigrant in Calgary to his entrepreneurial success with his global tourism company, G Adventures.

Poon Tip has journeyed the world, received numerous entrepreneurship awards, and experienced a wealth of business and personal success.

So, it's easy to see why his story (which starts with his journey from Port of Spain, Trinidad, continues with his rise as a business whiz kid in Canada, and then becomes an international success story) is a definite page-turner. The handsome immigrant of Chinese, Dutch, and Guyanese heritage even looks the part of a multicultural hero.

How did Poon Tip do it? It never occurred to him that he couldn't.

After the Poon Tip family (parents and seven children) immigrated to Calgary, Poon Tip watched as his parents struggled to make it. His father eventually bought and managed a gas station, while his mother also worked full-time.

After a relatively easy life in Trinidad, where the family's blended heritage was accepted in the multicultural country, the culture shock they experienced thickened the plot. "It was a real struggle when we came here. Calgary was a very tough city to [live in] in the early 1970s [for] a minority," says Poon Tip.

The Poon Tips were the only non-white family in their new neighbourhood. "I often tell this story of my mother's that when she got her first job, she had arranged over the phone for daycare…. When she got there, they told her they didn't take kids of colour. She lost her job."

These students are adventure tourists in Kashmir, India. The Kashmir government has been focusing on adventure tourism since the spring of 2010, with hope that tourism will help bring prosperity and peace to the region.

"I am going to start a business and take on the world."

He and his siblings were continually treated like "others." "My brothers were always fighting to protect our sisters. We were always being chased home from school," he says. "Lucky for us, we had a big family; it was like our own little city inside our house."

Later, the family moved to a better neighbourhood, but still Poon Tip was only one of two visible minority students in his new school. "I remember acknowledging each other and high-fiving each other." He chuckles at the memory.

Perhaps the cultural isolation a young Poon Tip felt is what prompted him to start dreaming up business ideas. At 12, he started a newspaper delivery business and hired younger kids to deliver the papers.

"That was a really defining time in my life that made me what I am today," Poon Tip says. "There was a lack of role models, of seeing someone who can represent what you are on TV and in school. I put all that energy into my businesses where I was a leader and people listened to me."

After some postsecondary education in business and tourism, Poon Tip moved out to Toronto at the age of 22. "I had $800 in my pocket, and was full of stupidity, really. I thought, 'I am going to start a business and take on the world.'"

Before taking over the world, Poon Tip travelled around Asia to experience it. "I saw there was a gap in the travel market for people like me.... I wanted a cultural-type holiday, where I could meet local people and really experience the culture."

Poon Tip returned from his trip with the inspiration to start G Adventures. "When I came back, I developed my first group tour to Belize, Ecuador, and Venezuela, booking local bed and breakfasts and arranging local transportation. It was really grassroots."

Poon Tip certainly found a gap in the market. His adventure travel business has grown steadily, to the point where his tours to more than 100 countries generate revenue of about $160 million a year.

"In my twenties and thirties, I was known as that 'wunderkind.' Now I'm an old has-been," jokes Poon Tip.

It's hardly time for his epilogue. With so much success achieved, Poon Tip now spends time giving back through his humanitarian organization, Planeterra.

PLANETERRA FOUNDATION

On its website, Planeterra Foundation is described as "a non-profit organization that helps empower local people to develop their communities, conserve their environment, and provide supportive solutions to local problems."

These adventure tourists are taking a camel ride in Wadi Rum, Jordan.

VISUAL LITERACY

Think about the types of images you associate with travel magazines or advertising. What do those images have in common? As you view this article, ask yourself: How do the images in this article reflect those codes, conventions, or techniques?

"Our company is so connected with people, so as we became more successful, it was a no-brainer for me to give back to those communities we visit. It was the right thing to do," says Poon Tip, who sets a good example for his two children, Jada and Terra with his wife, Roula. "I'm a really big karma guy. I believe that you get what you give."

While Poon Tip struggled to find role models that looked like him when he started on his Canadian journey, he's now proud to serve as an inspiration to today's immigrants.

His tips for today's newcomers? "The first thing is to embrace the country that is now your home. You have to have an open mind. You have to venture out," he says.

As for business-specific advice, he says, "Know what your motivation is; why do you want to be an entrepreneur? You also have to fully understand what it's going to take; it's not an easy road.... So, do what you love, be passionate about it, and don't be afraid to ask for help. Have the courage to get out there." ◆

RESPONDING

DISCUSSION QUESTIONS

MAKING INFERENCES
Create a graphic organizer to list Bruce Poon Tip's personality traits, both those that are stated explicitly and those that can be inferred. Support your observations with details from the text.

CRITICAL LITERACY
Compare how the people in Poon Tip's youth used their power to how he uses his power today. What does this reveal?

METACOGNITION
What connections did you make to Poon Tip's personal history or to the idea of ecotourism? How did your connections affect your personal or critical response to this article?

TASKS

DEBATING
Prepare a debate on the following proposition: "Travel companies should give back to the countries to which they send tourists." Develop your ideas by visiting websites for travel companies and looking for pages on corporate responsibility or core values.

RESPONDING CREATIVELY
Reread the text about tourism in the margin on page 88. What type of tourist are you or would you like to be if you were given the opportunity? Develop an answer in a form of your choice (e.g., magazine article, video travel blog, photo essay, or adventure story).

ABOUT THE AUTHOR
Margaret Jetelina is a writer and editor for numerous Canadian publications. She believes that "The right words make a difference; they evoke emotion ... inspire action ... encourage loyalty. They tell a story."

FOCUS ON genre

> "What a writer can do, what a fiction writer or a poet or an essay writer can do, is re-engage people with their own humanity."
> —Barbara Kingsolver

ANALYZING EXPOSITORY WRITING AND THE ESSAY

THE PARTS OF AN ESSAY

BEGINNING
The introduction tells readers about the essay's topic, purpose, and scope. It includes a thesis statement that states the main idea of the essay and tells readers what major points will be explored and supported in the rest of the essay.

↓

MIDDLE
The body consists of several paragraphs that explore in detail the points identified in the introduction. Transitions help to move readers from one paragraph to the next.

↓

END
The conclusion is a brief paragraph that summarizes the main points. Often, a writer will restate the thesis in different words, possibly recasting it in such a way that readers are left with a new perspective on the topic.

// **DEFINING TERMS**

An *expository essay* is an essay that is written to explain. *Expository writing style* is a way of writing that is used to explain, but can take a variety of forms, including an essay, report, or article.

ESSAYS

Essays are brief nonfiction compositions that explain, argue, or explore a subject or topic. The essay is a form of writing used in virtually every academic subject. Like most other forms of communication, an essay has a beginning, middle, and end. While essays may be written using an expository writing style, they may also use a narrative or persuasive writing style, depending on their purpose.

SAMPLE ESSAY TYPES	PURPOSE
Research Essays (usually expository writing style)	to inform or explain
Literary Essays (may be expository or persuasive writing style)	to analyze or argue
Descriptive Essays (usually expository writing style)	to inform or describe
Argumentative Essays (persuasive writing style)	to persuade
Personal Essays (usually narrative writing style)	to make a point through story

EXPOSITORY WRITING

The expository writing style is used to explain or give information, and can take the form of a paragraph, essay, or report. Successful expository writers do the following:

- express their purpose clearly
- craft attention-grabbing introductions and powerful conclusions
- construct paragraphs with relevant and distinct main ideas (topic sentences)
- use a variety of supporting details, including statistics and researched information
- use appropriate organizational structures that aid in understanding (for more on organizing your writing, see the Focus on Writing section on page 120 of this unit)
- provide the necessary background information to aid readers in understanding

DESIGN That Fits to a Tee

WHAT DO YOU THINK?

Today, the Internet is more about belonging to a community than finding information.

 STRONGLY AGREE   STRONGLY DISAGREE

Jake Nickell is the CEO of Threadless.

Article by Laura House, posted on the *American Institute of Graphic Arts* website

What began as a design submission for an online contest has spooled into the thriving T-shirt business and web-based community Threadless. Now a multi-million-dollar enterprise selling more than 120 000 tees a month, this is the little community-based design company that could.

Central to its success are its independent designers and supporting community. Here's how it works: the site holds ongoing open calls for T-shirt designs, which are then scored and critiqued by over 2 million registered users; next, the winning designs are printed and sold. This medium offers wide exposure for budding designers and an affordable way for people to support independent artists. And, of course, there's the benefit of having something unique to wear, cooler than the average mall gear.

//Threadless Gives Back

Threadless has launched a not-for-profit program, called Threadless Causes. It provides a platform for organizations to sell certain T-shirt designs to further their missions and causes. Up to 25% of all sales are donated to the sponsoring organization. So far, dozens of organizations, from the Ocean Preservation Society to UNICEF, have used Threadless Causes to further their goals.

This T-shirt celebrates the series finale of the TV show *Lost*. Many Threadless designers pay tribute to classic and contemporary popular culture in clever and humorous ways.

Jake Nickell, a self-described "entrepreneurial madman," is the founder and CEO of Threadless. In 2000, while a student at the Illinois Institute of Art in Chicago, Nickell entered a design contest on the now-defunct Dreamless website. The challenge was to create the official T-shirt for an event in London. His design won the competition—a perk for an art student. However, the greater reward was the exposure to a unique online community of designers.

The Dreamless website "was a great environment for hobbyists and professionals alike to unleash creativity," Nickell says. Artists chatted online, shared critiques, and bantered in mock design battles. It was through this online forum that Nickell met his first partner, Jacob DeHart. Although no longer with Threadless, DeHart was crucial to its inception.

Inspired by the London contest, Nickell and DeHart decided to host another design competition. They posted it as a thread on the Dreamless forum with the apt title "Threadless."

"We thought it would be a fun project that would give back to the community by actually making goods out of the work created by these artists," Nickell explains. "We started it as a hobby … just a way to enhance the Dreamless community."

The winning design was then printed on T-shirts and sold. Any profits were put toward hosting another competition and printing more winning designs. For the first few rounds, winning designers received a few free tees, but by 2002 Threadless was able to award a US$100 cash prize.

Nickell and DeHart each invested US$500 to fund these competitions, which they began hosting on the Threadless site. As Threadless expanded, they created the umbrella company skinnyCorp to launch other online projects and communities. "For those first two years, every dime we earned from selling tees just went right back into printing more of them," recalls Nickell. Not only were funds tight, but their free time was, too. They each worked full-time jobs while attending college and running the business on the side.

By 2003, it was clear that this was more than just a hobby. Nickell and DeHart scouted office space, quit their jobs, and even hired their first employee. Although not profitable yet, Threadless proved that they could build an e-commerce website.

By 2004, they had outgrown their roughly 275-square-metre space. Two years later, they were up to 18 employees and running the operation from a 7620-square-metre facility. The team took on an investor, Insight Venture Partners, to manage the rapid growth. Nickell admits, "I'm much more interested in the creative, fun side of the business. It's nice to have someone with expertise who is invested in the business to help us figure out all the boring stuff."

//Threadless Artists

Threadless allows artists from all over the world to express their creativity. For example, Priscilla Wilson from California is a full-time graphic designer who likes the freedom of designing T-shirts for Threadless as well as being part of a creative community online.

Anna-Maria Jung, also known as Queenmob, is a freelance illustrator from Austria. She is inspired by the Cartoon Network. About submitting designs to Threadless, she says, "Persistence and the will to learn and accept critique by others is vital. Open your mind for new concepts, but don't leave your own style and love for certain topics."

It seems like a simple concept, this T-shirt business, but visit the site to catch a glimpse of why this model has thrived. It doesn't float adrift in cyberspace. Threadless has sparked a vibrant, involved community with an inviting, friendly vibe. Members can check in on designers, keep up with celebrity tee sightings, rate submissions, or chat with other like-minded members. When asked if he ever dreamed the community would expand as it has, Nickell says, "I did not envision it to be as large as it is. I think that having a variety in the designs that get chosen is pretty important in keeping the community fresh. To be able to see design trends come and go is important, and we always need to be on top of what is cool at any given moment."

Today, winners receive a sizable cash prize (US$2000 plus either a US$500 Threadlesss gift certificate or another US$200 cash), get extra exposure with an interview slot on the site and, more importantly, get to see their designs everywhere.

The designer success stories are impressive, too. "Tokidoki is a great example of an artist who has gained huge exposure since being printed on Threadless," Nickell points out. He is referring to the Italian artist Simone Legno, who has gone on to collaborate with other manufacturers of commercial goods. Another success story is Glenn Jones, who "recently started up his own T-shirt site and left his full-time job due to his fame and success on Threadless."

Proving that commercial success need not be dull, the Threadless empire continues to evolve. In fall 2007, its first retail space, or community centre, opened in Chicago. There is a store at street-level and an interactive space upstairs used for gallery shows promoting independent artists, design classes, and other special events. The company has also created its own private label to further perfect the end product. As for the future, Nickell muses, "We plan to continue to grow the awesomeness levels to new, previously unreached heights." And as with all things Threadless, we users will be the judge. ◆

Threadless's new facility reflects the company's vibrancy and creativity.

RESPONDING

DISCUSSION QUESTIONS

ANALYZING WRITING
Identify the organizational structure used in this article. What transitional devices or organizational strategies does Laura House use? Is the organizational structure appropriate, given the article's purpose and audience? Support your response.

EVALUATING
What makes Threadless such an attractive "community-based design company" to so many people around the world? Why might some people not be comfortable doing business with Threadless?

TASKS

DESIGNING A T-SHIRT
Create a T-shirt design that could be submitted to Threadless. When completed, write an email or letter addressed to Threadless that explains the concept behind the design.

MAKING COMPARISONS
Compare and contrast Jake Nickell and his company to Bruce Poon Tip and his company (see "Top of the World," page 88). Use a graphic organizer to help organize your ideas.

WHAT DO YOU THINK?
If it's to be ... it's up to me.

Worldwide We

Expository Essay by Cheryl Gilbert

The Free The Children movement is a formidable force. At its core are groups of idealistic young people without whom change would not be possible.

Every social movement starts somewhere. This movement started with Craig Kielburger, a small group of Grade 7 students, and their initiative to stop child poverty and exploitation: Free The Children. Through empowerment programs and leadership training, Free The Children inspires more than one million young people to be socially conscious global citizens.

Today, the organization has two goals. The first is to free children from poverty by providing them with schools, clean water, healthcare, alternative sources of income, and other resources they need to live healthier lives.

The second goal is to free young people from the idea that they are powerless to effect positive change in the world. Often, people believe that only adults can make a difference. Kielburger and the team at Free The Children know this isn't true.

Craig Kielburger inspires people to take action that will lead to positive change.

1995
Free The Children begins. Kielburger and 11 of his Grade 7 classmates start a group dedicated to raising awareness about child labour.

1996
Kielburger holds a press conference urging Prime Minister Jean Chrétien to address child labour. The prime minister agrees to meet with Kielburger. Free The Children soon gains international recognition.

1999
Kielburger appears on *Oprah* to discuss his work with Free The Children. As a result, millions of people are inspired to end child labour.

2002
Free The Children is nominated for the Nobel Peace Prize.

These school children in the Kono District of Sierra Leone are a new hope for a brighter future. Free The Children has empowered this community, as well as hundreds of others. These communities have increased their level of education and introduced new projects for economic development.

The Fuel

According to Kielburger, the success of Free The Children is due to the idealism of youth. "People called us idealistic," he says of Free The Children in its early days. "We still are. In fact, we're shamelessly idealistic." That idealism was infectious. It spread from his small group to thousands of supporters in 45 countries. They all shared the same belief: their small actions would collectively change lives.

Eventually, they looked to the idealistic Me to We philosophy for inspiration. The philosophy is based on the belief that each choice a person makes doesn't just affect "me," it affects "we"—the world around us. Thanks to this philosophy, Kielburger's small spark spread into a fiery global initiative.

WHAT "WE" HAS ACCOMPLISHED

To date, Free The Children has accomplished the following:
- built over 650 schools and schoolrooms
- provided education to over 55 000 children
- shipped over $16 million worth of medical supplies
- built healthcare centres for over 512 000 people
- equipped more than 30 000 women to be economically self-sufficient
- improved access to clean water, healthcare, and sanitation for over 1 million people

ORGANIZING TEXTS

Headings organize a text and inform readers that a new point or idea is being introduced. In this text, the headings use the metaphor of fire to express how Craig Kielburger's message spread around the world. This metaphor also helps Cheryl Gilbert organize the text.

2006
Free The Children wins the World's Children's Prize for the Rights of the Child, also known as the Children's Nobel Prize. It recognizes Free The Children's outstanding contributions to the defence of children's rights.

2007
The first We Day event takes place in Toronto with 8000 students in attendance.

2011 and 2012
Free The Children is recognized as one of Canada's Top Employers for Young People.

2013
We Day continues to expand, holding its first events in Saskatchewan, Atlantic Canada, and the United States.

WE DAY TICKETS

Participants at We Day events have to be part of a school or youth group. Attendees often earn their spots through volunteering.

We Day is dubbed a "rock concert for social change." This innovative event educates and excites the young people that make this movement successful.

By taking on new challenges, Spencer West hopes to "motivate and inspire" others.

Fan the Flames

We Day is a series of annual events that celebrates the power of young people to change the lives of others and inspires youth to change the world. In 2013, over 100 000 students attended We Day events in eight cities, and millions more watched the webcast and TV broadcast.

Since it began, the intention of We Day has been to inspire and engage youth to take action for change. Events feature motivational speeches by social activists, famous leaders, and actors, and performances by singers. Speakers have included an impressive number of high-profile activists, politicians, authors, sports figures, and actors, such as writer and activist Robin Wiszowaty, Paralympian Chantal Petitclerc, TV host Jessie Cruickshank, activist Dr. Jane Goodall, author and activist Elie Wiesel, former child soldier Michel Chikwanine, and His Holiness the Dalai Lama. High-profile singers who have performed include Hedley, Jennifer Hudson, Jason Mraz, K'naan, Justin Bieber, Colbie Caillat, Nelly Furtado, and Marianas Trench.

One of the many inspirational speakers at We Day is humanitarian Spencer West. West was featured in media sources ranging from CTV to *People* magazine when he climbed Mount Kilimanjaro—the highest peak in Africa. West lost both his legs when he was 5 years old. He climbed the mountain on his hands. His efforts raised over $500 000 for Free The Children clean water projects. When students hear West's story, they know that anything is possible.

Every person who attends We Day commits to take steps for a better world. Since 2009, attendees of We Days have raised over $20 million for local, national, and international organizations. They have also donated over 3 million volunteer hours. As part of a network of students, facilitators, and educators, members of the Free The Children movement transfer their idealism into action and realize the power of young people to change the world.

Jordyn Harrison (far right) and Brooke Harrison stand with Gary Maracle in front of a trailer of goods they collected.

Sparks Spread the Fire

Free The Children regularly celebrates the accomplishments of its members. Each year, the *Canadian Living* Me to We Awards are presented to six Canadians who have dedicated their lives to improving the lives of others. Award winners are nominated by Canadians.

In 2012, Jordyn Harrison won a *Canadian Living* Me to We Award for starting Kids 4 Kids. This organization began when Harrison found out that many foster children in Ontario only have plastic bags to hold their belongings. He began to collect donations from people he knew to provide luggage and knapsacks, filling these with goods for the children. The organization has grown to the point where it now collects donations from corporations and the general public and is able to provide filled luggage to 23 Children's Aid Societies. In 2011, Harrison and his sister Brooke began to collect donations to purchase goods for children in need in First Nations communities in northern Ontario. They worked with Ontario Provincial Police Staff Sergeant Gary Maracle to transport these goods.

Free The Children believes in its youth members and other supporters. They celebrate their victories and use them to inspire others to join the movement. Every youth can be inspired to become socially conscious, engaged, and active in the quest to improve lives around the world. It all starts with a spark. ◆

RESPONDING

DISCUSSION QUESTIONS

EVALUATING
Why is idealism important to Craig Kielburger and the Free The Children movement? Do you think idealism is important to the success of any social movement? Explain.

ANALYZING ORGANIZATION
How is this essay organized? What textual evidence helped you determine the organizational pattern?

CRITICAL LITERACY
According to this text, what do Kielburger and his supporters value? Do most members of Canadian society share their values? Explain.

TASKS

CREATING A DIGITAL PRESENTATION
Create a digital presentation of this essay. Consider how to incorporate the essay's main ideas and concepts. Be mindful of the codes, conventions, and techniques associated with visual media. Share your presentation with others in your class.

ROLE-PLAYING
The youth who make up the Free The Children movement eventually become adults. Imagine a reunion of a group of adults who, as teens, went to Peru to build a school. With a small group, role-play the discussion these adults might have.

The Pocket Camera Moment

WHAT DO YOU THINK? + AGREE   − DISAGREE
Technological innovation does little to change basic human behaviour.

Essay by Jonathon Keats, from *Wired*, June 1, 2012

"Any schoolboy or girl can make good pictures," declared an Eastman Kodak ad for the Brownie box camera soon after it launched in February 1900. It was an astonishing claim, given the unwieldy equipment, arcane chemistry, and extravagant expense of nineteenth-century photography. Sold for a dollar and preloaded with film, George Eastman's ultra-portable, one-button cardboard shooter could hardly match professional rigs in image quality, but by sponsoring contests, starting clubs, and charging just pennies for prints, Eastman nurtured something else: photography as a social activity.

Eastman sold 150 000 Brownies in the first year. Within a decade, nearly a third of Americans owned a camera, and even those who didn't could not avoid the "Kodak freaks" who toted their Brownies everywhere and traded snapshots for their scrapbooks. The mania only intensified when Kodak introduced a folding pocket model that could print photos directly onto penny postcards. (More than 677 million postcards were mailed in 1907 alone.) By transforming how people engaged with photography, Eastman transformed how they engaged with one another. Shared experiences no longer had to be experienced together.

We're in the midst of another Brownie moment. Yes, we've had cellphone cameras for years, and they can't compete with specialized digital cameras on image quality. But, as with the Brownie, image quality is secondary to the social nexus. Always at hand, an iPhone camera is easy to use unobtrusively, and apps such as Instagram and Hipstamatic facilitate effortless sharing of images, automatically optimized as eye candy.

Instagram in particular is on fire. The free app doubled its audience to 27 million users in the first three months of 2012, and that was before the Android version. And before it was purchased by Facebook for a cool billion. Pre-Instagram, you could text a photo or email it from your smartphone and eventually post it on Flickr, but that all took effort. Instagram has made sharing compulsively easy.

ANALYZING WORD CHOICE

As you read, consider why Jonathon Keats chose phrases like *eye candy* or *secret sauce*. Make inferences about what such phrases can tell you about Keats.

Not only is Instagram a full-fledged social network—with users sharing and commenting on one another's images—but users can post Instagram images on other networks like Twitter, where photos are becoming as important as text as a mode of communication. "Pictures are the quickest way to grasp information," says Wikimedia Foundation researcher and avid Instagrammer Parul Vora. "There's a reason our brains have evolved to be more than 30 percent visual cortex."

The 17 preprogrammed Instagram filters are the secret sauce, cleverly designed to distract the eye from amateur compositional defects by exaggerating colour saturation or introducing flair. "The human desire to get noticed is now very much connected to the technological capacity to make something noticeable," says Andrew Clarke, head of strategy at ad agency Butler, Shine, Stern & Partners, where he's currently orchestrating the U.S. relaunch of Nokia. Filters can make mediocre shots look good and good shots look great, which helps engage strangers. More important, filters alter the mood, visually adding layers of meaning. (The '70s Instamatic colour gamut exudes nostalgia—even for people born in 1993.) You're sharing not just what you see but also how you feel about it, a crucial element of visual communication previously accessible only to pros with pricey equipment.

On assignment in Afghanistan to document the troops' daily life, *New York Times* photographer Damon Winter observed the ubiquity of smartphone photography among the soldiers—so he chose to take his pictures with Hipstamatic on his iPhone. Unencumbered by a specialized digital camera, he was able to make social connections with the enlisted men and women and capture more casual, unguarded moments. His choice was validated when a series of these images were awarded third prize by Pictures of the Year International in February.

Hipstamatic was just a one-time tool for Winter. But the convenience of iPhonography has proven decisive for reporters like the *Times*'s Ashley Parker, who supplements her writing on the presidential campaign by posting pics to Instagram. Through these channels, breaking news is folded into the social life of Instagrammers, adding to the communal experience shared at a distance—another upshot of George Eastman's vision.

Eastman's company ultimately lost that innovative streak. In 1974, a Kodak engineer named Steve Sasson built the world's first portable digital camera by cobbling together parts scavenged from a Super-8 and a cassette player. Baffled colleagues asked, "Why would you want to look at photos on a TV?" A company that once led a visual revolution got stuck in the status quo and today stands for nostalgia: an app developer called Taplayer now offers a filter that makes digital pics look like they were shot with a Brownie. ◆

Breaking news is folded into the social life of Instagrammers, adding to the communal experience, as in this photo taken at a basketball game.

THE MOBILE PHOTO EXPLOSION

Infographic by Over, Design by NowSourcing

BIRTH OF PHOTOGRAPHY

1826 — **FIRST PERMANENT PHOTOGRAPH**
VIEW FROM THE WINDOW AT LE GRAS BY NICÉPHORE NIÉPCE
Required an eight-hour exposure

HARRY RANSOM CENTER AND J. PAUL GETTY MUSEUM

1861 — **FIRST COLOUR PHOTOGRAPH**
ADDITIVE-PROJECTED IMAGE OF A TARTAN RIBBON
TAKEN BY SCOTTISH PHYSICIST JAMES CLERK MAXWELL

Kodak

- **1888** — **FIRST KODAK CAMERA** contained a 6-m roll of paper, enough for 100 6 cm diameter circular pictures
- **1889** — **IMPROVED CAMERA** with rolls of film, instead of paper
- **1900** — **KODAK BROWNIE** Box roll-film camera introduced—cost US$1

DIGITAL REVOLUTION

KODAK RESEARCH SCIENTIST STEVE SASSON INVENTED THE **FIRST FILM-LESS ELECTRONIC CAMERA** — **1974**

HOW MANY PHOTOS ARE TAKEN EACH YEAR?

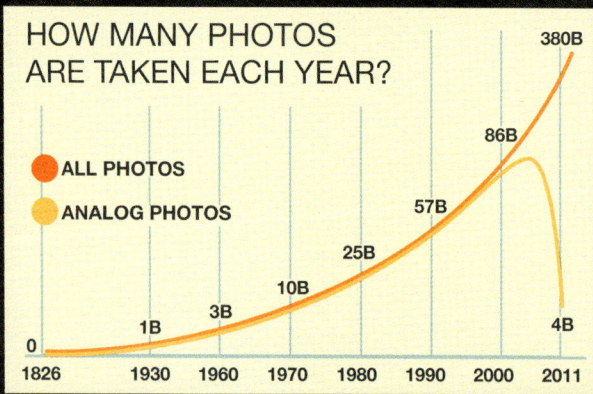

- ALL PHOTOS
- ANALOG PHOTOS

Year	1826	1930	1960	1970	1980	1990	2000	2011
Photos	0	1B	3B	10B	25B	57B	86B	380B / 4B

FIRST CONSUMER-LEVEL DIGITAL CAMERAS
WORKED WITH A HOME COMPUTER VIA SERIAL CABLE

Apple QuickTake 100
February 17, 1994

Kodak DC40
March 28, 1995

SOCIAL EXPLOSION

facebook

70% OF ALL FACEBOOK ACTIVITY IS BASED ON PHOTOGRAPHS.

In April 2012, Facebook bought Instagram for US$1.01 billion.

Instagram

TOP 4 FILTERS USED ON INSTAGRAM

- 44.5% NORMAL
- 11.1% EARLY BIRD
- 6.8% X-PRO II
- 4.2% RISE

26 PHOTOS are uploaded every second

TOP 5 #TAGS

#LOVE
#INSTAGOOD
#ME
#TBT
#CUTE

USERS

1 MILLION users in early 2011

27 MILLION users in March 2012

TWITTER VERSUS INSTAGRAM

6.9 MILLION ← DAILY ACTIVE USERS → **7.3 MILLION**

RESPONDING

DISCUSSION QUESTIONS

ANALYZING THESIS
How does the title "The Pocket Camera Moment" relate to Jonathon Keats's thesis? What is he saying about digital cameras and associated technologies?

ANALYZING WORD CHOICE
Keats uses the phrase *compulsively easy* to describe the use of Instagram. What is he implying about people who use apps such as Instagram? Explain why this implication is accurate or inaccurate.

RESPONDING CRITICALLY
Why did the editors of this selection use both an essay and an infographic? How does each piece support the other?

TASKS

WRITING A BLOG ENTRY
Write a review of Instagram (or Hipstamatic or another photo-sharing site you use) that might appear on a blog for people serious about photography as a social activity. In your review, include the features that make the app distinctive, the audience that would find the app appealing, and a rating for the app.

RESPONDING CREATIVELY
Choose either the essay or the infographic and produce a creative response using whatever media you wish. For example, you could create another type of infographic or a photo essay. Share your creative response with others and consider their feedback.

ABOUT THE AUTHOR

Jonathon Keats is a journalist, critic, and artist. His work has been published in *Wired*, *ForbesLife*, and the *Washington Post*.

WHAT DO YOU THINK? + AGREE — DISAGREE
Computer games help society.

Saving the World through Game Design

Blog Entry by Jane McGonigal

Jane McGonigal takes play seriously. She studies how games have an impact on the real world—and she creates mass role-playing games that do just that. Her projects include Superstruct, The Lost Ring, and World Without Oil.

McGonigal's games have near-future crisis settings, such as a world facing pandemics or mass migration. Hundreds or thousands of online players form cooperative networks and develop ingenious solutions to real challenges. Such gameplay has produced a precise forecast of social reactions. As a result, designers like McGonigal are moving computer games beyond entertainment; they are creating innovative ways to predict the future and explore solutions to real-world problems.

McGonigal has created games that encourage players to try to solve real-world problems, such as food shortages and global warming.

I'm a game designer, a games researcher, and a future forecaster. I make games that care. I study how games change lives. I spend a lot of my time figuring out how the games we play today shape our real-world future. And so I'm trying to make sure that a game developer wins a Nobel Prize by the year 2023.

OK, I had a revelation. Games like Superstruct and The Lost Sport and World Without Oil and Reverse Scavenger Hunts and Tombstone Hold 'Em and SF0 missions and The Go Game are "experience grenades."

That's a new term. I thoroughly Google-checked it.

Experience grenades: You play them, and that's like pulling the pin on the grenade.

Nothing has to happen right away. Nothing has to change or be solved right away. Then, you wait. It's later—an hour later, a day later, a week later, a month later—it goes off in your head, like the delayed explosion of a grenade.

You realize: You've learned something. Your cognitive patterns are different. Your view of the possibilities in the world around you has changed. Your sense of your own potential has changed. You're ready for something you didn't even know was coming. You understand something intuitively that seems alien or confusing to others.

... the games we play today shape our real-world future.

The thing is: This doesn't necessarily happen DURING the game. During the game, you might not believe the game is working. In the best-case scenario, you might think you're JUST having fun. Worse, the game might seem silly. You don't trust the design; it seems to be asking things of you that you don't naturally want to do. Or it might seem abstract—what's the practical takeaway? Or even worse, it might seem wonky or arbitrary or broken from your POV.

But it's working. If you're playing, the pin has been pulled. If you're really participating and immersed in the game, the work is happening in your brain. It just is. I've seen it again and again. The experience happens now, the payoff comes later.

Sometimes I know what the payoff will be; sometimes I just trust that a good game will produce something interesting. And the best thing that can happen in a game community is for players to trust that something interesting will happen, and to play as if it's an experience grenade, rather than expecting instant satisfaction.

SUPERSTRUCT

Superstruct was a forecasting game set in 2019. The citizenry (the players) tried to survive in the grip of several global SuperThreats. The game ran for three months in 2008 and more than 7000 players participated. The data collected will aid the Institute for the Future in making predictions about humankind's ability to cope with a variety of threats.

That's a strange thing to say about a game—something we play to produce in-the-moment fun. But some games are fun later. They just are. Like the trying adventures you have that you hate at the moment but that, looking back, are the adventures of your life, the stories you cherish, the bonds you made, and the way you discovered who you could be.

Yes, that's a different kind of fun, a different kind of payoff. But games can be that, and it feels different in the moment, different than immediate and obvious fun (like Rock Band or piñatas).

I see a new class of trusted game designers who are like personal trainers. The trainer tells you to do something, and you do it—even if it HURTS! Even if it isn't fun in the moment! And the benefits come later. Not necessarily during. You trust the trainer's process and you do it to be a better person and a happier person in the long run.

There are a few designers that I trust like this: Simon Johnson, who made The Comfort of Strangers and Hip Sync; the SF0 designers; Kati London at AreaCode. If they make it, I know I can show up and play it and I will have an experience that explodes later in my mind and stays with me. I trust them and don't care what they want me to do. I know they have a design process that works and that they're trying to make people happier and more aware of the possibilities in the world around them. And I am trying to be that kind of trusted designer myself to as many people as possible.

So I thank people who show up to play my games and trust the process. People who played Superstruct—I know that experience grenade will be going off literally for months and years to come. We've already celebrated how much we've achieved during the game—but the real effects will unfold for years. That's just how they work. That's just how they're designed.

Someday I hope game designers really are seen as trusted personal trainers, and that we have the chance to take people through proven processes that pay off in the long run. More gamesight, a surprising social safety net and support system, a more engaging environment, a higher quality of life. ◆

Some of McGonigal's games aim to help people improve their physical and psychological well-being.

VISUAL LITERACY

The designer of this selection didn't use real images from the games mentioned in this blog. Instead, he created his own images. Evaluate how well these images reflect the images from games you've played. Consider how game designers use certain codes, conventions, and techniques to make the game-playing experience a universal one.

FUTURE STUDIES

McGonigal works closely with the Institute for the Future (IFTF). The IFTF observes major societal trends, considers near-future scenarios, and—most importantly—researches what kind of images and positive visions help people take sound action toward a positive future.

These matters used to be dealt with only by a few avant-garde thinkers and high-level scientific institutions, pretty much disconnected from the rest of society ... but then along came McGonigal. She playfully interconnects four major fields: near-future scenarios, education/learning, positive action, and gaming. Gaming brings these fields together in a new, dynamic, participatory, inspiring experience!

SUPERBETTER

After sustaining a concussion, McGonigal began researching recovery strategies. She was struck by how similar they were to playing multi-player games. In response, she developed the online game Superbetter. Her hope is that the game aids in building real-life resilience in those who are unwell. So far, more than 120 000 players have used it to tackle challenges like depression, anxiety, insomnia, chronic pain, and traumatic brain injury.

RESPONDING

DISCUSSION QUESTIONS

ANALYZING VOICE
Compare the voice in Jane McGonigal's blog entry (pages 111 and 112) to the voice created in the paragraphs that introduce and conclude the selection (pages 110 and 113).

MAKING INFERENCES
What does this selection imply about what is important to users of McGonigal's games? What type of gamer might not find her games interesting? Explain.

ANALYZING LITERARY DEVICES
Identify two literary devices in this blog entry and analyze their purpose and effectiveness.

TASKS

DEVELOPING DIALOGUE
Develop a dialogue that McGonigal might have with a person who believes the only purpose for gaming is to entertain. What proof would each person present? Before drafting your dialogue, conduct research on the arguments that support each viewpoint. Be prepared to present your dialogue to your class.

WRITING TO RESPOND
After rereading the selection and visiting McGonigal's website, organize and write a response for her blog's comments section. Include some of the following:
- the reasons why you agree or disagree with her views on gaming
- a request to clarify any ideas that you find confusing
- any connections you made to her ideas

WHAT DO YOU THINK?

+ AGREE
− DISAGREE

"Part of the value of Pinterest is that it brings you out of yourself and into the world of things."

In Defence of Pinterest

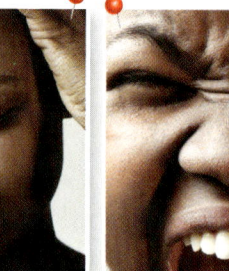

Virtual pin-up boards can be much more powerful than words
Article by Clive Thompson, from *Wired*, October 2012

Therapists often run into a curious problem during treatment: clients aren't very good at describing their emotions. How exactly do you express the nature of your depression?

So this spring, relationship counsellor Crystal Rice hit upon a clever idea. She had her clients use Pinterest, the popular picture-pinning social network, to create arrays of images that map out their feelings. It's a brilliant epiphany: While emotions can be devilishly difficult to convey in words, they're often very accessible via pictures. "This way, we can really identify what's going on," Rice says.

And Rice's idea, as it turns out, is a clue to a question that's been debated a lot: Why the heck is Pinterest so popular?

Critics love to hate the site, which lets you assemble collections of themed images. Because a significant majority of the first users were women—many of whom avidly set up boards to organize their weddings, fantasize about home décor, or store workout-inspiration photos—numerous observers have concluded that Pinterest is pure fluff. "Banal, girly crap," as one blogger posted.

Beyond that, there's also a gloomy suspicion that Pinterest, like Twitter before it, is an assault on literacy itself. Pinterest is for people who "will do anything to avoid having to read," as another critic complained.

This is almost certainly untrue (not least because women handily eclipse men in book reading). But these critiques are, inadvertently, on to something. As Rice discovered with her clients, Pinterest's appeal is that it gives us curiously powerful visual ways to communicate, think, and remember.

VIGILANCE AND SOCIAL MEDIA

Like most social media sites, Pinterest may be manipulated by marketing companies or organizations with special interests. Users of Pinterest need to question the purpose behind what they read, view, or watch.

> It's a brilliant epiphany: While emotions can be devilishly difficult to convey in words, they're often very accessible via pictures.

Pinterest encourages collecting photos based on a theme, and this in turn encourages categorical thinking—13 ways of looking at a blackbird. If you see one picture of a guitar, it's just a guitar, but when you see 80 of them lined up, you start to see *guitarness*. This additive power is precisely what helps Rice's clients paint their internal worlds.

What's more, Pinterest's glanceability makes it incredibly useful as a visual memory locker. Consider the case of Josh Hirschland, a 26-year-old heading off to grad school in Chicago. He realized, as he told me, "I'm going to be broke, so I'm going to be doing more cooking." So, like thousands of other folks, he began pinning recipe pictures and scanning others' food-related boards. He found that a grid of images is a better way to generate ideas—and to access what he has personally filed away.

I have used this memory function myself, by putting together a board for eBooks I've read—a virtual bookshelf for titles I don't physically possess. And I've discovered that glancing at it produces the same Proustian jolt I get from gazing at the spines of my "real" books: I suddenly remember a favourite passage.

Indeed, part of the value of Pinterest is that it brings you out of yourself and into the world of things. As the *Huffington Post* writer Bianca Bosker argued, Facebook and Twitter are inwardly focused ("*Look at me!*"), while Pinterest is outwardly focused ("*Look at this!*"). It's the world as seen through not your eyes but your imagination. "In such a self-obsessed society, this is a place where people are focusing attention on something other than themselves," says Courtney Brennan, an avid Pinterest user.

Granted, Pinterest encourages plenty of dubious behaviour, too. It can be grindingly materialistic; all those pins of *stuff to buy*! Marketers are predictably drooling, and as they swarm aboard, the whole service might well end up collapsing into a heap of product shilling.

But, I suspect we'll see increasingly odd and clever ways of using Pinterest. If a picture is worth a thousand words, then those collections are worth millions. ◆

RESPONDING

DISCUSSION QUESTIONS

EVALUATING
What is Clive Thompson's opinion of Pinterest? What evidence does he present to support his opinion?

CRITICAL LITERACY
Thompson notes in the article that one blogger suggests Pinterest is pure fluff because it is "banal, girly crap." By making this comment, what assumptions about males and females does the blogger make? What does Thompson think of this comment?

METACOGNITION
How well would a tool like Pinterest support your learning style?

TASKS

CREATING A VISUAL ESSAY
Create a visual essay to express your opinion about the value of a website like Pinterest. Include a caption with each image to help your audience understand how it relates to your thesis (your thesis can be stated either in the title or in a brief introduction, or can remain unstated but implicit in your choice of images).

DIGITAL LITERACY
Compare Pinterest to Instagram and Hipstamatic (websites mentioned in the selection "The Pocket Camera Moment," page 100). In what ways are the codes, conventions, and techniques used by the designers of these websites similar and different? Which one of the three websites most effectively appeals to its audience? Share your conclusions with a small group.

ABOUT THE AUTHOR
Clive Thompson is a Canadian freelance journalist, science and technology writer, and blogger. He writes about digital technologies and their social and cultural impacts.

Jeremy Gutsche: Mister Chaos

Newspaper Feature by Cathal Kelly, from the *Toronto Star*

WHAT DO YOU THINK?

"Invention, it must be humbly admitted, does not consist in creating out of void, but out of chaos."
—Mary Wollstonecraft Shelley

Jeremy Gutsche was raised in Calgary. He attended Queen's University and, within a few years, founded Trendhunter.

EXPLOITING CHAOS

Exploiting Chaos is Jeremy Gutsche's book about innovation in times of change. Since 2012, it has been available online as an interactive video. The Trendhunter website notes that the book has been translated into seven languages, downloaded 300 000 times, tweeted 100 000 times, and viewed as a 30-minute keynote 200 000 times.

Jeremy Gutsche is explaining how I should write my Jeremy Gutsche article.

"Now, you're going to do one article, an in-depth piece," says Gutsche. He is disappointed.

"The majority of your traffic comes from search engines. So one article, well, that's no good. You need to break the story into a Jeremy Gutsche interview, an *Exploiting Chaos* interview, a Trendhunter interview, and maybe a couple of other things. In a newspaper, it'd look ridiculous. Online, you've created four or five options for the search engines to find. That's the future, in a nutshell."

Gutsche is the founder of the Trendhunter website, a constantly changing site dedicated to identifying the latest big thing. And by "latest" we mean, like, 15 minutes ago.

While running a billion-dollar credit card company, Gutsche began building Trendhunter at night. He taught himself how to code and design. He hung in for "one last bonus" before heading out on his own three years ago.

Gutsche initially saw Trendhunter as a virtual community to discuss business ideas. He eventually realized the website was the idea. Today, 28 000 global "trend hunters" contribute ideas—from baby Jacuzzis to pet piercings. They are sifted by the Trendhunter staff, repackaged, resifted, and posted—100 of them every day. Recent contributions include 99 Bizarre Toys and TV-Themed High Tops.

For Gutsche, the site led to a regular spot as a *cultural futurist* (someone who predicts what popular culture might be like) in the mainstream media (TV, newspapers, radio). From that role, he launched his book *Exploiting Chaos*, a colourful, large-print collection of slogans. His former boss calls it "putting PowerPoint in book format."

For most businesspeople, Gutsche's ideas are scary. He encourages constant change, relentless questioning, and ignoring the rules. "Hire freaks," Gutsche advises on page 138. "Freaks are the only ones who succeed."

Gutsche's vision may be frightening to big businesses, but it addresses one of their current concerns. "The Nikes and Apples are paranoid about finding the next big thing," Gutsche says. "The more traditional companies are paranoid about reinventing. So now they're all worried, and they're desperately listening to the [chaos] message."

That nontraditional message comes across loud and clear in Trendhunter's office. There are no walls or desks. The dozen employees—half of whom are interns or students working on co-op placements—sit at long tables. Brainstorming sessions happen at a local coffee shop ("I'm going to have to start paying them rent," says Gutsche). Once a month the staff go on a group outing—next stop, African Lion Safari.

Gutsche's company operates as a testing ground for the creative workplace he advocates. The creative chaos extends beyond the office onto the Web. Trendhunter undergoes nearly constant tweaking. An entire site redesign is often done in a day. At a major corporation or a mainstream news site, that process takes months.

Speed is paramount. Trendhunter's senior editor, Bianca Bartz, recalls the thrill of being the first to post the news that Paris was allowing the only skyscraper development in the city's history. She found the news on a German site. Yahoo quickly picked up on the story, generating off-the-chart traffic at the Trendhunter website.

"It turned out to be a hoax," Bartz says, as an afterthought. "You know, a lot of people don't trust what we do. We aren't able to fact-check everything. But other newspapers or Yahoo or whoever are publishing what we find because they don't want to miss anything."

MEDIA LITERACY

When evaluating websites like Trendhunter, or articles about such sites, carefully consider the information that is included and what that suggests about what the producers value. Ask yourself what reality is created by these media texts and what place you have in that reality.

TRENDHUNTER TOPICS

On Trendhunter, readers can investigate a wide variety of innovative products, including the following:
- wooden bicycles
- techie sneakers
- radical sunglasses
- trendy visual art

Ian Berry uses denim to create monochromatic artwork. His work appears on the Trendhunter website.

As a content provider—Trendhunter's core mission—it sits at the contested intersection of old and new media.

Trendhunter (and similar sites, like The Daily Beast and Gawker) need old media for content. The old media—the established news organizations—increasingly need the new media to spread their messages. Depending on your perspective, it's a negative or positive relationship.

"In the long run, this is going to be a good thing for journalists, though many of them can't appreciate it right now," says Lisa George, an economist who studies the media at New York's Hunter College.

She points out, "Newspapers may or may not exist in the future. But there will be a market for individual content providers. However, this may well be a winner-take-all market. The journalists who are not as well known, the ones who can't generate traffic—they may not have jobs."

At this point, traffic is the greatest money-maker for Trendhunter. Internet ads bring in enough money that top contributors can earn up to $2000 a month, according to Gutsche. Trendhunter also does tailored trend reports for businesses like Microsoft, Holt Renfrew, and eBay. The $1500 fee for a single one of these pays a month's rent on the office.

As for the future, that's difficult to say. Remember—relentless change. Gutsche has already started a second book on a topic yet to be named. "Right now, this feels like a hobby," he says, shrugging. "If it ever gets boring, there's an opportunity to use Trendhunter as a launching point for some new product."

It's not difficult to bask in Gutsche's relentless positivity.

"You're going to be okay," Gutsche coos to me. "You've got 188 000 search engine hits on your name."

"Really?"

"Sure. You're easy to find at this point. You're a legend!" ◆

RESPONDING

DISCUSSION QUESTIONS

MAKING INFERENCES
What does the phrase *creative chaos* mean? Why might it be considered an appropriate description of Jeremy Gutsche's vision and business model?

CRITICAL LITERACY
Why might some people find Gutsche's philosophy about employees ("Hire freaks … freaks are the only ones who succeed") not only insensitive, but flawed? Do you agree or disagree with him? Explain.

EVALUATING
Trendhunter "sits at the contested intersection of old and new media." What does this statement mean? Why might such a position be considered an advantage or disadvantage?

TASKS

PRESENTING A SCRIPT
Develop a script that captures the energy and creative chaos that might unfold at a Trendhunter staff meeting. Decide the topic of conversation and create the dialogue and appropriate stage directions. Be prepared to perform your script.

DIGITAL LITERACY
Construct an online ad to attract new and creative employees to the Trendhunter team. Begin by reviewing online ads and evaluating their use of codes, conventions, and techniques. As you construct your ad, keep purpose and audience in mind.

FOCUS ON Writing

> " Organizing is what you do before you do something, so that when you do it, it is not all mixed-up. "
> —A.A. Milne

ORGANIZING IDEAS

The degree to which writers succeed in communicating ideas in nonfiction writing depends on how they organize their research and thoughts. A well-organized text makes it easier to clearly express and effectively communicate ideas.

When you write a paragraph, report, or research paper, the successful organization of ideas is dependent upon these interrelated skills:
- your ability to conduct and manage research
- your ability to construct a blueprint or outline for your writing

CREATING AN OUTLINE

Arrange your research notes into groups according to their content, for later organization into paragraphs. If you are writing an essay, compose a tentative thesis. If you are writing a paragraph, compose a tentative topic sentence. Your thesis or topic sentence will serve as a guide to help you construct your outline. Choose an appropriate organizational structure based on your topic and purpose.

// THE RESEARCH PROCESS

Research allows you to explore what others have said about a topic. What you discover can be combined with your own thinking or used as supporting evidence. A well-researched paper tells readers that you have a thorough understanding of your topic.

1. Use critical inquiry questions to guide your research.
2. Use credible sources.
3. Take notes, summarize ideas, and keep track of sources.
4. Reread your notes. Determine if additional research is needed.

COMMON TYPES OF ORGANIZATIONAL STRUCTURES USED IN EXPOSITORY WRITING

ORGANIZATIONAL STRUCTURE	DEFINITION	TRANSITIONAL DEVICES
Sequence	lists items or events in sequential or numeric order	first, second, third; next, then, finally
Comparison	explains how two or more things are alike and/or different	similar to, same as, like; unlike, on the other hand, in contrast
Cause and Effect	explains one or more causes and the resulting effect or effects	if … then; as a result; therefore; consequently; not only … but
Problem and Solution	states a problem and lists one or more solutions	the problem is, possible solutions include

The Writing Process

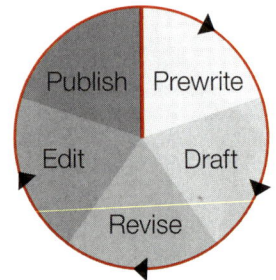

ORGANIZING WRITING FOR FICTION

When you write fiction, you may still need to research. As well, consider how to organize your ideas or the work generally; creating an outline is still a very useful tool. Fiction may start with exposition—telling readers about the characters and setting, and then introducing the problem. The story may then be told sequentially, sometimes with the use of flashbacks. However, many modern writers will play with the organization of events, perhaps beginning with the final event, or using a prologue that hooks readers by plunging them into the action.

Airbus
Plane of the Future

WHAT DO YOU THINK?
The sky is the limit when imagining the future of air travel.

👍 STRONGLY AGREE   👎 STRONGLY DISAGREE

Photo Essay by Alex Davies, from *Business Insider*, November 21, 2012

Airbus is an international aerospace company that produces airplanes for use by the military and civilians. The company developed a project called "The Future by Airbus" to answer the question "What will air transport look like in the year 2050?" The images in this selection are from videos that Airbus produced to share their vision.

Airbus is planning to change the future of flight. On top of imagining how to transform airports, the self-described "future-gazing Airbus" has come up with the plane of the future, and it is pretty wild.

The plane is nothing like what transports passengers today. On top of being more reliable, quiet, and fuel-efficient than current aircraft, it will have seats grown from plant fibres that harvest energy. Passengers can play golf and tennis on board, or have a virtual business meeting.

Of course, the concept relies on technologies that have not been invented, and the plane is unlikely ever to be built. But, as Airbus notes, it is a useful thought experiment that pushes aviation engineers to think outside the box and radically advance the air travel of the future.

> **// Analyzing Photo Essays**
>
> When analyzing photo essays, consider the reasons particular images were chosen, the way they were arranged or organized, their size, and the text that goes with them. Ask yourself: What is the overall message the writer wishes to send? How does the organization help to convey the message?

FORGET THE FLYING CAR

Airbus suggests that unless we develop flying cars, airbus planes like these will be the most efficient mode of travel in the future. An airbus like this one will be able to transform its shape as weather conditions change.

WINDOWS INTO A BRIGHTER FUTURE

Windows in the plane's floor will revolutionize sightseeing.

Forget tiny windows—the plane offers panoramic views.

MORE COMFORTABLE THAN STAYING HOME

The upholstery for the seats is organically grown from plant fibres. Seats rotate so passengers can enjoy the sunshine.

The seats are self-cleaning, and they morph to provide the perfect fit. Each seat has a large entertainment zone.

The seats collect body heat from passengers to power the cabin. When the sun goes down, the seats recline.

Airbus: Plane of the Future

ZONING IN ON YOUR NEEDS

The plane is divided into zones. Each interaction zone offers an individually tailored experience.

> //**Visual Literacy**
>
> When evaluating a photo essay, examine the images closely and consider how people are portrayed and who may have been left out. Reflect on how different groups might respond to the images.

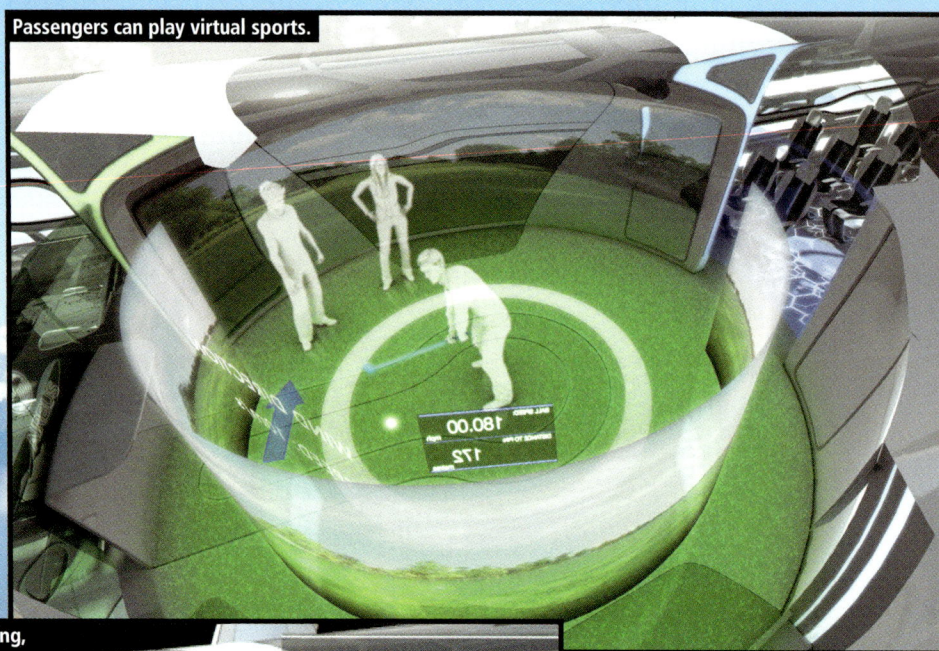

Passengers can play virtual sports.

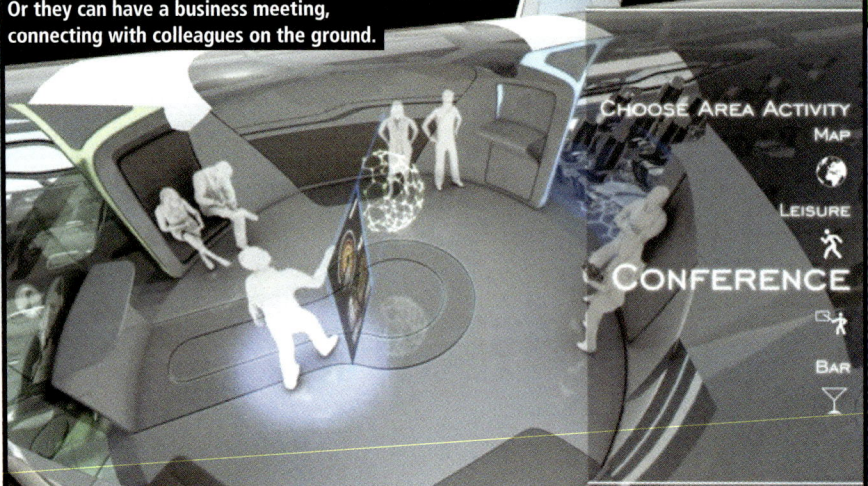

Or they can have a business meeting, connecting with colleagues on the ground.

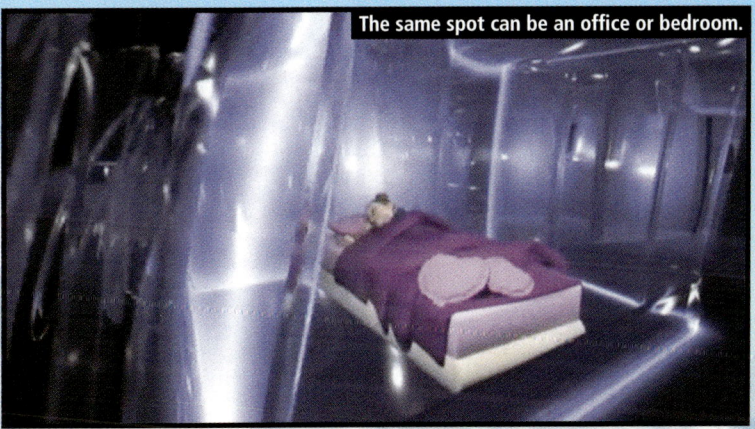

Personal spaces can also change functions. The setting morphs, thanks to holographic projections.

The same spot can be an office or bedroom.

Potentially, the plane could be filled with individual pods that continue their journeys by rail or road upon landing.

RESPONDING

DISCUSSION QUESTIONS

RESPONDING CRITICALLY
Choose one image from this photo essay to evaluate more closely. Analyze the purpose and ideas in the image. Explain how effectively the image conveys the overall message of the photo essay.

ANALYZING ORGANIZATION
Create a graphic to show how Alex Davies has organized his ideas. Does this organization support the message of the photo essay? Explain.

ANALYZING TECHNIQUES
What techniques are used in the images to help convey the sense of an unlimited future? How do those techniques affect the quality and the clarity of the images?

TASKS

BRAINSTORMING IDEAS
Work with a small group to brainstorm ideas for the future of air travel. Build on the ideas in this photo essay. Choose how you want to organize and present your ideas to your class.

DEVELOPING AN AD CAMPAIGN
Choose several images and use them to develop an ad campaign for the future Airbus. Who is your target audience? What message do you want your ads to send?

WHAT DO YOU THINK? + AGREE — DISAGREE

All human innovation, no matter what form it takes, must be outside the rules.

Top 25 Innovations

Online Article posted on *CNN*

TECH TERMS

Technophiles have a love of or enthusiasm for technology, especially computers and micro-technology. They see technology as a way of improving life and combatting social problems.

Technosis emerges when a person loses sight of where they end and technology begins. Symptoms of technosis include not knowing how to function successfully without technology.

Without the Internet, there would be no way to instantly find out which movie your favourite actor was in five years ago. You would need to brave the elements and the crowds to shop.

So, it should come as little surprise that the Internet topped the list of top 25 innovations created by a panel of technology leaders. In creating the list, the panel hoped to single out "25 non-medically related technological innovations that have become widely used since 1980. These innovations are readily recognizable by most people, have had a direct and perceptible impact on our everyday lives, and/or could dramatically affect our lives in the future."

The creator of the Web as we know it is Tim Berners-Lee. Frustrated by the variety of information systems that were complicated to access, Berners-Lee made a universal one that made information readily available. He created HTML (hypertext markup language) and its rules of usage (HTTP, hypertext transfer protocol) and in 1991 unveiled the World Wide Web. Like the Internet, other items on the top 25 list have changed the way people live and are so commonplace that they are almost taken for granted. For example, many people turn off their PCs (No. 3) and their plasma screen TVs (No. 18) and grab their cellphones (No. 2) and laptops (No. 7) as they leave their homes. Some check their email (No. 5) via short-range, high-frequency radio (WI-FI, No. 25) and their voice mail (No. 23), before heading off to an ATM (No. 14) for cash.

This photo shows a back view of the NASA space shuttle orbiter *Enterprise*, an early prototype for the space shuttle *Challenger*.

Among other uses, fibre optics allow for speedy Internet and phone services.

The technology that makes these items possible is taken even more for granted by the average consumer. For example, emergency phone calls are made possible by compact power sources, such as nickel-metal hydride and lithium-ion batteries (No. 15). Without them, cellphones would be far less dependable and not rechargeable. Also, flash memory (No. 22) has made the digital camera (No. 9) possible and has changed the way people transport data. Some of the inventions on the list have brought to life science-fiction concepts. Among them are the space shuttle (No. 20), which advanced space exploration, and hybrid cars (No. 16), which pollute less. Interestingly, the innovation that laid the groundwork for many of the inventions mentioned above is found underground, where fibre optics (No. 4) have helped turn the world into a global village. ◆

TOP 25 INNOVATIONS

1. the Internet
2. cellphones
3. personal computers
4. fibre optics
5. email
6. commercialized GPS
7. portable computers
8. memory-storage discs
9. consumer-level digital cameras
10. radio-frequency ID tags
11. micro-electromechanical system (MEMS)
12. DNA fingerprinting
13. airbags
14. ATMs
15. advanced batteries
16. hybrid cars
17. organic light-emitting diodes (OLEDs)
18. display panels
19. HDTV
20. the space shuttle
21. nanotechnology
22. flash memory
23. voice mail
24. modern hearing aids
25. short-range, high-frequency radio

RESPONDING

DISCUSSION QUESTIONS

CRITICAL LITERACY
What specific words or phrases suggest the author's viewpoint on innovation? Who might agree or disagree with the author? Explain.

MAKING INFERENCES
If people from your generation, the previous generation, and the generation before that read this list, how might their view of these innovations differ? How might their criteria for evaluating the list differ?

MAKING CONNECTIONS
Between technophile and technosis, where do you fall? Create a graphic to show how you view your position on a continuum that starts with technophile (or even before, with technophobe) and ends with technosis.

TASKS

CATEGORIZING INFORMATION
Sort the top 25 innovations into five or six groups. Give each group a title that describes how they are related and then number the groups in order of importance. In writing, explain why you have placed the groups in that order.

CREATING A MEDIA TEXT
Transform this text into another media form, such as a podcast, infographic, or digital documentary. Present the top 25 innovations in a unique and creative way. Share your work with your class.

> **WHAT DO YOU THINK?**
> When does technology go too far?

The Kitchen at the End of the Universe

Essay by Scott Feschuk, posted on *Maclean's*

Can't wait to watch *Glee* on a high-tech $1000 blender? No? You will soon be able to, anyway.

Good news, everyone: the age of the "connected home" is nearly upon us! Soon we'll be able to spend thousands of dollars on an Internet-linked washing machine, a Wi-Fi-enabled oven, and maybe a sentient, wisecracking toaster of some kind. Think of the benefits of making our household contraptions more advanced and connected: I for one can't wait to go online and read the Facebook status updates of celebrity-owned appliances.

No longer shall humans be forced to open the fridge door to see if there's milk left. This taxing ordeal will be replaced by the simplicity of logging the milk's arrival on a touchscreen keypad, typing in its expiry date, routinely taking note of its level, providing our cellphone number, and reading a text message sent by the fridge indicating it's time to buy more milk. What could be easier?

The dawn of connected appliances has been predicted, touted, and hyped for years now. Perhaps some figured that appliance manufacturers had given up on the idea—but no. GE, Sub-Zero, and others have never wavered in their quest to answer the vexing question that has long plagued us as a species: Why can't I use my dishwasher to tweet?

These new gizmos are a marvel to behold. Take Samsung's Internet-enabled refrigerator, which is expected to go on sale this spring for about $3500. It features a video interface that runs apps, displays news stories, creates to-do lists, and enables family members to post to Twitter. If Samsung engineers can somehow find room for a compressor, the fridge may even keep stuff cold. Amazing.

LG, meanwhile, is introducing an oven that can access a computer server, download preprogrammed recipes, and display them on a built-in screen. And thank heavens for that, because until now there has been no way to obtain recipes other than by computer, iPad, smartphone, book, magazine, cereal box, soup can, memory, guesstimation, or grandmother. And who ever has any of those handy?

LG's new refrigerators go even further. They allow you to use a "drag-and-drop" menu to keep track of precisely where each food item has been placed inside. This will be a godsend to all of us who store our butter at the middle of the Minotaur's labyrinth. And that's not all. An excited LG spokesman noted in a recent news story: "I have the ability to see what's in my fridge from my phone!" What a perfect tonic for those of us who get separation anxiety from our ham.

MAKING INFERENCES

When a writer uses sarcasm, you need to make inferences to understand what is really meant. As you read, consider both Scott Feschuk's tone and his real meaning. Pay attention to how his tone and voice are different from those in the direct quotations included in this essay.

The visionaries behind connected appliances are building their industry on the indisputable theory that if you take one good idea (household appliances) and combine it with another good idea (wireless Internet), you can't help but wind up with an idea that is, at minimum, double good.

Sure, maybe we ordinary folk have trouble seeing the merits of one day watching an episode of *Glee* on a $1000 blender. But that's our fault. As a news story recently put it: "It can be hard to explain to consumers all the promise of a Web-connected dishwasher or washing machine, but [an executive at Whirlpool] said they're inevitable." Got that? Inevitable. So stop not understanding why they're building it and start not understanding why you're buying it.

Those who question the viability of connected appliances just don't grasp how business works. It's about the relationship between supply and demand. When there is absolutely no demand, you need to compensate with an overabundance of supply.

It comes down to this twenty-first-century maxim: If something can be made with technology, it must be made—whether we want it or not. That's how we ended up with the Segway.

As one industry executive put it: "We're connecting devices that have never been connected before and we're connecting them to you." Why? Who knows. To what end? Who cares. The only certainty is that we won't stop there. Next, we're going to connect your toothbrush to your car engine. Then, we're going to connect your razor to your vacuum. It won't make your life any easier, but the devices will enjoy being able to talk about you behind your back. ◆

RESPONDING

DISCUSSION QUESTIONS

RESPONDING CRITICALLY
Identify Scott Feschuk's message. How effectively does he deliver his message?

ANALYZING ORGANIZATION
Create a graphic organizer to show how Feschuk has organized his essay. How else could the essay be organized?

TASKS

WRITING TEXT MESSAGES
Develop a dialogue that your toothbrush might have with your bicycle, or that your knapsack might have with your gym shoes. They should exchange at least five text messages.

PRESENTING A SPEECH
In role as a company executive, prepare a speech to present one of the innovations mentioned in this essay to a group of consumers (your classmates). Present your speech, being as persuasive as you can about the need for this innovation. Encourage the group to ask questions.

RESEARCH AND INQUIRY
Which of these real innovations are you interested in seeing and why? Or, what other innovation would appeal to you? Research to find out how close we are to achieving that innovation. Also, find out what its environmental or societal impact might be. Present your findings to your class.

Giving Garments a Second Chance

Sustainable fashion is the future, say eco-friendly designers

Newspaper Article by Patricia D'Cunha

> **WHAT DO YOU THINK?** + AGREE — DISAGREE
> The trend to recycle clothing is as important as any other recycling initiative.

Julia Grieve (bottom right) and Preloved staff model the store's clothing.

Kim Munson celebrates the end of an Orphanage Clothing fashion show.

RESPONDING PERSONALLY

A growing number of people are asking the following questions: Where were my clothes made? What are they made of? Who made the clothes and how were these workers treated? As you read, reflect on how concerned you are with the answers to these questions.

The fashion gods are all clear about one thing—clothes are designed to make people look good.

But what if looking good can also be eco-friendly? That's a concept some designers have embraced in recent years, but it's yet to envelop the mainstream.

Eco-friendly clothes are sustainable and recyclable in that something that was once a throwaway can now be turned into something new. "Sustainable clothing is a movement away from fashion as a disposable commodity," says Canadian designer Kim Munson, founder of Nova Scotia-based Orphanage Clothing. "In the case of Orphanage, one that is extending the life of used textiles."

But this concept is not only applicable to vintage clothing: it's also about not using synthetic fibres, which do not decompose. "Big box retail leads to the consumption of fashion, which in turn leads to more discarded clothing, which ends up in the landfills," Munson explains.

"My biggest thing with sustainability is that it's not a trend, it's very common and it's the future," says Julia Grieve, founder of Preloved, the store and fashion label that creates one-of-a-kind clothing from reclaimed vintage fabrics.

Grieve began her career as a model, and then started Preloved in 1995. Along the way, she also worked as a fashion editor and writer, and has made appearances on TV shows, such as *Diva on a Dime* and *Project Runway Canada*.

"I always call myself the accidental environmentalist," Grieve laughs. "We were doing all this good without even knowing it. In one season, we'll recycle over 80 000 sweaters just to produce our sweater collection."

Once a month, Preloved's employees root through thousands of kilograms of sweaters, looking for material to create one-of-a-kind items.

Grieve says that their line is fashion forward, with attention paid to style and detail. "Our line is always based on fashion first … the sustainable side is just the cherry on the top."

Munson, who actually worked at Preloved when she was fresh out of design school, calls the store the "grandfather" of the sustainable clothing method in Canada.

Her own clothing line was founded in 2003, and can be summed up as "edgy street wear"—timeless, with a flawless cut. Munson always had an affinity for changing up her clothing. Her mother had a clothing line as well, while her grandmother made clothes out of unwanted garments. "You could say it runs in the family," she explains.

Munson says most people think that sustainable clothing lacks in quality and style. But that misconception almost always turns into a pleasant surprise.

"You get the people who get freaked out that the dress they just purchased was once a trench coat worn by someone else," she says.

Grieve agrees. She says people are often over-the-top when they find out that a dress designed by Preloved is made from two different pairs of old trousers and two curtains. "Oh my god, it is so cool," customers often say to her.

While the clothing is eco-friendly, it does cost more to make fashion from reclaimed clothing. "There is a deconstruction phase that happens first. It's a whole other phase that doesn't happen when you're just using regular fabric," says Grieve.

But both Grieve and Munson say their lines of eco-friendly clothing are affordable for the everyday consumer. ◆

RESPONDING

DISCUSSION QUESTIONS

SYNTHESIZING
What does Patricia D'Cunha want readers to understand after reading this article? What personal connections helped you understand this message?

ANALYZING ORGANIZATION
Outline this article with the intent of showing how the main idea and conclusions are organized. Based on your map, what organizational structure is D'Cunha using?

TASKS

CREATING AN AD
Imagine you have been asked to create a 30-second ad that will appear on a youth TV channel. The purpose of the ad is to persuade teens that buying eco-friendly clothing is cool. Use dialogue, images, graphics, slogans, and/or endorsements that appeal to that audience. Share and compare completed ads.

RESEARCH AND INQUIRY
Research sustainable fashion by reading several news articles from reputable sources. What patterns in news reporting emerge? Is the reporting of this topic positive or negative? Why?

CONDUCTING A SURVEY
Design and conduct a survey on youth perceptions of the sustainable clothing movement. Do youth support the idea or oppose it, and for what reasons? Is there a difference between male and female perceptions of this type of clothing? Be prepared to present your findings and conclusions.

WHAT DO YOU THINK NOW?

Think back to your original response to this statement:

"What drives innovation?"

How has your thinking about this statement changed
since you began this unit?

Responding Personally and Creatively

In a small group, choose two selections from this unit that explore a similar theme or issue. Consider how this theme or issue relates to you and your group, to your family and peers, to your community and nation, and finally, to humankind. Present your ideas and analysis to your class using a digital format that includes audio and visual elements. While preparing your presentation, consider the oral and visual strategies you will need to effectively communicate with your audience.

Writing to Respond

Choose one selection in this unit that you responded to strongly (either positively or negatively). Write a report detailing your personal and critical response to that selection. Analyze how your personal and critical responses influenced one another. In your report, suggest three ways you could respond creatively to that selection—to show your personal or critical response. Choose one creative method of response and carry it out.

Creating a Media Text

The ideas explored in this unit serve many different purposes, but all of them are intended to help people in some way. Create one of the following media products to promote an idea from one selection in this unit:

- a video talk-show interview with the key character or person in the selection
- an infomercial that highlights the positive attributes of the person or organization
- a 30-second song in support of the idea that could be used on the person's or organization's website
- your choice of media or visual text

Writing an Expository Essay

Choose one selection from the unit that presents an idea or issue that you oppose. Conduct research on the idea or issue to support your viewpoint. In an expository essay, explain your reasons for opposing the idea, making specific reference to your research. Be sure to develop a clear thesis statement and to use an appropriate organizational pattern.

humour

WHAT DO YOU THINK?

+ AGREE
− DISAGREE

Humour is the most honest art form—you can't fake a response to it.

Unit Learning Goals

- constructing and extending meaning
- analyzing narrative and expository writing in scripts
- analyzing audience responses
- improving word choice

Talk About It

"They say jolliness skips a generation."

> **❝** Analyzing humour is like dissecting a frog. Few people are interested and the frog dies of it. **❞**
> —E.B. White

> **❝** Tragedy is when I cut my finger. Comedy is when you fall into an open sewer and die. **❞**
> —Mel Brooks

> **❝** Humour is a **rubber sword**— it allows you to make a point without drawing blood. **❞**
> —Mary Hirsch

Sharing a laugh with someone …

1. relaxes the whole body and reduces stress
2. increases creativity
3. improves bonding
4. elevates mood and increases self-esteem
5. enhances memory

> **❝** Laughter drives **shouting** away. **❞**
> —Indra Devi

Something went wrong in plane crash

Students cook and serve grandparents

Miners refuse to work after death

Thief gets 2 years in violin case

FOCUS ON reading

> "The kind of humour I like is [that which] makes me laugh for five seconds and think for ten minutes."
> —William Davis

CONSTRUCTING AND EXTENDING MEANING

Readers construct and extend meaning by thinking about how the writer provokes a response and crafts the text, as well as by reflecting on how the stylistic elements connect to the larger meaning of the text.

While reading, you might consider the following:

- how setting, character, plot, conflict, and point of view contribute to the meaning of a text
- how tone, word choice, sentence structure, organization, and stylistic elements reveal a text's purpose or underscore its message or theme
- the connections between the themes in two or more texts
- the impact of the text on its readers or society

After you have constructed meaning, confirm that the meaning makes sense and that your assumptions can be supported. You can confirm meaning by rereading, discussing, or questioning the text. Assess your interpretation of the text and the strategies you used to form that interpretation.

HUMOROUS TEXTS

When constructing and extending meaning for a text that is supposed to entertain, you must examine the use of stylistic techniques and the writer's voice or tone. You should also consider how your prior knowledge affects your response. Ask yourself:

- Why did you (or didn't you) find the text funny? What prior knowledge helped you get the joke? What devices or tools did the writer use?
- What was the writer's purpose for including humour (e.g., to entertain, to criticize, or to provide an emotional break after a tense or sad event)?

MEDIA AND VISUAL TEXTS

When constructing and extending meaning for media or visual texts, the same strategies and questions will apply. Ask yourself:

- How has the creator crafted the text to provoke a response?
- What contributes to the meaning of the text?
- What is the purpose of the text? How do I know?
- What connects this text to others?
- What impact will this text have?

// IRONY

When writing ironically, a writer focuses your attention on the juxtaposition between what is expected and what is occurring. Understanding irony in a text requires you to think beyond the literal meaning of the text.

SYNTHESIZING

Synthesizing is an essential strategy for constructing and extending meaning. When you synthesize, you connect ideas from multiple texts to come to a new understanding. You use your background knowledge, consider how the texts change your thoughts, perspectives, or conclusions, and gain new insight about the topic. Some of the skills you may call on when you synthesize or construct and extend meaning include:

- analyzing
- asking questions
- categorizing
- confirming
- connecting
- drawing conclusions
- hypothesizing
- inferring
- predicting
- reflecting
- summarizing

LITTLE RED RIDING HOOD

Fractured Fairy Tale by James Finn Garner

> **WHAT DO YOU THINK?**
> All traditional fairy tales are sexist.
>
> 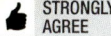 STRONGLY AGREE   STRONGLY DISAGREE

There once was a young person named Red Riding Hood who lived with her mother on the edge of a large wood. One day, her mother asked her to take a basket of fresh fruit and mineral water to her grandmother's house—not because this was womyn's work, mind you, but because the deed was generous and helped engender a feeling of community. Furthermore, her grandmother was not sick, but rather, was in full physical and mental health and was fully capable of taking care of herself as a mature adult.

So Red Riding Hood set off with her basket through the woods.

> **// Inclusive Language**
>
> The word *womyn* has been adopted by some feminist writers as a way to disconnect the word *woman* from the word *man*.

> ## //Stereotype or Archetype
>
> A fairy tale character like the Big Bad Wolf could be considered either a *stereotype* (a character who conforms to a widely held but fixed and oversimplified image) or an *archetype* (a recurrent character found throughout literature, such as the hero who goes on a quest). Writers can play with stereotypes and archetypes to create humour by making their characters act against type.

On the way to Grandma's house, Red Riding Hood was accosted by a wolf who asked her what was in her basket. She replied, "Some healthful snacks for my grandmother who is certainly capable of taking care of herself as a mature adult."

The wolf said, "You know, my dear, it isn't safe for a little girl to walk through these woods alone."

Red Riding Hood said, "I find your sexist remark offensive in the extreme, but I will ignore it because of your traditional status as an outcast from society, the stress of which has caused you to develop your own, entirely valid, worldview. Now, if you'll excuse me, I must be on my way."

Red Riding Hood walked on along the main path. But, because his status outside society had freed him from slavish adherence to linear, Western-style thought, the wolf knew a quicker route to Grandma's house. He burst into the house and ate Grandma, an entirely valid course of action for a carnivore such as himself. Then, unhampered by rigid, traditionalist notions of what was masculine or feminine, he put on Grandma's nightclothes and crawled into bed.

Red Riding Hood entered the cottage and said, "Grandma, I have brought you some fat-free, sodium-free snacks to salute you in your role of a wise and nurturing matriarch."

From the bed, the wolf said softly, "Come closer, child, so that I might see you."

Red Riding Hood said, "Oh, I forgot you are as optically challenged as a bat. Grandma, what big eyes you have!"

"They have seen much, and forgiven much, my dear."

"Grandma, what a big nose you have, only relatively, of course, and certainly attractive in its own way."

"It has smelled much, and forgiven much, my dear."

"Grandma, what big teeth you have!"

The wolf said, "I am happy with who I am and what I am," and leaped out of bed. He grabbed Red Riding Hood in his claws, intent on devouring her. Red Riding Hood let out a gigantic scream, which was heard by a passing wood-chopper-person (or log-fuel technician, as he preferred to be called). When he burst into the cottage, he saw the melee and tried to intervene. But, as he raised his axe, Red Riding Hood and the wolf both stopped.

> ## //Satire
>
> *Satire* is defined as the use of humour, irony, exaggeration, or ridicule to reveal undesirable aspects of people or society. As you read, consider how James Finn Garner uses satire and what undesirable aspects of people or society he wishes to reveal.

"And just what do you think you're doing?" asked Red Riding Hood. The wood-chopper-person blinked and tried to answer, but no words came to him.

"Bursting in here like a Neanderthal, trusting your weapon to do your thinking for you!" she exclaimed.

"Sexist! Speciesist! How dare you assume that womyn and wolves can't solve their own problems without a man's help!"

When she heard Red Riding Hood's impassioned speech, Grandma jumped out of the wolf's mouth, seized the wood-chopper-person's axe, and cut off his head. After this ordeal, Red Riding Hood, Grandma, and the wolf felt a certain commonality of purpose. They decided to set up an alternative household based on mutual respect and co-operation, and they lived together in the woods happily ever after. ◆

RESPONDING

DISCUSSION QUESTIONS

CONSTRUCTING MEANING
Explain the "commonality of purpose" the wolf, Grandma, and Red Riding Hood feel at the end of the story. Why is this sentiment a fitting conclusion to the satire?

CRITICAL LITERACY
Reflect on how James Finn Garner plays with the stereotypes of helpless girl, sick grandma, and evil wolf while embracing the stereotype of man as Neanderthal. How does playing with stereotypes affect readers?

SYNTHESIZING
What new understanding do you have after reading Garner's version of this old tale? Discuss this tale and other modern remixes that have made you think in new ways.

TASKS

DEVELOPING A SPEECH
In role as the wolf, develop a speech you might deliver to an audience of other wolves, cautioning them about the dangers of dealing with humans. Use humour to deliver this serious message. Be prepared to present your speech to others.

WRITING A FRACTURED FAIRY TALE
Create a fractured fairy tale based on another well-known tale. Consider satirizing the original tale's violence, sexism, stereotypical characters, or depiction of young people.

ABOUT THE AUTHOR

James Finn Garner's first book, *Politically Correct Bedtime Stories*, includes "Little Red Riding Hood" and several other fractured fairy tales.

Garner comments that, *"Politically Correct Bedtime Stories* arose out of a weekly cabaret I hosted back then. I learned very quickly that reading aloud (especially with an audience) will show you what is original and worthwhile with your writing, and what needs to be fixed or excised, so I recommend it to anyone who wants to get better at writing."

WHAT DO YOU THINK?
Humour can be found in conflict.

+ AGREE
− DISAGREE

Invasion of the Snotty Badgers

Flash Fiction by Karin Weber

A traditional short story follows a plot comprised of exposition, rising action, climax, falling action, and resolution (or denouement). Although "Invasion of the Snotty Badgers" falls under the genre category of short story, it is written in a specific form called flash fiction. Flash fiction tells a story in as few words as possible, leaving readers to make inferences about many story elements, including setting, problem, and characters.

ANALYZING SENTENCE STRUCTURE

Writers can create a strong voice by carefully choosing various sentence structures and sentence lengths. As you read this story, reflect on the effect of punctuation, clauses, short and long sentences, and sentence fragments.

At first she thought they were raccoons; the spilled garbage and nightly caterwauling under the hedge. The next morning clumps of grey fur were lodged in the armpits of her garden angel. Raccoons for sure.

Luckily they ignored her garbage, and went can tipping next door. Pizza rinds and baloney wrap festooned the shared chain link fence like punk Christmas lights. The neighbours cleaned up their side. They copied her garbage security system of bungee cords, yet night after night their garbage was chosen.

Actually it was irritating. Her can, with its smears of organic hummus and tofu, just didn't rate for raiding. She glared out the window at midnight. To her surprise the raccoons were flat and had stumpy tails. Badgers! In suburban Canada? How exciting!

Time to shop for new tactics: Froot Loops and Cheez Whiz.

She googled "badgers." They couldn't yawn but they liked corn and mushrooms. She made a portabella stew and promptly threw it out. The next morning an empty bacon package was left under her car. She felt angry.

She adored Nature, religiously recycled, shopped organically, left miniscule footprints wherever she trod, and the Peaceable Kingdom up and supped on crappy food next door.

She put out fresh corn only to be greeted by shredded Pop Tart boxes on her patio. She raged. Time to shop for new tactics: Froot Loops and Cheez Whiz. While mixing them in a big bowl, she casually licked a finger. Then, as if she had become someone else, she took another intoxicating taste. ◆

RESPONDING

DISCUSSION QUESTIONS

CONSTRUCTING MEANING
Explain how the structure and length of Karin Weber's sentences add to the story's meaning. Did her sentence choices help or hinder your reading? Support your response.

ANALYZING WORD CHOICE
How has Weber used word choice effectively to develop character? Identify specific details from the story that support your analysis.

ANALYZING LITERARY DEVICES
How has Weber used irony to satirize environmental trends, such as organic food and recycling? Identify the ironic elements and explain how they contribute to Weber's message.

TASKS

DEVELOPING ORAL READINGS
Create three different oral readings of one passage from this story. In your performance, demonstrate how a reader can alter the mood of a story. Experiment with various tones, such as desperation, fury, sarcasm, or sincerity.

DIGITAL LITERACY
Create an animated version of "Invasion of the Snotty Badgers." Begin by developing a storyboard. Try to capture the tone and message of the story.

ABOUT THE AUTHOR
Karin Weber is a Canadian writer and visual artist. Her work explores themes of nature and mythology. "Invasion of the Snotty Badgers" won the Writers' Union of Canada's postcard story competition (the competition is for flash fiction that can fit on a postcard).

WHAT DO YOU THINK?
What is a healthy way to vent your frustrations?

Really?!?

Blog Entry by Sabrina Jalees

Dear Automated Voice-Mail Coach,

ANALYZING LITERARY DEVICES

Sarcasm is an exaggerated form of irony that is intended to ridicule. Vocally sarcastic comments are often delivered slowly and with exaggerated pronunciation. But how do you convey a sarcastic tone in print? Some writers have suggested using the emoticons :-7 or :b to represent sarcasm, while others suggest a sarcasm font. The font uses italic letters leaning in the reversed direction: "That's really clever!"

We get it, lady. I didn't want to have to be the one to break it to you, but you've got to know the truth: you're useless.

Here's the thing, we all know how to leave messages. Believe it or not, we here in the flashy modern world had actually been leaving messages for dozens of years before your robotic voice was born. I don't mean to offend you (do robots have feelings?), but the only thing that your repetitive anthem has been accomplishing is the jacking-up of my daytime minutes.

If we're talking before 6:00 p.m., I wouldn't even let a friend-in-need yammer on for the length of time it takes you to spit out your useless instructions: "At the tone, please record your message; when you are finished recording, you may hang up or press pound for more options."

Really?!? I may hang up? Because for the longest time I was recording my messages and staying on the line with hopes of hearing my favourite podcast. Either that or I would duct tape my phone to a skateboard and physically push it toward the direction of the intended message recipient.

It's not just your worthlessness that bugs me; it's the way you deliver your lines. You'd think you were having an Oprah "Aha!" moment. "Extra, extra! Read all about it: Messages are left after tones and end with hang-ups! Also, the world is round, heroin is addictive, and women are more susceptible to pregnancy than men!" That's really groundbreaking stuff, Captain Obvious.

The only informative thing about your mini speech (and *informative* is a stretch) is your hint about pressing pound. Having the option to review, erase, or re-record our not-so-prolific messages is definitely useful. Then there's the less brilliant option to mark our voice notes as urgent. Isn't that extra label just one more piece of audio-fluff delaying the receiver from getting your urgent message? I'm pretty sure the only people that use this option are desperate ex-lovers who create fake reasons for calling in the first place ("Uh, yeah, I still have that box of stuff that belongs to you and it's totally cramping my apartment, so ... let's have coffee.").

I may hang up? Because for the longest time I was recording my messages and staying on the line with hopes of hearing my favourite podcast.

The thing is, that once would have been enough. Instead of clinging onto each of our voice mails, you should have dialled us all up individually and left us personal messages. It's not too late to do it. Just make sure before you start recording to wait for the tone. When you're finished leaving your message, hang up. Press pound for more options.

See how annoying it is?

Look, I know it's not your fault. You're probably stuck in some windowless cell and chained to a giant microphone. Your robot throat is probably bone dry, and you get little to no time to recharge. You may think, because of this letter's tone (stop recording—it's a homonym), that I'm hoping you'll power yourself down. I swear that's not my intention. I just think you could use some reprogramming.

Your booming voice of guidance could be put to better use. If you were on standby to help us through one of life's more complicated junctures, we could actually grow to appreciate you.

How about an automated break up speech? "Begin changing your Facebook relationship status at the tone. When you're finished, pack up my things and place them outside of your house. Withhold belongings for more options."

I apologize if this note made you feel like a broken tape deck, but I couldn't sit here day after day listening to you embarrass yourself. If you want to go for coffee some time, I've got some other career suggestions I'd like to go over with you. It's urgent.

Love,
Sabrina Jalees

RESPONDING

DISCUSSION QUESTIONS

EXTENDING MEANING
Discuss whether or not you found this blog entry funny and the role prior knowledge may have played.

COMPARING TEXTS
Compare the organization, voice, and word choice in this blog entry to Rick Mercer's rant on page 13.

TASKS

PERFORMING A SCENE
With a small group, create a short scene featuring robots discussing Jalees's blog entry. How will the robots respond to her sarcastic rant? Be sure your scene reaches a conclusion. Present your scene to another group.

WRITING A STORY
Write a short story told only as a series of voice mails. Be sure to create unique characters with distinctive voices.

DEVELOPING A BLOG ENTRY
Write a passionate blog entry using one of the following titles:
- Best Day Ever!
- Worst Purchase Ever!
- Are You Kidding Me?!
- Take That, World!

Demonstrate effective word choice and a distinctive voice. Convince your readers you have strong feelings about your topic. Consider including visuals or audio files to support the blog entry.

AUTHOR THE AUTHOR
Sabrina Jalees is a Canadian comedian, actor, and writer based in Brooklyn, New York. As a stand-up comic, she's toured North America, England, and South Africa. She has played the prestigious Just For Laughs Festival and appeared on *Last Comic Standing*, *Flashpoint*, and MuchMusic's *Video on Trial*. She was nominated for a Gemini and an international Emmy as the host of YTV's *In Real Life*.

WHAT DO YOU THINK?

Some subjects are just too serious to be treated humorously.

+ AGREE
− DISAGREE

Novel Excerpt by John Green from *The Fault in Our Stars*

ANALYZING INTENT

Keep the following quotation from John Green in mind as you read his excerpt: "Remember that people who are sick and people who are dying aren't dead.... Sometimes we forget that, and we treat the sick and the dying so gingerly and so carefully, when often what they most want is to be alive while they are alive.... I've known a lot of young people who were very sick but also very, very funny, and often in dark, dark ways."

Late in the winter of my seventeenth year, my mother decided I was depressed, presumably because I rarely left the house, spent quite a lot of time in bed, read the same book over and over, ate infrequently, and devoted quite a bit of my abundant free time to thinking about death.

Whenever you read a cancer booklet or website or whatever, they always list depression among the side effects of cancer. But, in fact, depression is not a side effect of cancer. Depression is a side effect of dying. (Cancer is also a side effect of dying. Almost everything is, really.) But my mom believed I required treatment, so she took me to see my Regular Doctor, Jim, who agreed that I was veritably swimming in a paralyzing and totally clinical depression, and that therefore my meds should be adjusted and also I should attend a weekly Support Group.

This Support Group featured a rotating cast of characters in various states of tumour-driven unwellness. Why did the cast rotate? A side effect of dying.

The six or seven or ten of us walked/wheeled in, grazed at a decrepit selection of cookies and lemonade, sat down in the Circle of Trust, and listened to Patrick recount for the thousandth time his depressingly miserable life story—how he had cancer and they thought he was going to die, but he didn't die, and now here he is, a full-grown adult in a church basement in the one hundred thirty-seventh nicest city in America, divorced, addicted to video games, mostly friendless, eking out a meagre living by exploiting his cancertastic past, slowly working his way toward a master's degree that will not improve his career prospects, waiting, as we all do, for the sword of Damocles to give him the relief that he escaped lo those many years ago.

AND YOU TOO MIGHT BE SO LUCKY!

Then we introduced ourselves: Name. Age. Diagnosis. And how we're doing today. I'm Hazel, I'd say when they'd get to me. Sixteen. Thyroid originally but with an impressive and long-settled satellite colony in my lungs. And I'm doing OK.

Once we got around the circle, Patrick always asked if anyone wanted to share. And then began the Circle of Trust: everyone talking about fighting and battling and winning and shrinking and scanning. To be fair to Patrick, he let us talk about dying, too. But most of them weren't dying. Most would live into adulthood, as Patrick had.

(Which meant there was quite a lot of competitiveness about it, with everybody wanting to beat not only cancer itself, but also the other people in the room. Like, I realize that this is irrational, but when they tell you that you have, say, a 20 percent chance of living five years, the math kicks in and you figure that's one in five ... so you look around and think, as any healthy person would: I gotta outlast four of these kids.)

The only redeeming facet of Support Group was this kid named Isaac, a long-faced, skinny guy with straight blond hair swept over one eye.

And his eyes were the problem. He had some fantastically improbable eye cancer. One eye had been cut out when he was a kid, and now he wore the kind of thick glasses that made his eyes (both the real one and the glass one) preternaturally huge, like his whole head was basically just this fake eye and this real eye staring at you. From what I could gather on the rare occasions when Isaac shared with the group, a recurrence had placed his remaining eye in mortal peril.

Isaac and I communicated almost exclusively through sighs. Each time someone discussed anticancer diets or snorting ground-up shark fin or whatever, he'd glance over at me and sigh ever so slightly. I'd shake my head microscopically and exhale in response.

So Support Group blew, and after a few weeks, I grew to be rather kicking-and-screaming about the whole affair. In fact, on the Wednesday I made the acquaintance of Augustus Waters, I tried my level best to get out of Support Group while sitting on the couch with my mom in the third leg of a twelve-hour marathon of the previous season's *America's Next Top Model*, which, admittedly, I had already seen, but still.

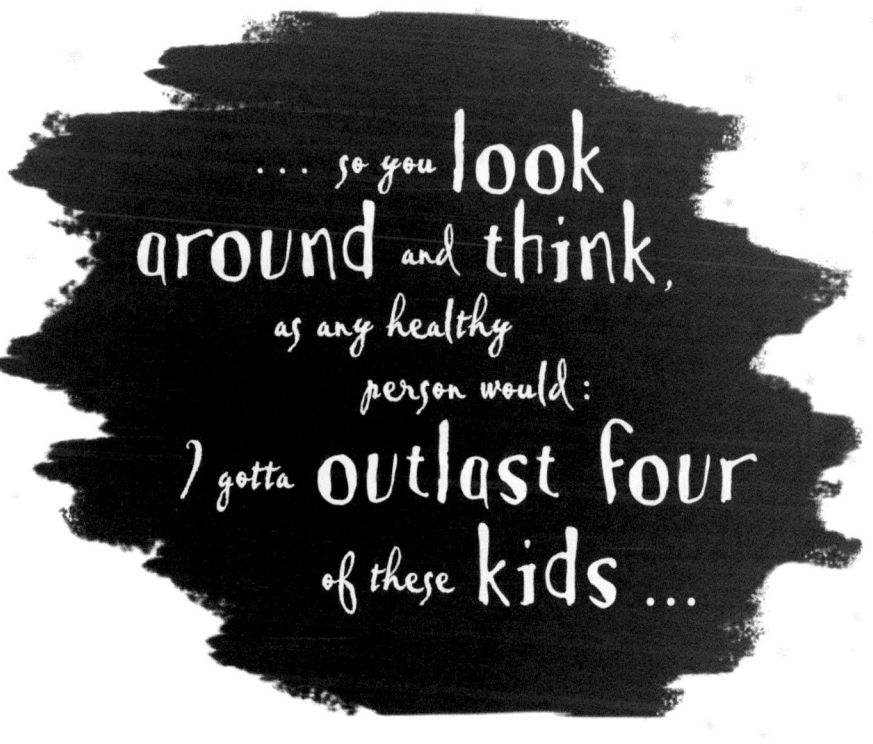

... so you look around and think, as any healthy person would: I gotta outlast four of these kids ...

DAD: (*offscreen*) OK, I've found the device.

OTHER OFFICER: (*offscreen, over radio*) COPY.

Cut to exterior car. Dad takes off his helmet and analyzes the bomb; daughter reads from a Take-Your-Daughter-to-Work-Day form, while filming father with her phone.

DAUGHTER: What's your official job title?

DAD: Could we do this afterwards, sweetie?

DAUGHTER: Can I take this helmet off?

DAD: Absolutely not.

DAUGHTER: It's hurting my face.

DAD: So would shrapnel. And third-degree burns.

DAUGHTER: You took your helmet off.

DAD: Just try to relax and watch your dad defuse this bomb—

DAUGHTER: (*looking at the bomb*) Shouldn't I be standing back with the motorcade during this—?

DAD: No, absolutely not. You're perfectly safe—(*into radio*) I'm looking at six sticks of construction-grade dynamite, two propane tanks, and two containers of what's gotta be gasoline—

DAUGHTER: If I'm totally safe, why can't I take my helmet off?

//Analyzing Voice

As you read the lines for each character, try to hear his or her voice in your head. Make connections to infer what that voice sounds like. For example, how do you think the daughter sounds when she says "It's hurting my face"? What connections help you figure that out?

Driver is seated absolutely still in the front seat, wires hang down the back of his seat.

DRIVER: Am I gonna blow up?

DAD: You're doing great, son. Hang in there— (*to Daughter*) You can keep filming me, though—

DAUGHTER: You didn't really answer his question—

DAD: (*into radio*) Got a timer counting down, probably started when device was armed—

DRIVER: How long does the timer have?

DAD: Stay calm, son— (*into radio*) Driver must've armed it when he sat down. Probably rigged to go if he tries to get up—

DRIVER: So I should keep sitting here—

DAD: One second, son— (*looks to Daughter*) What are you doing—?

DAUGHTER: Haley texted me, I'm just responding to her real quick.

DAD: Right now. Seriously.

DAUGHTER: Almost done—

DAD: Is she with her dad today, too?

DAUGHTER: Yeah.

DAD: And what does he do?

DAUGHTER: He's a writer.

DAD: Oh. So he's saving lives, too.

DAUGHTER: No, he … oh.

She gives Dad a look. He smiles. She goes back to texting. He's losing her.

DAD: You know what, let's do the form now. I can do two things at once.

DAUGHTER: Are you sure?

DAD: Let's do this, Barbara Walters.

She picks up the form, opens her visor—Dad promptly shuts it— and she starts to read aloud while he goes about disarming the bomb.

DAUGHTER: Describe your work, what you do during the day, and why you chose this profession—

DAD: One question at a time—

DAUGHTER: That's the first question.

DAD: That's, like, seven questions—

DAUGHTER: I didn't write it—

DAD: I certainly hope not, you're smart enough to know basic math—

DAUGHTER: Describe your work—

DAD: I defuse bombs.

DAUGHTER: What you do during the day—

DAD: I defuse bombs.

DAUGHTER: Why you chose this profession—

DAD: Because the bombs need to be defused.

DAUGHTER: Can you maybe elaborate just a little bit?

DAD: Because the bombs need to be defused or they'll explode.

DRIVER: The bomb's gonna explode!?

DAD: Not yet, son … Just quiet down—

DRIVER: Why do I have to be quiet? Is the bomb triggered by sound?

DAD: (*beat*) Yep.

Driver buys it.

DAUGHTER: What is the best advice you can give a young person thinking about his or her career?

DAD: Go to college. For forever.

DAUGHTER: Oh my God—

DAD: Gosh—

DAUGHTER: On the job, are you part of a team?

DAD: Sure.

OTHER OFFICER: (*apparently been there the entire time*) YES—

DAD: Right. Yeah.

DAUGHTER: If yes, please explain your role on the team—

DAD: To defuse the bombs.

DAUGHTER: Roughly how much money does a person make in your occupation? High, medium, or low?

OTHER OFFICER: High—

DAD: Enough.

DAUGHTER: (*looking at phone*) Wikipedia says around $46 000.

OTHER OFFICER: Wait, seriously—?

Dad motions to change the subject.

OTHER OFFICER: That sounds really high—

DAD: (*to Other Officer*) Go check on the driver, will ya?

Other Officer goes.

DAUGHTER: What education prepared you for your work?

DAD: A full four years of college.

DAUGHTER: Are you kidding me, Dad—

DAD: Plus maybe even graduate school.

DAUGHTER: Dad—

DAD: All within a 30-minute radius of my hometown.

DAUGHTER: OK, got it—

DAD: And I got straight As the whole time—

OTHER OFFICER: So if I had gone to graduate school, would I be making $46 000 a year—?

DRIVER: EVERYONE'S BEING WAY TOO LOUD!!!

//Script Conventions

Punctuation in a script may be used in unconventional ways. Here, the use of a dash shows how the actors are interrupting or talking over each other. This gives the actors a sense of how quickly paced the scene will be. The effect is to create chaotic, yet realistic, dialogue.

Camera closes in on Dad framed by wires.

Dad: THERE YOU ARE. I've located the timing circuit and I'm bypassing it—

Other Officer: Sir, don't you think—

Dad: You watching, honey?

Other Officer: Yes, but—

Daughter: I'm watching …

Other Officer: Oh, you were talking to—

Dad: (*connecting the jump wire*) Just … like … that—

Cut to the timer, which flickers OFF. Then it comes back ON, and the countdown accelerates. Everyone panics.

Dad: That wasn't it. Timer is now accelerated.

Driver: What'd he say?

Other Officer: Nothing. It's … code.

Dad springs into action, trying to fix what he did.

Daughter: OK, if it helps, I already have "disarming a bomb" pulled up on Wikipedia—

Dad: Not now, honey—

Driver: What does it say?

Daughter: A lot— but apparently half the page needs to be verified—

Dad: OK, fine, read it aloud to me—

// Analyzing Literary Devices

The bomb disposal team trying to decide which wire to cut is a stock scene that appears in many TV shows and movies. In this case, the scriptwriters are using this overused scene purposefully for comic effect.

> **// Script Conventions**
>
> Often, a script will tell the actors how something should be said by using parenthetical notes before the words to be spoken. For example, "DAD: (*impatiently*) I know what I am doing." In this script, the scriptwriters also use all caps, for example, "BOMB," to show the tone of voice the actors will use.

OTHER OFFICER: Sir, shouldn't our priority be—

DAD: I've got this under control, son—

DAUGHTER: Dad, are you sure you even know what you're doing—?

DAD: YES. I know what I am doing—

DAUGHTER: I thought when you got promoted, you stopped having to do this kind of stuff—?

DAD: (*impatiently*) I know what I am doing.

DAUGHTER: I thought you worked behind a desk now—

DAD: Honey—

DAUGHTER: When was the last time you actually disarmed one of these things?

DAD: I said—

DAUGHTER: Can I at least go back to the motorcade?

DAD: You're safe right here—

DAUGHTER: With the BOMB?

DAD: WITH ME—

Beep beep beep—it's been there all along, but suddenly it's all Dad can hear. The quiet ticking of the timer—the objectivity light in his brain switches on. What is he doing here?

DAD: (*to Other Officer*) I think it'd be a good idea for you to take my daughter and get to safety now. I'll stay with the device—

OTHER OFFICER: Like that scene in *Armageddon*—

DAD: No, it's not—

OTHER OFFICER: Don't worry, sir. I'll take good care of your daughter—

DAD: On second thought, this is a terrible idea—

DAUGHTER: Dad—

Daughter grabs Dad and pulls him aside. She opens her visor. Dad promptly shuts it.

DAUGHTER: Let the other techs do this. Stop trying to impress me.

DAD: I'm not trying to impress you.

DAUGHTER: I don't know how you think I see you, Dad, but there's nothing unheroic about leading from behind a desk.

DAD: I know that—

Meanwhile—

OTHER OFFICER: Hey, guys, you're totally cool, um I'm just gonna go ahead and disarm this bomb—

Dad looks at Other Officer, then Daughter, then back to Other Officer.

DAD: No. You started to say it earlier and I cut you off. Our priority is the driver.

Dad and Other Officer spring into action, working together.

DAD: Which of these have you already checked?

OTHER OFFICER: I marked 'em. So far they just loop back to each other or to nothing. Except these—(*points*)—I can't verify them.

DAD: (*to Other Officer*) What's your gut tell you?

OTHER OFFICER: To vomit. Just everywhere.

DAD: Your other gut.

OTHER OFFICER: That, that's the one. (*He points.*)

DAD: All right, then set it.

OTHER OFFICER: Yes, sir.

Dad looks up at Daughter—

DAD: The yellow one. Your favourite colour.

DAUGHTER: That's not— Yes.

Other Officer carefully sets the jump wire.

OTHER OFFICER: We're CLEAR—

They both reach in to get Driver out.

DAD: (*to Other Officer*) Good work. (*hand on Other Officer's shoulder*) You have permission to date my daughter.

OTHER OFFICER: Thank you, but I'm married—

DRIVER: I'll do it.

DAD: Too loud, son, the bomb can still hear you—

They go to pull Driver from the car, when …

DAD: WAIT—

They stop.

Dad is staring down at a small, nondescript antenna attached to the roof of the car.

DAD: Do you have a CB radio in there, son?

DRIVER: No. Do I need one?

DAD: Don't get out yet.

Dad walks over to antenna.

DAD: That antenna has no reason to be here.

OTHER OFFICER: Unless the bomber's got a remote—

DAD: No … he's got all the people around this car he's gonna get before it blows. If he had a remote, he would have pulled the trigger by now.

OTHER OFFICER: Then what else could it be for?

Dad realizes—

DAD: No— There's a remote—

Dad starts following wires.

DAD: But the bomber doesn't have it …

He follows wires to UNDERNEATH THE CAR—where he finds a transmitter attached to the underside of the vehicle.

DAD: … we do.

Other Officer and Daughter get down beside him.

OTHER OFFICER: Oh my God—

DAUGHTER: Gosh—

OTHER OFFICER: Sorry—

DAD: It's his backup device on the driver's seat. I need my tools.

Other Officer hands Dad the tools he needs. Dad proceeds to very quickly set the jump wire as the timer closes in. Daughter, still wearing the helmet, stays down on the ground beside him.

DAD: (*working fast*) Sweetie, I'm glad that you finally wanna watch your dad work, but I need you to get to a safe place.

DAUGHTER: I am in a safe place.

Dad looks at Daughter.

DAD: Your head is stuck, isn't it.

DAUGHTER: Can't move. It's like I'm part of this car now.

He reaches across and unhooks her helmet for her. He turns back and sets the jump wire and pulls himself up, leaving the helmet behind.

// **Script Conventions**

Movie scripts use words and phrases like *cut*, *pan*, and *fade out* to describe how a scene is being shot. Consider the effect these techniques will have on the audience.

Cut to Other Officer standing. He pulls Driver from the car as Dad and Daughter rise up into frame.

DAD: Let's go—

They run for cover.

Cut to point of view from Daughter's phone, looking at her feet as they all run, until finally camera pans back to show the car being blown to kingdom come. Pans over to Dad, watching.

DAUGHTER: (*offscreen*) So, Dad, what is your official job title?

He turns to camera.

DAD: I'm Lieutenant—

DAUGHTER: (*offscreen*) No, Dad—

She drops the camera, whispers something. Camera comes back up.

DAD: I defuse bombs.

A small explosion in the background.

DAD: Except that one.

End credits. A silhouette of everyone watching the explosion. Driver looks around.

DRIVER: Can I get a ride home …?

Fade out. ◆

RESPONDING

DISCUSSION QUESTIONS

ANALYZING GENRE
Identify at least three of the visual jokes in this script. Consider how the jokes might have been written in a short story version of the script.

MAKING INFERENCES
What inferences do the scriptwriters expect the audience to make about the relationship between the father and daughter? Support your analysis with specific details.

CRITICAL LITERACY
How have the scriptwriters used stereotypes for comic effect? Identify specific details and explain how the scriptwriters use the audience's expectations to create humour.

TASKS

WRITING IN ROLE
Writing in role, create the "Take Your Daughter to Work Day" report that the daughter might produce after the events in the script. Reflect details and events from the script, capturing her voice and her relationship with her father.

CREATING A MONOLOGUE
Choose one of the characters and decide what he or she would say to a loved one at the end of this traumatic day. Develop and present a monologue.

The World Ends on WEDNESDAY

Skit by Tim Cooper

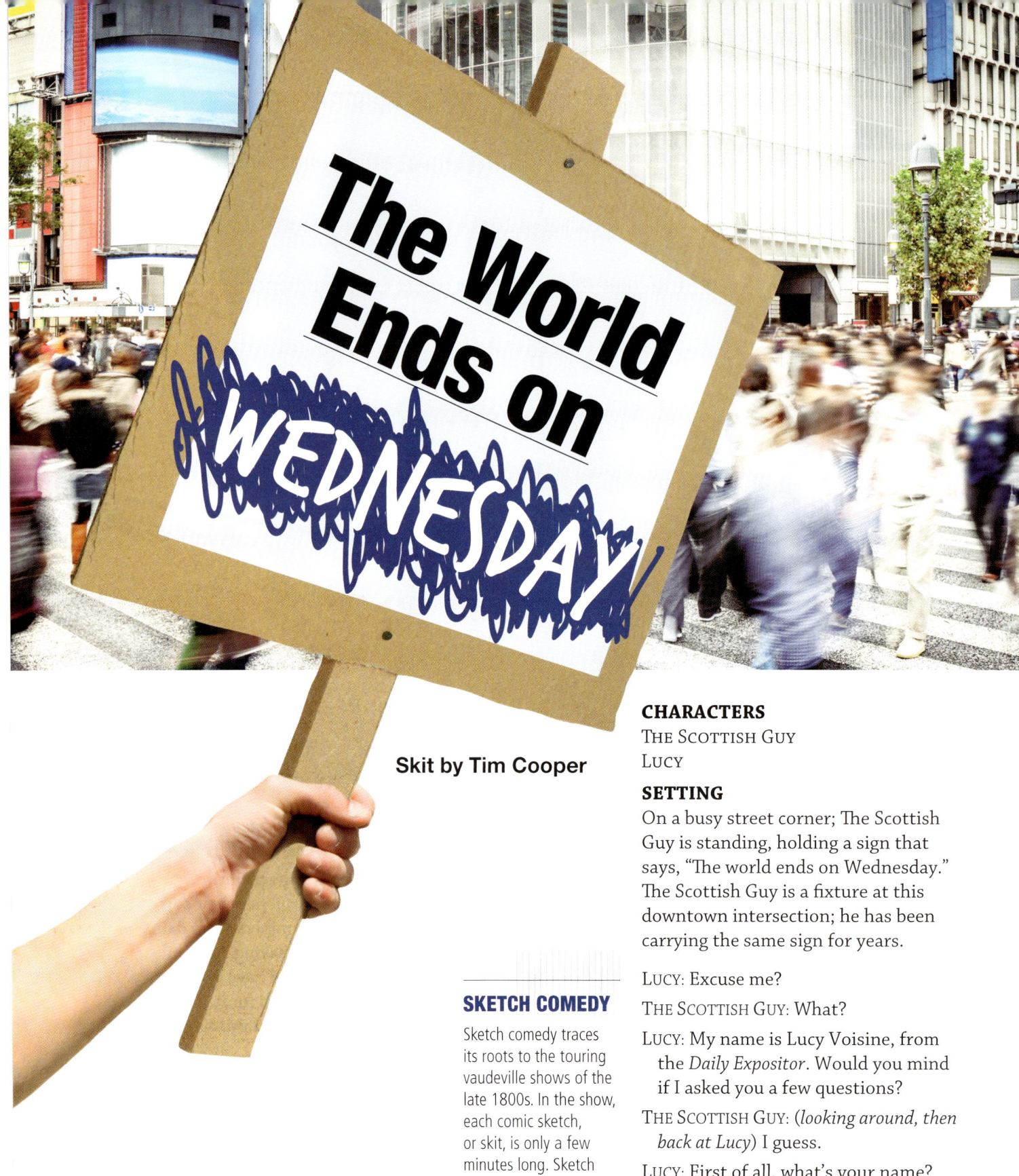

SKETCH COMEDY

Sketch comedy traces its roots to the touring vaudeville shows of the late 1800s. In the show, each comic sketch, or skit, is only a few minutes long. Sketch comedy troupes use popular characters or situations.

CHARACTERS
The Scottish Guy
Lucy

SETTING
On a busy street corner; The Scottish Guy is standing, holding a sign that says, "The world ends on Wednesday." The Scottish Guy is a fixture at this downtown intersection; he has been carrying the same sign for years.

Lucy: Excuse me?

The Scottish Guy: What?

Lucy: My name is Lucy Voisine, from the *Daily Expositor*. Would you mind if I asked you a few questions?

The Scottish Guy: (*looking around, then back at Lucy*) I guess.

Lucy: First of all, what's your name?

The Scottish Guy: Bodo Mueller.

Lucy: That's not exactly a Scottish name.

The Scottish Guy: Why would I have a Scottish name? I'm Austrian.

Lucy: So what's with the kilt?

162 Nelson English Unit 3: Humour

THE SCOTTISH GUY: Hey, not only the Scottish can wear kilts! Kilts are convenient. And cheap. And I have the legs for it.

LUCY: (*scribbling every word in her notebook*) Legs for it, this is great. About the sign—

THE SCOTTISH GUY: What about it?

LUCY: "The world ends on Wednesday." You've carried that message for years.

THE SCOTTISH GUY: I don't follow.

LUCY: Why Wednesday?

THE SCOTTISH GUY: The world has to end someday. Why not Wednesday?

Lucy is speechless.

THE SCOTTISH GUY: Do you gamble? Play the lottery?

LUCY: Sometimes.

THE SCOTTISH GUY: OK. The odds of winning the lottery are really, really small. Same with the world ending— I have a one-in-seven chance of being right.

LUCY: OK, now I don't follow.

THE SCOTTISH GUY: People guess about stuff all the time, mostly the future. I don't know, like retirement or did they marry the right person. They don't know the truth, so they guess. I guess, too, but about the end of the world.

LUCY: So why the sign?

THE SCOTTISH GUY: I wanna be on the record.

LUCY: But what if you're wrong?

THE SCOTTISH GUY: Who's gonna know? The world's over.

LUCY: (*thinking for a moment*) Can't argue with that. Thanks. I think I have what I need. I'll write up an article and pitch it to the paper.

THE SCOTTISH GUY: Sounds good. Oh, can you do me a favour?

LUCY: What's that?

THE SCOTTISH GUY: Could you publish the story by Tuesday? The world's gonna end on Wednesday. ◆

ANALYZING WORD CHOICE

Consider how scriptwriters use language to make their characters sound natural. They may use contractions, dialect, slang, and even grammatical errors. "Who's gonna know?" sounds more natural than "Who is going to know?"

RESPONDING

DISCUSSION QUESTIONS

EVALUATING
How funny are these skits? Explain your analysis with specific references.

ANALYZING HUMOUR
Most humour is fast-paced. Count the number of lines in each skit and the number of jokes. How effective is the pacing of each skit?

CRITICAL LITERACY
Evaluate the use of stereotypes in "The World Ends on Wednesday" and explain how different audiences might respond to these stereotypes.

TASKS

PERFORMING A SCENE
Create and perform a sequel to either skit. How could Tim Cooper further develop the narrative? Remember that your skit must end with a punchline.

RESEARCH AND INQUIRY
Research to find a funny skit. Share the skit with others and explain why you think it is funny.

WRITING TO PERSUADE
What fictional character would you want to be named after? Write a persuasive essay to your parents or guardians trying to convince them that you should change your name.

AUTHOR NOTE

Tim Cooper lives in Hamilton, Ontario. He says of his writing, "The stories I write are borne out of my observations of everyday life and the conversations that invariably blossom in my imagination. I'm curious to see how very different people would interact if brought together in unusual circumstances. Humour is the inevitable result. I cannot remember a time when I didn't write. I suppose I've always seen the world as a very funny place."

ANALYZING AUDIENCE RESPONSES

The audience is the only critic that matters. When creating media texts, producers must be very aware of their intended audience at every step of the production process. Analyzing audience responses to media texts requires a clear understanding of the audience's prior knowledge, culture, and context.

// SATIRE VERSUS PARODY

Satire is a form of humour intended to provoke a strong audience response. When creating satirical texts, producers might exaggerate the characteristics of a person or a situation in order to reveal a problem. Politicians and public figures are frequent targets of satire.

Parody is a simpler form of humour with one purpose: to entertain. Successful parodies require that the producers and audience share a prior knowledge of the subject being mocked. Unlike satire, parody does not concern itself with addressing political or social issues.

CONSIDERATIONS WHEN ANALYZING AUDIENCE RESPONSES

Prior Knowledge and Experiences
How an audience responds to any media text depends on what that audience already knows about a topic or how it feels about an issue. This knowledge becomes especially relevant when a media text uses humour. When an audience fails to respond to humour, it may be due to the media producer making a wrong assumption about what the audience knows or how it feels. Ask yourself: What does an audience need to know to appreciate this media text? What elements in the media text might an audience not like and why?

Culture
All media texts are culturally biased; the bias might be reflected in the clothing, music, language, or even the depiction of relationships. For example, consider how a Bollywood movie might differ from a movie made in Canada. As well, how the audience responds to these different movies will depend on the culture of the audience. Ask yourself: How might the cultural background of audience members influence their responses to this media text? What elements in the media text might appeal to this audience?

Context
All media texts are created within a particular context. The context in which a media text is viewed also influences the audience's response and ends up influencing how the audience interprets the meaning of the text. Ask yourself: How would an audience of my peers respond? How might the audience response change over time or in different situations?

Creation Context
Who created this media text?
When and where was it created?
Who was it created for?
Why was it created?

+

Viewing Context
Who is watching this media text?
Where and when?
Is the current audience the intended target audience?

=

Audience Interpretation
What does the text mean to its audience?
How would the intended audience respond to this text?
How does context affect the audience's interpretation of the text?

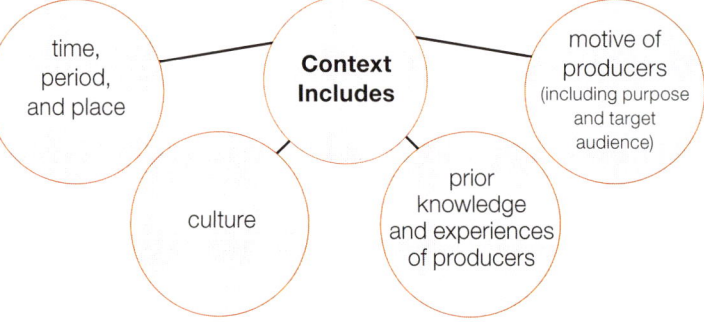

Context Includes:
- time, period, and place
- culture
- prior knowledge and experiences of producers
- motive of producers (including purpose and target audience)

Campaign Emails from the Donahue Family Pet Debate

WHAT DO YOU THINK?
How democratic should families be?

Story by Johnny McNulty

✉ **From:** Martin
Subject: One Step Closer

Dear Family,

I've just come from a spirited but productive Family Meeting. We can now finally repair the dog-shaped hole in the hearts of the majority of family members. The cat campaign was skillfully waged, but ultimately the dog had the day. Myself, Dad, and Kevin voted for a dog, and Mom and Laura voted for a cat.

Now, the boys understand our sister's preference for a cat, and we're totally up for talking about that later, after the dog settles in. But Laura's claim that a dog will be given her room is fear-mongering hyperbole. Any hint we gave that that was true was just teasing. As for Mom's assertion that Dad got to pick the car so she should pick the animal that stays home with her all darn day, I appeal to her sense of democracy and respect for majority rule.

And Kevin, while getting a Rottweiler would be nice, it's unlikely, and the point of this process is getting a terrific canine pet, not one specific option.

Let's advance with respect and optimism as we begin the search for the right dog for our family. We rightfully had a vigorous debate, but now we must unite to accept this puppy into our home.

Sincerely,
Martin Donahue
Eldest Sibling

From: Laura
Subject: Nuh Uh

Dear Family,

No way did we decide to get a dog tonight. There were two votes for cat, two votes for dog, and Kevin voted for a Rottweiler.

On a multiple-choice test, if the options are either A or B, and you write down Rottweiler, you don't get credit. Kevin did not vote for a dog. Kevin voted for a Rottweiler. Since we're never going to get a Rottweiler, Kevin's vote doesn't count.

We'll vote again at next week's Family Meeting. Tonight didn't count. We should spend as much time on the issue as it takes to realize we need a cat.

Dogs are big, smelly, and dumb. I don't want one. Mom doesn't want one. It's the wrong decision. What's happening to the family we used to know?

Plus, Dad, I looked on the Internet, and dogs are way more expensive than cats. Remember that whole big talk about saving money, and you told Mom you'd cut golfing next, promise? Maybe she and I would forget you said that with a cat. Or I could give up my phone! I would!

If we get a cat, it will love us and you can even take pictures of it and put them on the Internet if you want.

<3<3<3<3
Laura Donahue
Travel Team Soccer Captain

P.S. Martin, once "the dog settles in," we'll have to "get you a car" or "send you to college." The pet window is now, and you're 15. You're gone in three years; you're too old to vote. This is NOT over. We are GETTING a NICE, FLUFFY KITTY.

From: Susan Donahue
Subject: Go to bed.

We are not talking about this anymore tonight.

—Mom

✉ **From:** Kevin
Subject: Facts

Facts:
- Rottweilers originated during the Roman Empire.
- Rottweilers herded the cattle that armies brought along for food.
- Our Rottweiler would let you lay your head on his belly next to a fire.
- Rottweilers worked as draught animals to haul carts.
- Rottweilers were also police and military dogs.
- Our Rottweiler, Jake, could jump out of bushes and scare Timmy Delarosa when he teases me.
- Despite their fierce reputation, Rottweilers are simply very loyal and like to work a lot.
- Rottweilers were the most popular dog in America during part of the 1990s.
- Rottweilers are awesome.
- Rottweilers are the best kind of dog, so why would you get a different dog?
- Cats are lazy and boring.

Rottweiler,
Kevin

✉ **From:** Laura
Subject: Why Are We Even Talking About This?

Dear Family,

Once again, Mom says stop, and one of the boys disobeys and spouts pro-dog nonsense anyway. We are not getting a Rottweiler. Both Mom and Dad said so, and Tina's dad got a Rottweiler and now she said his assurance rates went up.

I don't care if Kevin reads Rottweiler books all day, that's not a reason to bring a murderer into the house. You're gonna be upset when the Rottweiler eats me, Dad.

Kevin only wants a Rottweiler. We can't get a Rottweiler, so he doesn't count as a dog vote.

<3<3<3<3
Laura Donahue
Travel Team Soccer Captain

ROTTWEILER

WHY WOULD YOU GET A DIFFERENT DOG?

// **Analyzing Literary Devices**

The *epistolary form* is a type of story told using a collection of documents, usually letters or emails. The word *epistle* is Greek for *letter*. The epistolary form was used by Mary Shelley in *Frankenstein* and by Bram Stoker in *Dracula*. The inclusion of "real" letters and reports helped make these fantastical stories more believable.

Campaign Emails from the Donahue Family Pet Debate

✉ **From:** Martin
Subject: Pot and Tea Kettle

Dear Family,

Laura is obviously talking just as much as Kevin after Mom said not to. And it's *insurance* rates. Maybe you and Kevin are just too young to weigh in. So it's still 2–1, me and Dad versus Mom.

We both know that Kevin will go for a dog over a cat. Stop trying to divide everybody.

Taking the high road,
Martin

✉ **From:** Susan Donahue
Subject: RE: Go to bed.

GO TO BED. WE ARE NEVER GETTING A PET. IF ANYTHING, I'M DEBATING DECREASING HOW MANY THINGS LIVE IN THIS HOUSE.

—Mom

✉ **From:** John Donahue
Subject: Come downstairs

Hey guys, sorry I've been gone all night but I've got a surprise for you! It's either a dog or a sweet science experiment, but there's definitely a chocolate lab downstairs!

Love,
Dad

✉ **From:** Martin Donahue
Subject: RE: Come downstairs

Dear Family,

WOOOO! Let's all get behind our new dog!

Sincerely,
Martin

//Analyzing Literary Devices

In selections intended to amuse, writers often use literary devices like hyperbole and understatement. Hyperbole can help set up a joke, while understatement is frequently used in punch lines. Consider how this story uses both hyperbole and understatement to structure its humour.

✉ **From:** Laura
Subject: Re: RE: Come downstairs

This isn't over. That dog is illegitimate.

✉ **From:** Kevin
Subject: Re: Re: RE: Come downstairs

Although I still believe that a Rottweiler is the best option, I have no choice but to admit this dog is pretty awesome. Thanks, Dad! I guess.

—k

✉ **From:** Susan Donahue
Subject: Re: Re: Re: RE: Come downstairs

John,

I believe there's a summit of the G2 powers upstairs right now, discussing the possibility of sleeping-on-the-couch sanctions.

✉ **From:** Buddy
Subject: Re: Re: Re: Re: RE: Come downstairs

Did I miss something? I'm in trouble, aren't I?

RESPONDING

DISCUSSION QUESTIONS

MAKING INFERENCES
What events and discussions does the reader have to infer took place prior to the first email?

ANALYZING VOICE
How does Johnny McNulty use ideas, word choice, and sentence fluency effectively to create each character's unique voice?

CRITICAL LITERACY
Identify the stereotypes in this story. Is it possible to maintain the humour in the story without relying on stereotypes? Explain.

TASKS

PERFORMING A SCRIPT
Write and rehearse a script of voice-mail messages that tell the story of the family's first week living with the dog. Be sure to maintain the voices of the characters.

WRITING AN EPISTOLARY STORY
Use this story as a model to write your own story using letters, emails, or instant messages. Consider what situation or problem will require a series of communications. Who will be communicating about the problem? How will you use ideas, word choice, and sentence fluency effectively to create voices for your characters?

AUTHOR NOTE
Of this story, Johnny McNulty says, "I wrote 'Campaign Emails From The Donahue Family Pet Debate' in November, 2009 as a satire of the vicious battle over President Obama's health care proposals. While political satire has always been my favorite form of humour, comedy is challenging enough to be rewarding on even the stupidest subjects."

"It's sad to see how out of line so many people's basic priorities are."

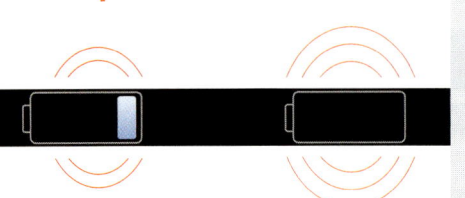

HOW LOYAL ARE iPHONE CUSTOMERS?

A survey conducted by Protect Your Bubble, an insurance company, revealed that over 50% of iPhone customers would rather lose their wallet than their iPhone.

The iPhone's owner issued a statement through her attorney:

"My client deeply regrets the incident, and wishes to express a sincere apology to the police, the community, and the fine manufacturers at Apple," said lawyer Henry Durst, who was retained by the suspect following her arrest. "My client is remorseful and clearly emotionally distraught. This is her first iPhone."

Nonetheless, local government officials remain disturbed by what they are calling "inhuman" treatment of the iPhone.

"My husband and I have been trying for months, but so far, we've been unable to have an iPhone," town assemblywoman Janet Nuetreer said. "But if we did, we would understand that there is nothing more important."

"Sadly, this sort of mistreatment of iPhones is more widespread than people think," said Dr. Jordan Heimlich, director of Winnetka Community Services, who is currently supervising the iPhone's care. "People leave their iPhones precariously perched on the edges of counters; they forget to charge them; they even fail to provide them with basic necessities like a decorative carrying case. I've even heard of iPhones being dropped."

"But I've never seen anything like this happen here in Winnetka before," she added. "It's sad to see how out of line so many people's basic priorities are."

Authorities added that it was "just sheer luck" that the toddler who was also left in the car was unconscious at the time, as otherwise he could have potentially damaged the iPhone. ◆

RESPONDING

DISCUSSION QUESTIONS

ANALYZING FORM
Identify the elements in this parody that combine to mimic a news article. Which of these elements contributes the most to the success of the parody? Support your response.

ANALYZING THEME
Identify the theme, purpose, and subject of this news parody and explain how all three are connected. What or whom does the article parody? What is the purpose in creating this news parody?

CRITICAL LITERACY
Some readers find the final paragraph of the selection to be in bad taste. Do you agree or disagree? Explain and defend your judgment. How do you think *The Onion* expected the audience to respond?

TASKS

DEBATING
Debate one of the following statements. Before you begin, choose a side and jot down some ideas for your topic.
- Electronic gadgets are overvalued.
- Most people's basic priorities are out of line.
- Electronic gadgets have greatly improved the lifestyle of the average Canadian.
- Canadians are generally materialistic.
- Canadians are stereotyped as being materialistic.

CREATING A VISUAL REPRESENTATION
Create a visual representation for the ideas or theme of this parody. You may include words or phrases from the text. Convince viewers of the seriousness of the issues you are raising.

FOCUS ON Writing

> "The ill and unfit choice of words wonderfully obstructs the understanding."
> —Francis Bacon

IMPROVING WORD CHOICE

Choosing the right words transforms tired, drab prose into writing that's powerful and alive. The words writers use help to make their voices distinct.

STRATEGIES FOR IMPROVING WORD CHOICE

STRATEGY	ASK YOURSELF
Match word choice to your purpose and audience.	Are my words entertaining, persuasive, or informative? Will my readers be frustrated by any of the vocabulary I'm using?
Choose strong, evocative words.	How will readers visualize what I've just described? Have I created clarity? Have I used a strong voice?
Use synonyms for overused or vague words.	Can I replace words such as *say*, *go*, and *like* with more specific synonyms?
Choose the exact word you want.	Does the word have both the denotation and connotation I want? Is the connotation of the word wrong or awkward? Will my readers make the inferences I want them to make?
Play with language.	How can I use idioms, similes, and metaphors to make my voice stronger? Will my readers still understand what it is I am trying to say?
Show, don't tell.	Is there a way to show my readers what my characters are like without telling them directly?
Reread your work. Check to see if you can eliminate some words or if you need to add more description.	Do I have so many words that I'll bore my readers? Or so few words that my readers are puzzled?
Begin to refine your word choice as you edit and revise.	How will my readers respond? Is that the response I want? Does my word choice reflect my purpose and audience, and the voice I want my work to have? Am I communicating clearly and effectively?

SAMPLE TEXT

"Our cell number is on the fridge," the escaping parents called out, without a backward glance at their spawn or the new babysitter.

Sarah cast a weary and wary glance at the six anklebiters sitting quietly in front of the TV. As soon as the door closed, they swarmed her, a tsunami of grubby, yowling urchins.

// DENOTATION AND CONNOTATION

Denotation is the most specific or direct meaning of a word. *Connotation* is the emotional associations a word has beyond its meaning. For example, while the words *youngster*, *anklebiter*, *progeny*, *bambino*, *little one*, *wee one*, *whippersnapper*, *rugrat*, *brat*, and *spawn* can all be used to mean *child*, some of these words have negative connotations, some have positive connotations, and some are neutral. The context in which a word appears will also affect its connotation.

// CONFUSABLE WORDS

Make sure you choose the words you want, and not words that are spelled somewhat like the words you want. Examples of confusable words include *affect* and *effect*, *complement* and *compliment*, *allude* and *elude*, *lose* and *loose*, *choose* and *chose*, *compose* and *comprise*, *elicit* and *illicit*.

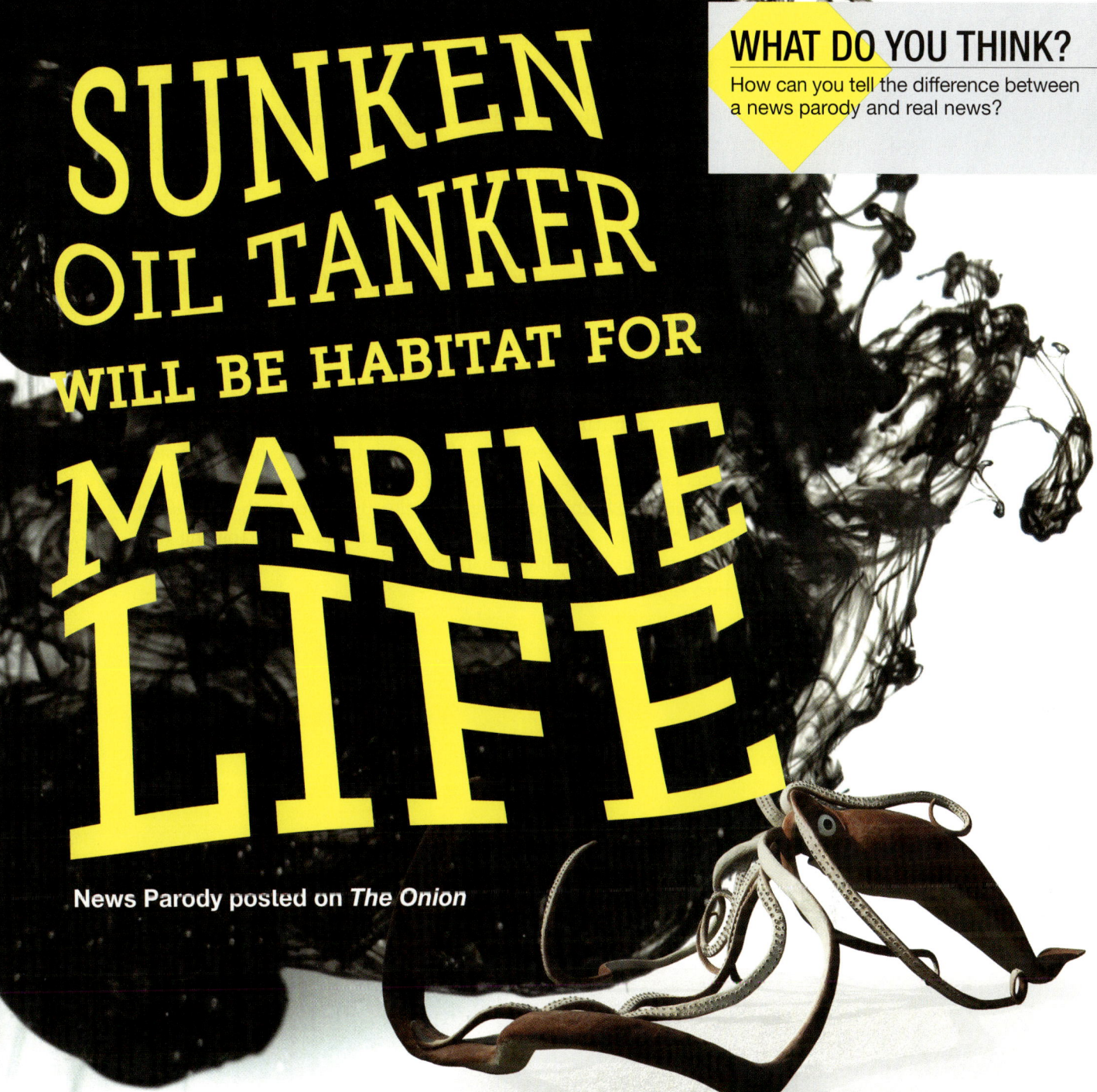

SUNKEN OIL TANKER WILL BE HABITAT FOR MARINE LIFE

News Parody posted on *The Onion*

WHAT DO YOU THINK?
How can you tell the difference between a news parody and real news?

// **Analyzing Word Choice**

When reading parodies, paying careful attention to the writer's word choice can be particularly important. Consider how phrases such as *with a straight face* and *without a trace of irony* can help readers understand this selection.

HOUSTON, TX—The 329-metre, 270 000-tonne oil tanker the Shell *Global Explorer*, which sank off the coast of Newfoundland and Labrador last month, will provide a welcome habitat for many diverse species of endangered marine life, Shell Oil Company executives announced with a straight face Tuesday.

"In its new resting place, far beneath the surface of the North Atlantic, the *Global Explorer* is host to countless fish and an infinite variety of marine vegetation," a press release from Shell read without a trace of irony. "A ship that once helped run life above the waves now houses life beneath them."

The reading of the press release preceded public statements from Shell executives.

"We in the petroleum industry have long believed that we have a responsibility to protect and conserve the environment in our daily business operations," said Shell CEO Steven L. Miller to reporters in the face of all available evidence. "We view this commitment to projects that will conserve and protect the marine ecosystem as an important investment in our future."

"At Shell, we're proud to provide a niche for the struggling denizens of our oceans," said Shell vice-president of international shipping Dennis Gallsworthy, who apparently intended his words to be taken seriously.

Somehow maintaining his composure despite being able to hear the things he was saying, Gallsworthy added, "We have a strong commitment to protecting and preserving sea life."

Radio messages from the tanker indicated it had suffered extensive damage to its hull following an explosion, which pierced its overloaded crude-oil tanks. By the time the ship slid to the bottom, Shell public relations officials were touting its potential as an artificial habitat, often while looking straight into reporters' eyes.

//Public Relations

Multinational oil giant British Petroleum recently introduced a new logo for the company. The new logo looks like a flower, or as the company describes it, "a sunburst of green, yellow, and white symbolizing dynamic energy in all its forms. It was called the Helios after the sun god of ancient Greece."

"The many species of fish native to Newfoundland's Grand Banks have, in recent years, increasingly struggled to find feeding and breeding grounds," Miller said, as if Shell were deeply concerned with these circumstances and not, in fact, partially at fault for them. "We must take all available steps to help re-establish these species in their native waters."

Hoping to both deflect blame and take an opportunity for self-promotion, Miller took aim at the commercial fishing industry without so much as a smirk.

"The *Global Explorer's* new resting place will provide shelter for countless threatened, often over-harvested fish," he said. "At Shell, we're proud to use our multi-billion-dollar, globe-spanning resources to aid a worthy environmental cause."

Not all press reaction has been positive.

"Once again, Shell has demonstrated its unique brand of environmentalism, this time to the life of our planet's oceans," *Mother Jones* environmental reporter Neil Taylor said Tuesday. "The sunken hulk of the Shell *Global Explorer*, which hauled billions of gallons of crude oil during its operational lifetime, will have an impact on aquatic life for hundreds of years to come."

Shell reacted quickly to these and other statements, working with mainstream news sources to tell its side of the story.

"Once again, Shell has demonstrated its unique brand of environmentalism, this time to the life of our planet's oceans," read a full-page ad from Shell that will appear in Wednesday's edition of *USA Today*. "The sunken hulk of the Shell *Global Explorer*, which hauled billions of gallons of crude oil during its operational lifetime, will have an impact on aquatic life for hundreds of years to come."

"We're proud of what we've done for the planet," Miller said, possibly truthfully. "And believe me when I say that at Shell, we're committed to changing our world forever." ◆

RESPONDING

DISCUSSION QUESTIONS

CONSTRUCTING MEANING
Explain how the tone, word choice, and stylistic elements in this news parody reveal its purpose and underscore its message.

ANALYZING PERSPECTIVES
This news parody is not based on any actual oil spill. What do you think motivated the editors at *The Onion* to produce and publish this article? Why might a Shell executive in Calgary feel more personally criticized by this article than a Shell oil rig worker in the Atlantic?

EXTENDING MEANING
Discuss how this news parody uses quotations that have a double meaning. For example, "... at Shell, we're committed to changing our world forever."

TASKS

PERFORMING A SCENE
Think about an industry that creates products that have consequences harmful to the environment. What would a corporate spokesperson for that industry say to a group of journalists? Perform a scene that includes both the spoken words (the corporation's official message) and thought bubbles that reveal the true thoughts of the spokesperson. Be prepared to answer questions from your audience.

WRITING A NEWS PARODY
Examine how "Sunken Oil Tanker Will Be Habitat for Marine Life" and "iPhone Left in Hot Car," on page 178, use parody. Identify a cause that is currently being discussed in the news and write a parody to highlight the issues around that cause.

WHAT DO YOU THINK? + AGREE − DISAGREE
The best way to correct bad behaviour is to make a joke about it.

I See You Think I'm Not Very Interesting

An open letter to the person with whom I was having a nice conversation until he looked down at his phone and started pecking away at the keyboard for, like, 10 minutes.

Open Letter by Scott Feschuk

Dear Señor Jerkface,

I'm not a big "manners" person. I don't care which fork you use to eat your salad, so long as it's not mine. But while you and I are dining together, perhaps you would deign to keep your hands and eyes off your mobile phone for more than 30 seconds at a time.

No? Very well—might I see your device for a moment? How sleek and stylish! And how very clumsy of me to accidentally drop it into my soup, then drop the soup into a crocodile, then push the crocodile out of a helicopter.

Don't get me wrong: I understand how important it is for you to stay in constant, utterly relentless touch with your many friends, avatars, and close, personal LinkedIn contacts. I grasp what a gruelling ordeal it now will be for your Twitter followers to go 90 whole minutes without knowing precisely where you stand on quantitative easing or the introduction of Cousin Oliver on *The Brady Bunch*. On the other hand: I AM SITTING RIGHT HERE.

Ah, I see you have a second phone. And I am all out of crocodiles. So be it.

Forgive me for interjecting as you enter the third exciting minute of "texting a buddy," but perhaps you have heard of a new gimmick meant to restore actual human eye contact to meals. Upon arriving at a restaurant, all those who are dining together must place their phones in the middle of the table: The first person to reach for his or her device is obliged to pick up the entire dinner tab. I for one think this is a great idea but would add one small tweak: Everyone at the table should also get to stab that person in the hand with a fork.

I take it from your reaction that you don't support this—and also that my fork hurts.

Let me assure you, dear friend, that I am not blind to the virtues of the smartphone. It empowers instant communication. It enhances workplace productivity, especially if your company is in the business of obliterating green cartoon pigs. Plus, as you have demonstrated, it provides a convenient way to let people know they are not very interesting.

This used to be much harder in the olden days, when you'd have to use subtle signals like theatrical yawning. Now, when your friends start telling you about the accomplishments of their children, you can simply glance at your device. It's a real time saver.

Ah, your phone is vibrating yet again. I sense my opportunity approaching.

YOU: Sorry, I just need to ...
You lapse into silence.
ME: Hey, can I have one of your kidneys?
YOU: (*distracted*) Mmm hmm.
ME: Great!
YOU: (*looking up*) Sorry, what did you just say?
ME: (*reaching for scalpel*)

I agree you are by no means alone in your habits. In the days before the last federal election, I sat down for drinks with five Ottawa journalists—and at one point, ALL OF THEM lapsed into silence, staring into their phones. I didn't know what to do. Should I look at my phone and pretend I had an urgent message to return? Would five smartphones even fit inside a crocodile?

Perhaps you've been led to believe that your station in life is of sufficient importance that you are justified in the comically habitual checking of your emails and texts. And maybe you're right! After all, there are three groups of people who get a free pass to constantly gaze at their phones during dinner:

1. Brain surgeons who abruptly left in the middle of brain surgery and are checking in to see if maybe they ought go back and finish the brain surgery.
2. Current presidents of the United States of America (basketball scores only).
3. Cuba Gooding Jr. (When so few job offers come your way, you simply can't be tardy in replying.)

If you don't fit into one of these categories, perhaps you could hold off on using your phone until you pretend to need to go to the bathroom, but later I discover you were actually in there re-tweeting the results of Tony Clement's squash game. ◆

ANALYZING CONVENTIONS

Consider the various ways writers can emphasize certain words, such as using all caps, italic, or boldface. Ask yourself: How does Scott Feschuk expect his readers to read the words in all caps? What other words in the letter could have been treated the same way?

RESPONDING

DISCUSSION QUESTIONS

SYNTHESIZING
Reread this letter to determine just how serious Scott Feschuk is about the issue of people using cellphones when they're with someone else. What details in the text indicate the depth of his feelings about the issue? What new ideas or understanding do you have about this issue after reading his letter?

ANALYZING FORM
Discuss what the characteristics of an open letter might be, considering the model provided by Feschuk. What is the purpose of this form? Who is the audience?

METACOGNITION
Identify the allusions to people or events in this open letter that you understand and those that you don't. How does understanding or not understanding an allusion affect your response to the letter?

TASKS

DEVELOPING A SCENE
Create a script based on this letter in which Feschuk and his dinner partner have a conversation before, during, and after the cellphone incident. Base your dialogue on what you can infer about their personalities. Rehearse and present your scene.

WRITING AN OPEN LETTER
Based on this letter, consider how Feschuk would respond in similar situations (e.g., if someone cuts in front of him in line for a movie, or if a store clerk is talking on the phone while ringing up his purchase). In an open letter, explore the situation and respond to it as if you were Feschuk. Try to capture his tone, but use your own words and ideas to respond.

WHAT DO YOU THINK? + AGREE − DISAGREE

Traditions should be respected, not made light of.

Not Enough

Horses

Short Story by Thomas King

When Clinton Merasty showed up at Sarah Heavyman's place with the box, Sarah's father, Houston, was not particularly impressed.

"Kittens?"

"Kittens," said Clinton. "I want to marry your daughter."

"That's the way we used to do it in the old days, all right," said Houston.

"Yeah," said Clinton. "I know."

"Times change, I suppose," said Houston. "In the old days, when a man wanted to marry a woman, he'd bring horses."

When Clinton rang the doorbell on Saturday, he was carrying four boxes of honey-garlic sausages in his arms.

"Happy Canada Day," Clinton told Houston.

"Holy," said Houston, when he saw the sausages. "These are my favourite."

"They're from Rowe Meats."

"They're the best," said Houston. "You still want to marry my daughter?"

"You bet."

The following week, Clinton drove up with a brown Naugahyde recliner. Clinton and Houston set it on the sidewalk in front of the house.

"This looks just like the chair your father has in his den."

"That's the one," said Clinton. "Dad said I could have it, if I thought it would help."

"What's your father going to sit on?"

"He bought a leather recliner at The Brick's half-price sale."

Houston eased himself into the chair and leaned back so he could catch the sun on his face.

"It's got this lever," said Clinton. "When you pull it, a footrest pops out and holds your feet up."

"It's comfortable, for sure," said Houston. "But your father's right. There's nothing like leather."

MAKING INFERENCES

Thomas King's writing style could be described as sparse; it requires readers to make inferences. For example, you must infer that there are kittens in the box, that Clinton has brought the kittens as a gift to Houston, and that the gift is connected to Clinton wanting to marry Houston's daughter.

A few days later, Clinton came by with a snow blower in the back of his truck.

"It's July," said Houston. "You know something I don't?"

"Hard to find a snow blower once winter sets in," said Clinton.

"Is it new or used?"

"Used," said Clinton, "but it's got an eight-horsepower engine, six forward gears, and a 66-centimetre clearing path."

"Eight horses, eh?"

"That's right."

"She's a good cook," said Houston. "I guess you know that."

"I do," said Clinton.

"And she's got a university degree in biology." Houston rolled the snow blower back and forth to check the balance. "Those things don't come cheap."

"I had the blades sharpened and the spark plug replaced."

"You love her?"

"Absolutely," said Clinton.

"You know," said Houston, "you've been by four times now."

"Yes, sir," said Clinton.

"And four's an important number to Native people."

"Like the four directions?" asked Clinton.

"That's right," said Houston. "A lot of the songs we sing are sung four times through, and a lot of the dances are done four times. Sometimes when we pray for something, we say the prayer four times."

"So, can I marry Sarah?"

"You should probably ask her."

"I have."

"What'd she say?"

"She keeps saying no," said Clinton. "I thought maybe you could talk to her."

"Yeah," said Houston, "that's what I would have said, too."

Clinton and Sarah were married in September. Houston would have preferred a traditional wedding on the reserve, but Clinton's parents were Catholic. Afterwards, Houston took Clinton off to one side.

"I'm curious," he said. "How'd you get my daughter to marry you?"

"It wasn't easy," said Clinton. "I can tell you that."

"She ask about horses?"

"Yes, sir."

"What'd you tell her?"

> **ANALYZING CONVENTIONS**
> King doesn't always tell you who is speaking. Consider the effect this has on readers.

"**Welcome to the family. You're smarter than you look.**"

"I told her there weren't enough horses in the world, but that I'd keep trying."

"Welcome to the family," said Houston. "You're smarter than you look."

That evening Houston relaxed on the recliner in front of the television with a plate of sausages on his lap, while the kittens fought over a twist-tie. He wasn't sure about the Catholic ceremony. A little too long, perhaps. A little too pretentious. But all in all, it had been a fine wedding. Enough to eat, enough to drink. Plenty of cameras.

It was too bad about the horses, though. As Houston watched Tiger Woods sink a 45-foot putt, he wondered what it must have been like for his grandfather to stand in front of his lodge and feel the land tremble, as young men, wild for his approval, galloped by, driving strings of ponies through the prairie grass.

A snow blower was a fine thing, to be sure, but where was the romance, where was the tradition? Still, Houston had to admit, it did have an eight-horse motor, six forward gears, and a 66-centimetre clearing path. And maybe tomorrow, if the weather took a turn for the worse, he'd run it out to the backyard and start it up. Just to hear the motor rumble. Just to feel the earth move under his feet. ◆

RESPONDING

DISCUSSION QUESTIONS

ANALYZING CHARACTER
How does Thomas King intend for his readers to feel about Houston? Identify specific details from the story that reveal Houston's character traits.

CRITICAL LITERACY
Reflect on the characters that appear in the story (Houston and Clinton) and the characters that don't appear (e.g., Sarah, her mother, or other family members). Why do you think King chose to tell the story with just Houston and Clinton speaking? What effect does that create for readers?

ANALYZING HUMOUR
How is humour created in this story? What is King's message? How effectively is that message delivered?

TASKS

WRITING A STORY
Rewrite the story from the point of view of either Clinton or Sarah. Be sure to maintain the integrity of the characters as King created them. Reveal how Clinton or Sarah may feel about the traditions and changes that Houston reflects on in the story.

RESEARCH AND INQUIRY
Research and analyze either birth, coming of age, wedding, or funeral ceremonies from cultures around the world. Create an infographic that explains what the ceremonies have in common and what makes each one unique.

> **ABOUT THE AUTHOR**
>
> Thomas King is an award-winning novelist, broadcaster, and director. King is of Cherokee and Greek descent, and his work frequently examines First Nations experiences in popular culture, protest, history, and politics. King has been nominated for a Governor General's Award and the Commonwealth Writer's Prize, and is a member of the Order of Canada.

WHAT DO YOU THINK NOW?

Think back to your original response to this statement:

"Humour is the most honest art form— you can't fake a response to it."

How has your thinking about this statement changed since you began this unit?

Writing and Presenting a Script

Imagine that the authors of two of the texts from this unit met backstage at an award ceremony. Each author is about to receive an award for writing. Write a script in which the authors discuss their work and their use of humour. Remember to

- create distinctive voices for each of your characters;
- create an interesting plot for your scene;
- reference specific details from the author's texts; and
- demonstrate your understanding of the role that humour played in their texts.

Once the script is finalized, rehearse and present it to others. Consider how you will use diction and devices to enhance your characterizations.

Creating a Media Text

Demonstrate your deeper understanding of the role that humour can play in promoting change, dealing with tragedy, and providing entertainment. Beginning with examples from the selections in this unit, create a media text (in a form of your choice) that illustrates what you've learned about humour in our society. Remember to

- provide an analysis of the texts you reference;
- use appropriate language;
- choose effective examples to demonstrate your analysis; and
- make effective use of technology to develop your media text.

Writing an Essay

Write an essay in response to one of the following prompts:

- Humour is an effective form of criticism.
- Satire is an effective rhetorical device.
- Humour helps us to understand tragedy.

Create a clear thesis statement, and organize your ideas effectively to support your thesis. Use quotations and refer to specific examples to support your ideas. Use a strong voice and effective word choice to convince your readers.

perspective

WHAT DO YOU THINK? + AGREE
— DISAGREE

It is impossible to be completely objective.

Unit Learning Goals
- evaluating to form opinions
- analyzing persuasive writing and the opinion piece
- evaluating production perspectives
- creating fluency

Talk About It

Perspective—A Story

Marie opens her locker door and sees a large box sitting on her shelf.

"What's in the box?" her friend Melanie demands.

"Could be a gift from Drake."

"That's great! Open it."

"Or it could be payback for my practical joke on Laura. You know I filled her locker with bubbles last week."

"So open it and find out."

Marie closes her locker door.

"Nope, I'd rather leave it unopened and think it's a gift than open it and find out it's not."

Perspective Box of a Dutch Interior, 1663, by Samuel van Hoogstraten is an oil painting created within a box. The image is viewed through peepholes, allowing viewers to see a three-dimensional interior.

> "Art and life are subjective. Not everybody's gonna dig what I dig, but I reserve the right to dig it."
>
> —Whoopi Goldberg

Visual Perspectives

If you look the right way ...
by writer Frances Hodgson Burnett and designer Trinh Truong

I will not draw in class
by writer/designer Maria A. Dietz

What you got. What you want.
by writer/designer Chank Diesel

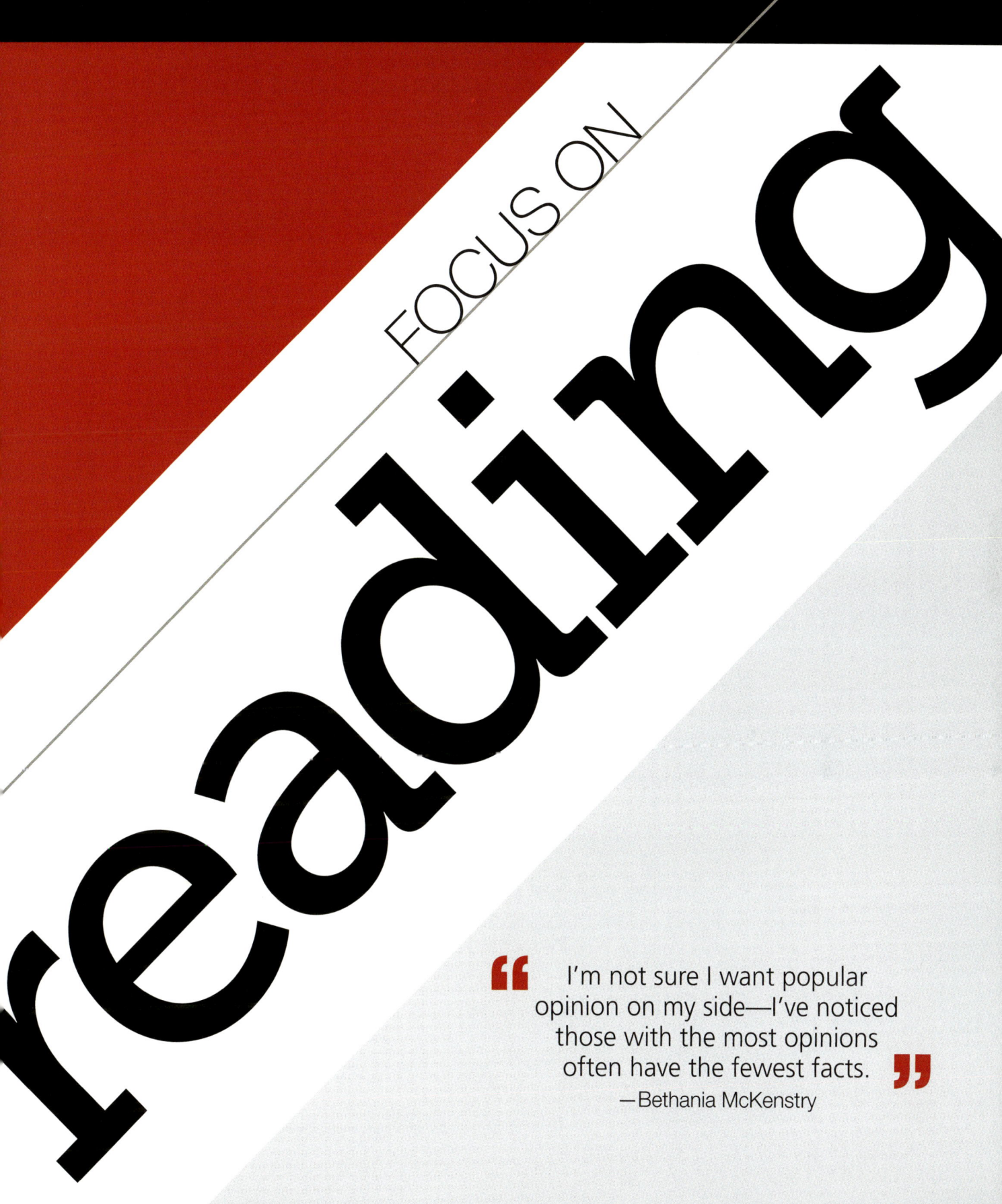

Focus on reading

> " I'm not sure I want popular opinion on my side—I've noticed those with the most opinions often have the fewest facts. "
> —Bethania McKenstry

EVALUATING TO FORM OPINIONS

As a critical reader, you must constantly evaluate and form opinions about both the content of what you are reading and how well the writer presents that content.

WHAT TO EVALUATE	NONFICTION: WHAT TO ASK YOURSELF	FICTION: WHAT TO ASK YOURSELF
Purpose and Intended Audience	Am I the intended audience? How relevant is the text's purpose to my needs or my purpose for reading?	How well does the text align with my interests? Who is the intended audience?
Ideas or Theme	How accurate are the writer's ideas? How clearly does the writer explain the ideas? Are the ideas biased? Whose point of view is presented?	How original are the writer's ideas, or the way those ideas are expressed? How have the writer's values influenced those ideas?
Organization	Does the text have an organizational structure that helps me find the information I need?	Does the organization increase or decrease my appreciation of the text?
Voice, Mood, and Tone	Is the voice, mood, or tone of the text appropriate for the writer's purpose and intended audience?	Does the writer's or the narrator's voice resonate with me? Is the mood or tone of the narrative one I can appreciate?
Sentence Fluency, Word Choice, Conventions, and Techniques	Do I find the text engaging? Is the vocabulary appropriate for the intended audience?	How well does the writing flow? Do I need to reread sections? Does the writer use literary devices effectively?
Features or Details	How helpful are the headings and subheadings? How well is the text supported (e.g., with photos or diagrams)? Does the writer provide the degree of detail that I require?	How engaging and well defined are the characters? What details help me visualize the characters or setting? What connections can I make?

EVALUATING THE RELIABILITY OF ONLINE SOURCES

Evaluating is an essential strategy for the research process. Consider the following tips when conducting online research:

1. Refer to online databases that your school subscribes to first. Online databases curated by professional librarians are generally more reliable than the results of an Internet search engine.
2. When using public websites, search for respected sources first. Websites owned by well-known organizations (e.g., universities, large media organizations, or governments) are generally more reliable than websites created by individuals.
3. Check how current your sources are.
4. Cross-reference information that you find. However, be aware that if you find a second source that repeats information verbatim from another site, you may have just discovered an error that has spread.

WHAT DO YOU THINK?
How much privacy do students deserve at school?

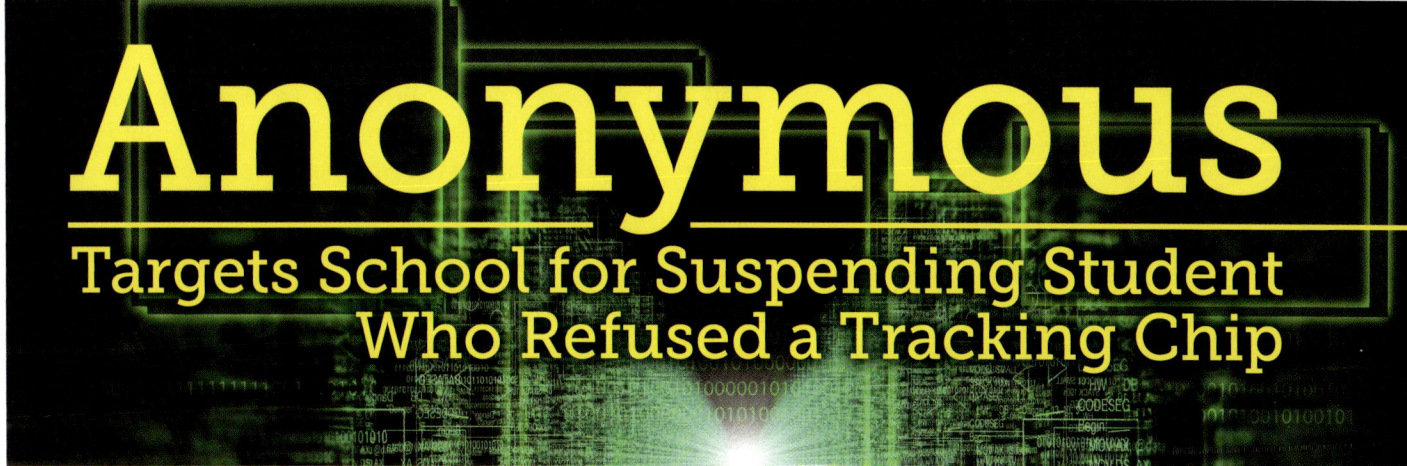

Anonymous
Targets School for Suspending Student Who Refused a Tracking Chip

Article by Liat Clark, posted on *Wired*, November 27, 2012

Hacktivist group Anonymous has taken down the website of an entire Texas U.S. school district in response to the news that a student was suspended for refusing to wear a Radio-Frequency Identification (RFID) chip tag around her neck.

The takedown of San Antonio's Northside Independent School District's website began late on 23 November and, despite reports that it was up and running on 26 November, it appeared to still be down at the time of writing. The action has been a typically defiant retaliation on behalf of student Andrea Hernandez, who, after refusing to wear the ID tag on religious and privacy grounds, was suspended by John Jay High School's Science and Engineering Academy and threatened with expulsion following several months of back and forth with the board.

A judge has since issued a temporary restraining order to stop the school from removing Hernandez from its grounds so she can finish her studies before the matter is settled.

That hasn't stopped Anonymous.

//**Hacktivists**

The term *hacktivist* refers to someone who uses technology hacking to effect social change. Although some hacktivists express their anger with disruptive activities, such as crashing a government website, there are others who attempt to use their technological skills in a positive way. Random Hacks of Kindness events held in Canada have tackled problems such as access to clean water in First Nations communities.

> **//Analyzing Allusions**
>
> *Panopticon* is an eighteenth-century prison-design concept in which all the cells are observable by one guard, without the inmates knowing whether or not they are being observed. Consider why this allusion is used and what effect it has on Liat Clark's argument.

Anonymous is a group of hackers who are not officially affiliated with one another and who use their hacking knowledge for social activism. Their actions and beliefs are often controversial, and at times illegal. Those who wish to associate themselves with Anonymous wear this mask as a sign of their involvement with the group.

"These 'student locator' programs are ultimately aimed at getting students used to living in a total surveillance state where there will be no privacy, and wherever you go and whatever you text or email will be watched by the government," announced tr1xxyAnon, claiming to be part of the hacktivist group, in a statement that mirrored one by president of the Rutherford Institute John Whitehead. The Institute is responsible for helping the Hernandez family in its legal action.

"I sincerely hope you have noticed that I took down your website for a reason, and that reason is stripping away the privacy of students in your school. What was going through your mind when you had this idea?" he added.

We do, in fact, know what was going through John Jay High School's mind when it began implementing the modern-day surveillance equivalent to Jeremy Bentham's Panopticon at the start of the school year in September. Along with Anson Jones Middle School, the state school decided to launch the $500 000 Student Locator Program to secure a steady flow of state funding. If any student is not present for the daily morning roll call, regardless of whether they are on the premises or simply running a little late, the school loses its daily funding for that pupil.

By embedding RFID chips in each student ID and forcing them to keep it visible at all times, the school has guaranteed proof that a pupil did attend that day; they just missed the morning call.

This is on top of the ID already featuring a student photo and barcode attached to the individual's social security number. The school claims the RFID chip only tracks students while on the premises, but it could stalk them wherever they went, if it so chose. The school even went so far as to use guilt to ensure no other guardian dare stray from the course, saying in a letter issued to every parent: "You expect school staff to always know where your children are during the school day ... think how important this will be in the case of an emergency."

Hernandez, who claimed students even need the ID to access the bathrooms (it's used for everything from school election voting to library access), took a proactive approach that Anonymous would be proud of, handing out flyers protesting against the tags (the school subsequently quashed this freedom of expression before suspending her).

Andrea Hernandez was 15 years old when she refused to wear a school ID tag that could monitor her whereabouts.

"I feel it's an invasion of my religious beliefs," she told *Infowars*. "It's also an invasion of my privacy and my other rights. I feel it's the implementation of the Mark of the Beast [the Hernandez family are Christian]." Since her protest is on religious grounds, John Jay High School is taking a particularly ballsy stance by throwing out the First Amendment to the Constitution, which protects the right to freedom of speech, religion, freedom of the press, to assemble, and to petition government.

The school had said it would reinstate Hernandez and agree to remove the chip, however, only under the understanding that she and her family would stop speaking out against the RFID chip project.

"I told [the Deputy Superintendent] that was unacceptable because it would imply an endorsement of the district's policy and my daughter and I should not have to give up our constitutional rights to speak out against a program that we feel is wrong," said the girl's father.

Regardless of the furor, the Texas school board plans on implementing the strategy across 112 schools—that's 100 000 students.

Remarkably, it's neither the first time U.S. school bodies have tried this, nor the worst method of implementation. In 2010, a preschool in Richmond, California, began embedding the chips in regulation clothing, totally bypassing any chance of the child carelessly leaving a tag at home and ensuring everyone learns their ABCs that week.

Another plan to use the same system was scuppered by concerned parents as early as 2005 in Sacramento, California.

"We are conditioning kids to live in a surveillance state," said Whitehead. "The court's willingness to grant a temporary restraining order is a good first step, but there is still a long way to go—not just in this case, but dealing with the mindset, in general, that everyone needs to be monitored and controlled."

A hearing will be held in a few days to consider whether the temporary injunction should be upheld or made more permanent. ◆

RESPONDING

DISCUSSION QUESTIONS

EVALUATING
Examine the ideas and quotations in this article, and consider its organizational structure. Is the article balanced or one-sided? Justify your evaluation.

DRAWING CONCLUSIONS
Should schools in Canada be allowed to limit students' rights simply because schools are responsible for their safety and security?

ANALYZING SENTENCE FLUENCY
How effective is the article's sentence fluency? Support your response.

TASKS

EVALUATING PODCASTS
Find at least two audio podcasts that address the issue of the loss of privacy in society. Evaluate which one makes the most convincing emotional argument, which one makes the most convincing intellectual argument, and which one provides the most balanced discussion of the issue. Create a chart to report your evaluations.

WRITING A SPEECH
Imagine you are a student at Andrea Hernandez's school. Write a speech to give to the school board or parent council that either supports or opposes her protest against the ID tags.

WHAT DO YOU THINK?

Students are some of the "most surveilled people in the world."

W1NSTON

Novel Excerpt from *Little Brother* by Cory Doctorow

COMPARING TEXTS

As you read, reflect on how this fictional narrative connects to the previous nonfiction text about Andrea Hernandez.

I'm a senior at Cesar Chavez High in San Francisco's sunny Mission district, and that makes me one of the most surveilled people in the world. My name is Marcus Yallow, but back when this story starts, I was going by w1n5t0n. Pronounced "Winston."

Not pronounced "Double-you-one-enn-five-tee-zero-enn"—unless you're a clueless disciplinary officer who's far enough behind the curve that you still call the Internet "the information superhighway."

I know just such a clueless person, and his name is Fred Benson, one of three vice-principals at Cesar Chavez. He's a sucking chest wound of a human being. But if you're going to have a jailer, better a clueless one than one who's really on the ball.

"Marcus Yallow," he said over the PA one Friday morning. The PA isn't very good to begin with, and when you combine that with Benson's habitual mumble, you get something that sounds more like someone struggling to digest a bad burrito than a school announcement. But human beings are good at picking their names out of audio confusion—it's a survival trait.

I grabbed my bag and folded my laptop three-quarters shut—I didn't want to blow my downloads—and got ready for the inevitable.

"Report to the administration office immediately."

My social studies teacher, Ms. Galvez, rolled her eyes at me and I rolled my eyes back at her. The Man was always coming down on me, just because I go through school firewalls like wet Kleenex, spoof the gait-recognition software, and nuke the snitch chips they track us with. Galvez is a good type, anyway, never holds that against me (especially when I'm helping get with her webmail so she can talk to her brother, who's stationed in Iraq).

My boy Darryl gave me a smack on the ass as I walked past. I've known Darryl since we were still in diapers and escaping from playschool, and I've been getting him into and out of trouble the whole time. I raised my arms over my head like a prizefighter and made my exit from Social Studies and began the perp-walk to the office.

I was halfway there when my phone went. That was another no-no—phones are *muy prohibido* at Chavez High—but why should that stop me? I ducked into the toilet and shut myself in the middle stall (the furthest stall is always the grossest because so many people head straight for it, hoping to escape the smell and the squick—the smart money and good hygiene is down the middle).

I checked the phone—my home PC had sent it an email to tell it that there was something new up on Harajuku Fun Madness, which happens to be the best game ever invented.

I grinned. Spending Fridays at school was the suck anyway, and I was glad of the excuse to make my escape.

I ambled the rest of the way to Benson's office and tossed him a wave as I sailed through the door.

"If it isn't Double-you-one-enn-five-tee-zero-enn," he said. Fredrick Benson—Social Security number 545-03-2343, date of birth August 15, 1962, mother's maiden name Di Bona, hometown Petaluma—is a lot taller than me. I'm a runty 5'8", while he stands 6'7", and his college basketball days are far enough behind him that his chest muscles have turned into saggy man-boobs that were painfully obvious through his freebie dot-com polo shirts. He always looks like he's about to slam-dunk your ass, and he's really into raising his voice for dramatic effect. Both these start to lose their efficacy with repeated application.

"Sorry, nope," I said. "I never heard of this R2-D2 character of yours."

"W1n5t0n," he said, spelling it out again. He gave me a hairy eyeball and waited for me to wilt. Of course it was my handle, and had been for years. It was the identity I used when I was posting on message boards where I was making my contributions to the field of applied security research. You know, like sneaking out of school and disabling the minder-tracer on my phone. But he didn't know that this was my handle. Only a small number of people did, and I trusted them all to the end of the earth.

"Um, not ringing any bells," I said. I'd done some pretty cool stuff around school using that handle—I was very proud of my work on snitch-tag killers—and if he could link the two identities, I'd be in trouble. No one at school ever called me w1n5t0n or even Winston. Not even my pals. It was Marcus or nothing.

ANALYZING CHARACTERS

As you read, compare Marcus to other characters and people you know. Consider whether Cory Doctorow has created a realistic voice for his character. If he has, think about how that voice is achieved.

ANALYZING WORD CHOICE

Doctorow uses expressions such as *tell, bad rap, perp-walk,* and *sweet hack* to establish the narrator's voice and set the tone of the novel. Consider how the use of formal and informal language, including slang and jargon, affect the voice and tone of this novel excerpt, as well as the effect they have on you as a reader.

Benson settled down behind his desk and tapped his class ring nervously on his blotter. He did this whenever things started to go bad for him. Poker players call stuff like this a "tell"—something that lets you know what was going on in the other guy's head. I knew Benson's tells backward and forward.

"Marcus, I hope you realize how serious this is."

"I will just as soon as you explain what this is, sir." I always say "sir" to authority figures when I'm messing with them. It's my own tell.

He shook his head at me and looked down, another tell. Any second now, he was going to start shouting at me. "Listen, kiddo! It's time you came to grips with the fact that we know about what you've been doing, and that we're not going to be lenient about it. You're going to be lucky if you're not expelled before this meeting is through. Do you want to graduate?"

"Mr. Benson, you still haven't explained what the problem is—"

He slammed his hand down on the desk and then pointed his finger at me. "The *problem*, Mr. Yallow, is that you've been engaged in criminal conspiracy to subvert this school's security system, and you have supplied security countermeasures to your fellow students. You know that we expelled Graciella Uriarte last week for using one of your devices."

Uriarte had gotten a bad rap. She'd bought a radio jammer from a head shop near the 16th Street BART station and it had set off the countermeasures in the school hallway. Not my doing, but I felt for her.

"And you think I'm involved in that?"

"We have reliable intelligence indicating that you are w1n5t0n"—again, he spelled it out, and I began to wonder if he hadn't figured out that the 1 was an I and the 5 was an S. "We know that this w1n5t0n character is responsible for the theft of last year's standardized tests." That actually hadn't been me, but it was a sweet hack, and it was kind of flattering to hear it attributed to me. "And therefore liable for several years in prison unless you cooperate with me."

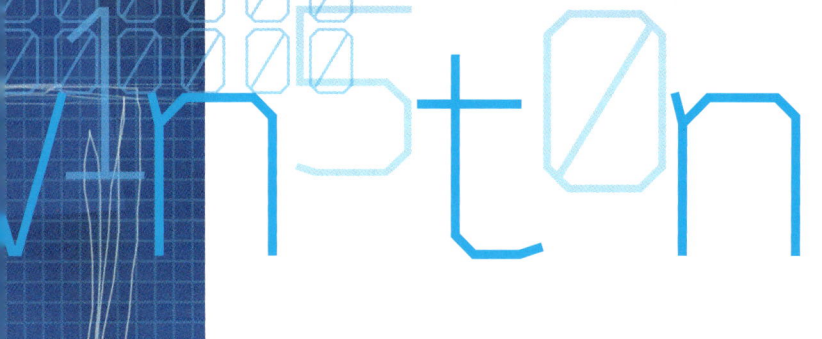

"You have 'reliable intelligence'? I'd like to see it."

He glowered at me. "Your attitude isn't going to help you."

"If there's evidence, sir, I think you should call the police and turn it over to them. It sounds like this is a very serious matter, and I wouldn't want to stand in the way of a proper investigation by the duly constituted authorities."

"You want me to call the police."

"And my parents, I think. That would be for the best."

We stared at each other across the desk. He'd clearly expected me to fold the second he dropped the bomb on me. I don't fold. I have a trick for staring down people like Benson. I look slightly to the left of their heads, and think about the lyrics to old Irish folk songs, the kind with three hundred verses. It makes me look perfectly composed and unworried.

And the wing was on the bird and the bird was on the egg and the egg was in the nest and the nest was on the leaf and the leaf was on the twig and the twig was on the branch and the branch was on the limb and the limb was in the tree and the tree was in the bog—the bog down in the valleyoh! Highho the rattlin' bog, the bog down in the valleyoh.

"You can return to class now," he said. "I'll call on you once the police are ready to speak to you."

"Are you going to call them now?"

"The procedure for calling in the police is complicated. I'd hoped that we could settle this fairly and quickly, but since you insist—"

"I can wait while you call them is all," I said. "I don't mind."

He tapped his ring again and I braced for the blast.

"*Go!*" he yelled. "Get the hell out of my office, you miserable little—" ◆

RESPONDING

DISCUSSION QUESTIONS

ANALYZING VOICE
How effectively does Cory Doctorow use word choice and sentence fluency to create distinctive voices for Marcus and Mr. Benson? Support your response with specific details from the text.

DRAWING CONCLUSIONS
Based on this novel excerpt, what values or ideas does Doctorow seem to be advocating? Refer to specific details in the excerpt to support your analysis.

CRITICAL LITERACY
Evaluate the stereotypes Doctorow uses in this excerpt. What elements in the characters of Marcus and Mr. Benson would you consider stereotypical? Support your evaluation with specific details from the text.

TASKS

CREATING A MEDIA TEXT
Read the About the Author information below and decide how you would remix this selection. What media text (or "cool junk") will you create in response to the issues raised in this excerpt?

DIGITAL LITERACY
Research the arguments for and against the use of digital devices in schools. Prepare notes to debate the proposition: "Digital devices have a place in the classroom."

ABOUT THE AUTHOR
Cory Doctorow is a science-fiction author, activist, journalist, blogger, co-editor of Boing Boing, and author of adult and young adult novels. Born in Toronto, Canada, he now lives in London, United Kingdom.

Doctorow wants readers to think about the issues he raises. He publishes his stories under a Creative Commons copyright license that empowers readers to, as he says, "Mix it up. Send them to your friends. Get creative. Tell me about it. Make cool junk."

NO WORD FOR …

Blog Entry by Sheila North Wilson

> **WHAT DO YOU THINK?** + AGREE − DISAGREE
> The language we speak has inherent bias.

Former CBC reporter Sheila North Wilson was asked to translate the script of We Were Children *from English to Cree. This docudrama examines the experiences of two Residential School survivors. The image above shows one of the main characters, Lyna Hart.*

ANALYZING FORM

In a personal essay, an author shares anecdotes to support the essay's thesis. Personal essays can be found in magazines, on blogs, and in promotional material.

Savage.

One of the words I had a hard time translating from English into Cree.

Most of the lines were for two particular children: a four-year-old girl who played the young Lyna Hart, one of the main characters in *We Were Children*, and a teenage boy who played an altar boy. My task was to simply translate the words so that the actors could use them on set. I was invited on set to coach the kids, too.

I was pretty excited to be asked in the first place, but as soon as I got the script and began trying to formulate the English words into Cree, my excitement turned to grief.

Emotional grief. Gradual grief.

It became heavier and heavier with every word—especially when I came across words and phrases like *savage*, *dirty*, and *evil ways*.

Since there are no Cree words for these, I had to dig deep into their meaning and come up with descriptive terms. For example, for *savage* I wrote *muh-cha-tis*—the literal Cree translation being, someone who is not living right or someone living an evil existence.

But before I could even teach the actors to say words like *savage*, I had to figure out a way to say them, so I tried to imagine how I would speak to my late grandparents. I called my parents for help, but even they had a hard time defining the concepts behind some of the words.

When I finally finished translating the lines and coached the actors on how to say them, hearing them back was interesting. The impact of the words really hit me when I got home and thought about what I heard. Powerful, painful words to hear, especially in your own language.

Weeks went by and I thought I was done with *We Were Children*, but then I was asked to coach the actors in post-production, so I did.

Once that was done, I was asked to take the whole script, translate it all into Cree, and then voice it. This is where the work got extremely heavy for me. The few lines that I had a hard time with before were now magnified into nearly 40 pages of script. Again, I struggled with some of the words, but thanks to my parents and siblings, I got through it.

Where I hit the wall and felt the most stress was translating Prime Minister Stephen Harper's apology into Cree. "To kill the Indian in the child" was by far the hardest part of the speech to say; the phrase just hit the deepest part of my emotions. It made me realize how close our people came to being wiped out.

Sitting in the sound booth by myself and formulating the ideas in my head brought back images and feelings for Residential School victims like my mother and aunts. I felt so sorry for them; it broke my heart to imagine how they must have felt.

I broke down, cried silently. It took every ounce of strength I had to gain my composure and finish the words. The producer, the sound guy, and my sister were sitting on the other side of the glass, unaware of how hard that day actually was for me. Their hugs immediately after helped, but the pain of the words affected me for weeks. Physical pain formed on my hands, my arms, and shoulders. It wasn't until I prayed over and over again that the pain finally left.

We Were Children is an important project and I'm very proud that I was involved in a very small way. ◆

AN APOLOGY

In his 2008 apology, Stephen Harper said, "The Residential Schools system [was] ... based on the assumption that Aboriginal cultures and spiritual beliefs were inferior and unequal. Indeed, some sought, as it was infamously said, 'to kill the Indian in the child.'... We now recognize that it was wrong to separate children from rich and vibrant cultures and traditions, that it created a void in many lives and communities.... We are sorry."

RESPONDING

DISCUSSION QUESTIONS

DRAWING CONCLUSIONS
Why is it significant that the Cree language does not have a word for the English word *savage*? Explain how this contributed to Sheila North Wilson's emotional response to translating the script.

ANALYZING FLUENCY
How effectively do the first four paragraphs use sentence fluency?

EVALUATING
How effective is this blog entry in helping you understand the lasting impact of the Residential Schools system? Support your evaluation.

TASKS

PREPARING A PRESENTATION
Research the use of Truth and Reconciliation commissions around the world. Discover the origins and purposes of these commissions. Synthesize your findings and prepare a presentation using effective visuals to support your ideas.

RESPONDING CREATIVELY
Imagine that the federal government has decided to construct a memorial to the victims of the Residential Schools system. Create a proposal for an appropriate monument that both remembers the victims and educates future generations about the mistakes of the past.

ABOUT THE AUTHOR
Sheila North Wilson is the chief communications officer for the Assembly of Manitoba Chiefs and a reporter for CBC Manitoba. She lives in Winnipeg, Manitoba.

WHAT DO YOU THINK?

"Perspective gives us the ability to accurately contrast the large with the small, and the important with the less important."
—John Sununu

HeartBEAT

Flash Fiction by Dan Evon

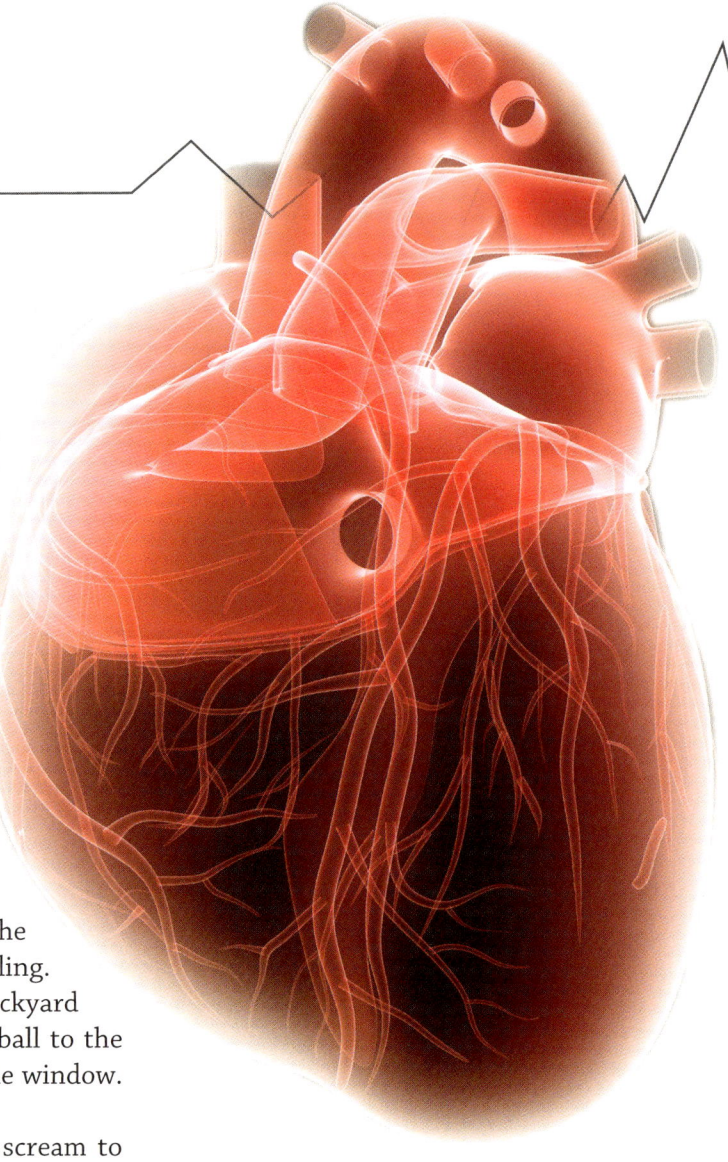

ANALYZING LITERARY DEVICES

As you read this story, consider how effectively Dan Evon uses repetition and sentence structure to develop the story.

He would have been 15. He would have been on the football team. They were having a good year. He would have played wide receiver.

She sat with her hands folded in her lap in the sunlight that came from a large glass window that overlooked the runway. Her eyes were closed. The airport moved around her. She thought about her son.

He would have been 15. She could see his face. He was smiling. He was standing in the backyard with no shoes on, throwing a ball to the dog. She was watching from the window. He loved that dog.

There was a loud and giddy scream to her left and she watched as two women flung their arms wide, shuffled their feet, and embraced. She smiled and looked down the long hall that was filled with people moving. With people smiling. With people rushing. She looked for a face she would never see again, then closed her eyes, and thought about her son.

He would have had a girlfriend. She would have been cute. They would have sat on the couch downstairs and kissed. She would have turned on the lights and walked down the stairs real slow, and they would have pretended that they were really enjoying the movie.

It broke her heart.

BASED ON A TRUE STORY

This piece of flash fiction is based on a true story. Evon was inspired to write "Heartbeat" by a photo in the news. He has fictionalized what the mother, April Beaver, felt and thought as she waited to meet the man who had her son's heart.

An unfamiliar voice called her name. She opened her eyes. There was a man standing in the busy hall, a brown suitcase at his feet, and a quivering smile across his face. He wiped something from his eye and shook the emotion from his body with a deep breath of airport air.

"April Beaver?" he said again. "Is that you?"

Her hand slowly rose to her chest and she nervously thumbed the silver cross that hung around her neck. She nodded and breathed in the same airport air as she rose to her feet.

The man stepped forward, then stopped, then bent down and opened the brown bag at his feet. He pulled out a stethoscope, wiped another tear from his eye, then turned with a big smile toward the woman.

"Ma'am," he said. "There's something I'd like for you to hear."

He put the stethoscope around her neck. He placed the cool steel underneath his shirt and the woman placed the rubber pieces into her ears.

They stared at each other. She placed her hand on his heart. The rhythmic beating of her son's life filled her ears and an overwhelming ball of joy, grief, and hope knocked her to her knees.

He would have been 15 years old. ◆

RESPONDING

DISCUSSION QUESTIONS

EVALUATING
How would this story be different if it were told from the transplant recipient's point of view? What impact would have been gained or lost had Dan Evon chosen an omniscient point of view?

ANALYZING SENTENCE FLUENCY
Analyze the sentence fluency in this selection. How does sentence fluency support the character development and pacing of the story? Refer to specific details from the text.

TASKS

CREATING A RADIO AD
Create a 30-second radio ad about organ donation. Use sound effects, dialogue, and accurate information to inform people about their options.

DIGITAL LITERACY
Research how social media has been used to increase participation in organ donation programs in Canada and around the world. Identify notable projects and assess their effectiveness. Choose an online tool to report your findings.

WRITING FLASH FICTION
Research to find a news item (with photos) that interests you. Use it as inspiration for writing a work of flash fiction. Share the news item and your work with others, discussing the choices you made.

WHAT DO YOU THINK?   **+ AGREE**
"No one really dies online."   **− DISAGREE**

Would You Like to

TWITTER

Since its launch in 2006, Twitter has gained over 500 million registered users who microblog over 340 million times a day. Twitter has become an instant news source, distributing on-the-scene information and images.

No one really dies online. It's a truth I'm only just starting to learn. What seems wholly ephemeral is stored away forever there, hidden perhaps, but recoverable for those who really want to find these little slices of the past, these flashes from the archives of oblivion.

I first joined Twitter two years ago as a means of keeping in touch with my son. That was Charlie; 19 years old; away at university. We'd always been close, and I'd always known his absence would leave a hole, but not the size or depth of it; the hours spent waiting for him to call, that perpetual sense of anxiety. Not that there was anything to fear; but to be without him, alone in this house, was worse than I'd expected.

It's a big house, perhaps too big for just a mother and her son. Four acres of garden; a paddock; a wood; a river running through it. But Charlie managed to fill it somehow; to make it come alive, to explode, to buzz with restless energy.

But then my son introduced me to the world of social media: Facebook, YouTube, and most importantly, Twitter, which I had at first dismissed as the most trivial of all, but which, I now realized, was to become a lifeline. To have my son at my fingertips; to know what was happening in his world; to connect whenever I wanted—these things were far from trivial, and in spite of my technophobia, I embraced it for his sake.

My online name was @MTnestgirl, a play on his love of musical theatre as well as my maternal role. Charlie's name was @Llamadude, a name I found ridiculous, but somehow oddly like him.

"I'll always stay in touch," he said. "Wherever I am, I promise I will."

And he did: from university; from Internet cafés around the world; from his phone; from his BlackBerry; from concerts and campsites and festivals. It isn't always easy to find a good wireless connection, but Charlie kept his promise and always tweeted every day. A moment is all it takes; a hundred and forty characters, or the time that it takes to click on a link or send a picture from your phone—

Reconnect?

 **Short Story by Joanne Harris**

And suddenly, I was not alone; I was *there*, with Charlie and his friends. I went to their lectures, watched their films, listened to their music. Charlie used Twitter to connect with a wide variety of people: some friends of his in real life; some stage performers he'd never met; actors; singers; writers; technicians. These virtual friends became mine as well. I visited their websites and blogs; watched clips of their concerts; shared in their lives. Through a glass, darkly, I watched my son and all his interactions. I couldn't be with him in the flesh, but I was in everything he did; a loving presence; a watchful eye; a ghost in the machine.

News breaks fastest on Twitter. Hearts can be broken as quickly. A winter's morning, an icy road, an oncoming truck, and my son on his bike, the bike I'd bought him a year ago, for his eighteenth birthday—

A hundred and forty characters is more than enough to end the world. First came the scatter of messages all across my timeline and his—

> OMG, is it true about @Llamadude? What's the news? Does anyone know? Has anyone heard from @MTnestgirl?

Death should be silent, I told myself. Death should be a black hole. But the news of Charlie's death was propelled by Twitter's morphic resonance, that mystic and mysterious force that holds flocks of birds together, shaping them into a widening gyre of screeching semi-consciousness—

Before Charlie's death, I'd had only about a dozen followers. Now, total strangers were following me. Hundreds of them. What did they want? To offer sympathy, to gloat, to share in a real-life tragedy?

I told myself I should go offline. My timeline was almost unbearable. The terrible news of Charlie's death had taken only minutes to spread. Thousands of Twitter users reached out. Strangers sent their condolences; singers and actors my son had followed posted words of sympathy. It was more than I could bear, and yet I couldn't turn away.

ANALYZING CONVENTIONS

Joanne Harris ends a few paragraphs with a dash. Consider why she has done so and what that suggests about how the narrator is feeling. What other punctuation does she use unconventionally?

GRIEVING AND SOCIAL NETWORKS

For many friends and families who have experienced a loss, social networks have become a central part of the grieving process. Social media provides us with the ability to
- express shock, sorrow, and other difficult feelings
- provide and receive emotional support anywhere, anytime
- maintain the memory of a friend or family member

I considered deleting his account. But I would have needed his password for that. It was equally true of all his accounts; his Facebook page was still open, his wall covered in messages. His YouTube channel was still alive with videos of Charlie, and when I logged into Twitter again, the first thing I saw was a recommendation, listing *@Llamadude* among the people I might like to follow.

Even worse were the emails. Automatically generated, they arrived in my inbox at intervals:

> An account you have been following (@Llamadude) has not posted in 14 days. Would you like to reconnect?

At first, I deleted the emails. I tried to disable the messages. But Charlie had set up my account, and I didn't know how to alter it.

Would you like to reconnect?

I thought about closing my account. But Twitter, for me, had become much more than just a means of staying in touch. It was here I felt closest to Charlie. Here among his virtual friends. People here still mentioned him; when they did, his name would appear on my timeline. Sometimes, whole conversations would be tagged with Charlie's name; and it was easy to picture him there, listening, taking part. It was their way of keeping him alive, I suppose; of making sure we remembered him.

"You ought to go out more," my mother said. "It isn't healthy moping around the way you do. And spending hours on that Twitter isn't going to bring our Charlie back—"

Well, of course it wasn't, Ma. But—

The Egyptians had their pyramids; the Victorians, their marble. And Charlie had Twitter; unhealthy, perhaps, but here was where my son lived on; cached, encrypted, stored away. I found myself including him in everything I tweeted. My comments filled up his timeline. Steadily, my followers increased. I now had over two thousand.

Only those automated emails reminded me of that other world.

> An account you have been following (@Llamadude) has not posted in 40 days. Would you like to reconnect?

This time, I clicked the option: Yes.

And then, one day, in my mailbox, there came a notification:

> @Llamadude has replied to your tweet.

Of course, it was impossible. It must be a mistake, I thought. No one else used Charlie's account.

My son had been meticulous about online security, his passwords carefully chosen to defy any attempt at hacking. I logged on to my Twitter account and rapidly scrolled down my Mentions page.

There! There it was. From @Llamadude—a wink, with a little smile, beside my dead son's avatar.

> ;-)

For a long time I just stared at it. That cluster of punctuation points. Of course, I knew it wasn't my son; but part of me didn't believe it. Tests on Twitter users have proved that we experience the same surge of endorphins when looking at a friend's avatar as when we see them in the flesh—and this was Charlie, smiling at me, somehow, from beyond the grave—

Someone must have hacked the account. Either that, or one of Charlie's friends had somehow got hold of his password. Anxiously, I awaited the inevitable wave of junk mail that would follow if his Twitter account had been hacked; or worse, drunken ramblings of some flatmate assuming his identity. But nothing happened. Just that smile—

;-)

No one else seemed to have noticed. Most of Charlie's friends had moved on. My followers, too, were drifting away, their attention claimed by riots and wars. I told my mother, who urged me to seek some kind of bereavement therapy.

But something had changed inside me. My mother would never have understood. The message from my son's account had changed the texture of my grief. Something I'd believed was lost had slowly emerged from the darkness—

It's not always easy to stay in touch. The Internet, for all its complexity, is still a work-in-progress. In the remotest parts of the world, you can still wait for minutes—even hours—to make that vital connection.

The thought was almost too absurd for me to put it into words. And yet, as I sat at my desk at night staring at the computer screen, there was something compelling about the idea. Charlie had promised to stay in touch. He'd just taken longer to get online.

> An account you have been following (@Llamadude) has not posted in 90 days. Would you like to reconnect?

I waited for confirmation. It came at last, in the form of a link, a complicated chain of code that had been abbreviated to fit Twitter's 140-character requirement.

> @Llamadude has sent you a link.

I clicked on the link. The screen went blank. For a moment I thought: It's a virus. Then an hourglass icon appeared, and I realized that I was waiting for a picture to load. It took a few minutes; then, reading the script at the top of the screen, I saw that the link had taken me to a page from Google Earth, taken from the air, I could see a house; some trees; a little stream—

That's my house, I realized.

My house captured on a day when the trees were beginning to turn, my car parked outside; and there, on the ground at the edge of the lawn, something bright that caught the sun—

It was Charlie's bike, I knew. The one he'd been riding the day he died. And now I also knew exactly when this picture had been taken: September 2009, just before he'd started college. A helicopter had flown overhead—you could just see part of its shadow in the photograph as they'd taken the picture, and Charlie and I had been sitting there in the shade of the big trees. If you could look through the canopy, you'd even be able to see us there, tiny, hopeful figures, frozen in eternity.

ANALYZING SETTING

For this story, part of what makes the setting realistic is the detail the author provides about the online world. Creating a realistic setting impacts how readers respond to events in stories.

I found myself beginning to shake. Why had he sent me this picture? No message had come with the link, not even an emoticon. What was he trying to tell me? That nothing need be lost for good? That somehow, I could reach him?

I stayed at my computer all night; I was afraid that if I logged off, or navigated away from the page, I would never find it again. I slept a little in my chair, ate a sandwich, checked my mail, opened a window to Twitter. I found that I could do this without losing my link to Charlie. I stayed at my desk all day, all night, waiting for instructions. Outside, the days and nights flashed by like windows on a passing train.

A hundred days since Charlie's death. Most of my followers are gone. I don't really care about that any more, as long as I still have Charlie. I'm starting to feel slightly faint whenever I stand up from my desk. Maybe I'm not eating enough. I don't seem to have any appetite. But looking at Charlie's picture helps; the one of our house seen from above, like an angel's-eye view of a loved one—

And if I really concentrate, I can sometimes believe the picture has changed; a blur in the far left corner, a flash of colour through the trees. And wasn't Charlie's bicycle lying flat at the side of the lawn when now it's standing against the wall? Wasn't it? I'm sure it was.

> *An account you have been following (@Llamadude) has not posted in 120 days. Would you like to reconnect?*

;-) ◆

VISUAL LITERACY

Consider how the designer of this selection has created mood through the use of visuals and design elements. Ask yourself: What mood is created? How does that mood affect my response to the story?

RESPONDING

DISCUSSION QUESTIONS

EVALUATING
What explanation for the @Llamadude tweets might there be, beyond the supernatural one? What does Joanne Harris intend for her readers to believe? Support your analysis with details from the text.

ANALYZING POINT OF VIEW
Why does Harris choose to tell her story in the first person, from the point of view of the mother? How effective would the story have been if it had been told from the third-person point of view?

COMPARING TEXTS
Compare "Would You Like to Reconnect?" with "Heartbeat," on page 208. Consider message, tone, fluency, word choice, and theme.

TASKS

RESPONDING CREATIVELY
Read the Author Note below. Create your own social media ghost story in the form of your choice (e.g., graphic short story, video, or podcast). What perspective on social media will your work take?

RESEARCH AND INQUIRY
Research the ghost story genre. Find another story to share with your class. Identify the techniques ghost stories commonly use.

AUTHOR NOTE
Of this story, Joanne Harris writes, "To me, the Internet seems the natural place for a certain kind of ghost story.... I found myself becoming increasingly fascinated by our growing dependence on the virtual world; the relationships we build there; the communities we create; the connections we make with people we may never meet in real life. This world can be a feast of friends, or the loneliest place on the planet. It's all a matter of perspective."

FOCUS ON genre

One question trumps all when analyzing an opinion piece: Were you persuaded?

ANALYZING PERSUASIVE WRITING AND THE OPINION PIECE

The persuasive writing style can use a variety of forms, tools, and devices to persuade an audience to do or believe something.

There are many different forms of persuasive writing. For example:

- A personal essay attempts to connect with and persuade its audience in a very direct way with humour and/or emotion.
- A newspaper editorial uses arguments, facts, examples, or reasoning to support its opinion and persuade its audience.
- A print ad uses a variety of techniques (some textual, some visual) to persuade.
- A rant uses passion and an appeal to emotion or justice to persuade.

OPINION PIECES

An opinion piece is a type of persuasive writing that can take many forms—from reviews to rants, from speeches to editorials. Opinion pieces try to persuade an audience to believe something or to take action. Most opinion pieces use facts, examples, or reasoning to support ideas and persuade an audience.

Use the structure of the opinion piece to help you locate the writer's opinion and support. Opinions are usually stated within the first paragraph. Support for the writer's opinion usually follows in body paragraphs. The opinion may be restated in the concluding paragraph.

As you read, remember to distinguish between what is opinion and what is fact. Sometimes it is easy to identify the opinion, because expressions like the following are used: *in my opinion, I believe, I feel*. Question whether the facts support the opinion. Analyze how the writer uses rhetorical devices to support his or her opinion.

SAMPLE

opinion — Social media is antisocial.

facts — In a recent study, more than 65% of people reported that they would rather spend time online chatting with people they don't know than actually talking with people they do know. Interestingly, 10% of the "people" they're speaking with are actually computers or robots!

RHETORICAL DEVICES

Hyperbole	Analogy	Repetition	Statistics	Rhetorical Questions
Hyperbole can make an argument more convincing, but it should be reserved for informal writing.	An analogy can support the emotional aspects of an argument. If a writer can convince you that the analogy is true, then you are moving toward agreeing with the writer's opinion.	Repetition is a powerful tool when used effectively. When used ineffectively, repetition can annoy readers and work against the writer's efforts to persuade.	Statistics are effective rhetorical tools because people associate numbers with facts. An idea supported by a statistic feels true. However, statistics are only as reliable as their sources.	Writers use rhetorical questions to invite their readers into a conversation about a topic.

WHAT DO YOU THINK?

Customers are always right, even when they're wrong.

 STRONGLY AGREE   STRONGLY DISAGREE

My Challenge to You:

Only Speak Like a Human

Opinion Piece by Daniel H. Pink, posted on the *Telegraph*

One night, a Virgin Atlantic flight left Heathrow Airport bound for Newark, New Jersey. As the plane neared the Eastern Seaboard, bad weather forced the flight to divert to Hartford, Connecticut, some 171 kilometres north of its destination. The plane sat on the runway there for four hours—without air conditioning, food, or water—as babies wailed and adults languished in the darkened cabin.

The next day, the airline, which explained that the Hartford airport lacked the customs personnel to process an international flight, offered this response: "Virgin Atlantic would like to thank passengers for their patience and apologize for any inconvenience caused."

Jason Fried, co-founder of the American software firm 37 Signals and co-author of *ReWork: Change the Way You Work Forever*, finds the language of that statement almost as inhuman as the problem that prompted it.

Not too long ago, Fried saw a similar, though less calamitous, disaster in a Chicago café. A woman had just purchased a large cup of coffee. On the way to sit down, she tripped and spilled the entire contents all over another customer.

// **Euphemisms**

A *euphemism* is a seemingly inoffensive word or phrase used in place of more direct or accurate words. Euphemisms are often used to speak about difficult topics in a gentler manner. They have also been used by governments and corporations to avoid speaking about a sensitive or unpopular topic directly. Examples include *collateral damage* to describe civilians killed in war and *right-sizing* to refer to the firing of employees.

Here's what she said: "I'm so sorry. I'm so, so sorry."

"If someone is really, truly sorry," says Fried, "that's how they respond."

But, in business, we rarely talk like that. Instead, we resort to a weird and inadvertent bilingualism. We speak human at home and "professionalese" when dealing with business.

Go back to that all-too-common phrase: "We apologize for any inconvenience this might have caused." Would you say that to your daughter when you were late picking her up from football practice? To your neighbour when your dog trampled his flowerbed?

"Any inconvenience" is emotionally anemic and lacks the specificity to make it meaningful. "We apologize" isn't much better. It's distancing almost to the point of dismissiveness. "When you say, 'I'm sorry,' you're owning," Fried explains. "When you say 'I apologize,' you're renting."

Professionalese is a renter's language. It doesn't expect to be around for very long and has no stake in the long-term prospects of the neighbourhood. It says, "mistakes were made" rather than "we messed up," and claims to "take responsibility" instead of acknowledging "it's my fault."

Using business-speak rests on the notion that the distance of professional language is inherently strong—and the closeness of personal language inherently weak.

But this idea may be wrong.

Behavioural economist Dan Ariely has conducted research showing that when people are treated rudely, they're more likely to behave vengefully—for instance, by not saying anything when they're given too much change in a transaction. But when rudeness is followed by a clear and simple "I'm sorry," the annoyance dissipates and people tend to behave as honourably as they do in ordinary circumstances.

> //**"United Breaks Guitars"**
>
> Persuasive writing comes in many different forms. When Canadian musician Dave Carroll's guitar was damaged by baggage handlers for United Airlines, he complained for nine months without result. Finally, Carroll created a song and music video about the incident called "United Breaks Guitars," trying to persuade the airline to pay for his broken guitar. Over 150 million views later, Carroll is in high demand as a speaker about customer service and United has changed its customer service policies.

Or consider medicine. In the United States, where physicians fret that every patient is a potential plaintiff in a malpractice lawsuit, lawyers counsel doctors never to admit a mistake. But evidence shows that when doctors apologize for an error and show how they'll avoid it in the future—that is to say, when they talk and act like human beings—aggrieved patients think more highly of the physician and are less likely to sue.

In 2006, Threadless, an online T-shirt company, confronted a case of technological malpractice. While upgrading its computer system, the company accidentally deleted all of the blogs that its customers had maintained for several years. Yet when Threadless, instead of hiding behind the stilted language of "inconvenience caused," explained its errors, apologized directly for them, and even invited comments on the blunder, customers reacted with surprising empathy.

"The best way to figure out if you're running a good company is to figure out if your customers trust your apology," says Jeffrey Kalmikoff, who was Threadless's chief creative officer during the snafu.

Like any valuable relationship, the ones we have in business hinge on trust. And trust depends on openness, respect, and humanity. Yet we often resist taking that approach in our professional lives, even though we know it would be absurd to do anything else in our personal lives.

For instance, suppose I'm talking on my mobile phone—maybe doing an interview for this column—when my wife calls. I can't speak with her at the moment—I'm on deadline—so I say to her: "All of my brain is busy right now, so please hold and I'll be with you shortly. Your call is very important to me."

I guarantee that my customer satisfaction scores at home would suffer.

But if that's true, why not re-craft the waiting message in our call centres so that it's more like what we'd say to our spouses? "We know it's frustrating to wait on hold—but we're swamped right now answering other calls. We'll get to you as soon as we can—probably in about [insert an accurate number] minutes. We're sorry for making you wait."

In a world awash in information and choices, clarity is now a source of competitive advantage, says Fried. "The real winners in business are going to be the clear companies. Clarity is what everybody really wants and appreciates."

So try an experiment. For the next seven days, go monolingual and speak only human at all times.

It might startle people at first. But I suspect that they'll reply in the same vernacular—and you might start actually understanding each other and getting something done.

However, if I'm mistaken—and this test flops—I apologize in advance for any inconvenience caused. ◆

Ways to Say You're Sorry … That May or May Not Get You Out of Trouble

1. I'm incredibly sorry I lost the only photo of your grandmother accepting the Nobel Peace Prize. Here's a really cute photo of a kitten playing with socks.
2. I'm terribly sorry I missed your graduation. Please let me take you to dinner—but could you lend me 20 bucks?
3. Please accept this used Frisbee as a sign of how sorry I am for forgetting to pick you up at the hospital.
4. These roses are my way of saying please forgive me. I'll never again suggest we play Scrabble without any rules.
5. I'm sorry I forgot you were allergic to roses. Please accept this bottle of antihistamines that I found in my cupboard.
6. I'm really and truly sorry I offended you. As I said last time, I'll never do it again.
7. You were wrong, but I'm sorry I called you a fool.
8. Sorry for being myself.
9. My bad!

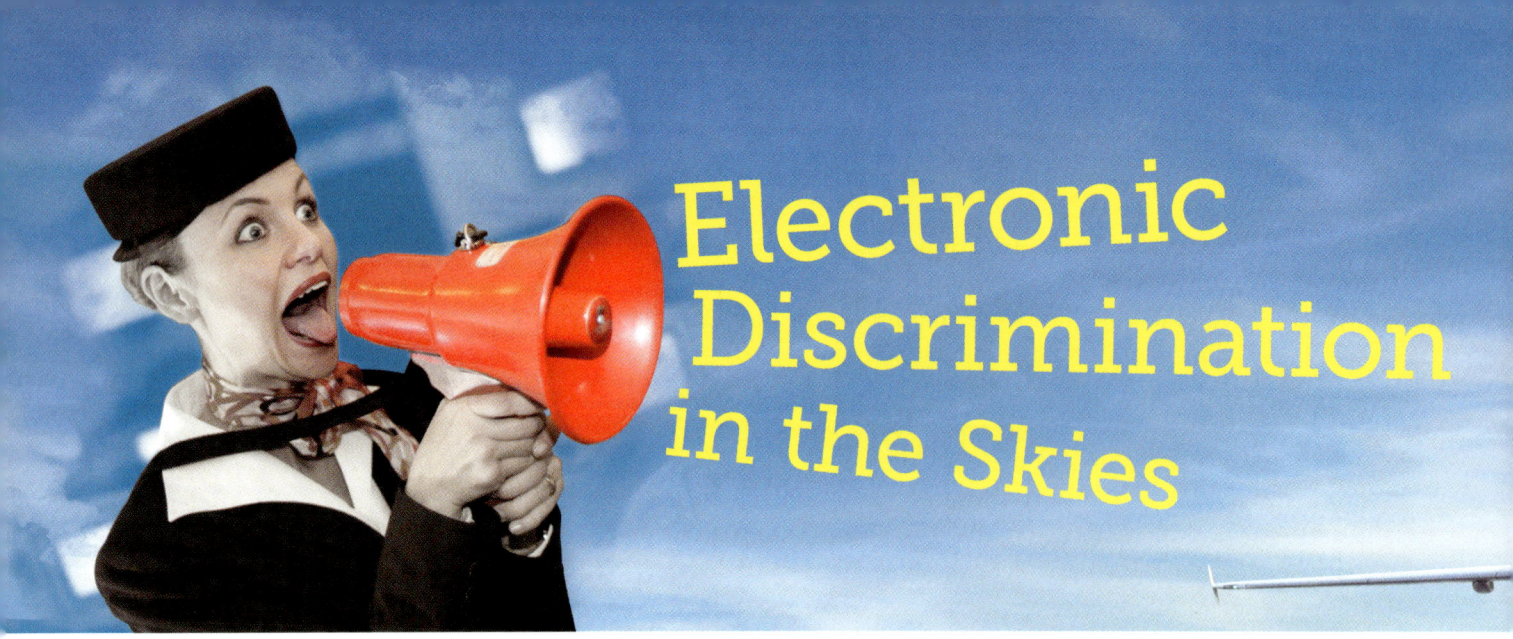

Electronic Discrimination in the Skies

Opinion Piece by Peter Nowak, posted on *Maclean's*

If you've ever been on a plane, you've probably heard those announcements right before takeoff and landing asking passengers to turn off all electronic devices. For kicks, I sometimes refuse to, just to hear what excuses flight staff come up with for why I should.

There's the popular one, about how electronics with connection technologies—cellphones, laptops, iPads—can interfere with the plane's navigational systems. If that were true, I don't know why would-be terrorists would go through the trouble of smuggling in shoe bombs or explosives packed in liquid containers when all they would need to do to cause catastrophe is turn on their phones.

I looked into this a couple years back while I was at the *National Post* and found that the real reason cellphones can't be used on planes is because, in the event that their signals are strong enough, they play havoc with networks on the ground. Because planes move so fast, phones can jump quickly from cell tower to cell tower, which can ultimately cause a big roaming mess. Cellphone carriers wouldn't know how to bill their customers. That's why the Federal Communications Commission bans their use on planes, unless such connections run through special in-flight systems.

ABC News had a recent story on a confidential airline industry report that questioned whether using cellphones on board is safe but, as a former air force and commercial pilot put it, there is no proof either way. In any event, I've never actually tried to use a cellphone on a plane, and not because of the potential interference issue. Sitting next to someone on a bus while they chat away is annoying enough; having to do it on a plane would be intolerable. My mom raised me to have better manners than that.

But what happens when the particular gizmo you're using doesn't have any sort of wireless connection, or it's turned off or in airplane mode? Why, in that case, do the flight staff still want you to shut it down?

//Irony

Irony is an important way in which writers develop deeper levels of meaning that are richer than the literal meanings of the words they use. Irony is used with particular effectiveness by writers of satire and by those seeking to bring about social or political change. Irony is often viewed as a provocative literary device because it can bring a reader new understanding in an often subtle and humorous way.

Such was the case Thursday night when I was flying back to Toronto from a PlayStation press event in New York. I was reading a book on my iPad when the flight attendant told me to turn it off. I ignored her and, when she returned and told me again, I asked her why. She whipped out another excuse I've heard before, which is that the device could fly out of my hands while landing and nail someone in the head.

True enough, but so could a book. Getting beaned with a hardcover copy of *Sex, Bombs and Burgers* hurts just as much (trust me, I tested it—and yes, that is a cheap plug).

Failing that, she tried another excuse—that the staff needed my full attention while landing in case of emergency. Again, fair enough—but, I asked, why weren't the people reading books and magazines asked to put those away? Her answer made me chuckle: apparently, any flight attendant who didn't ask passengers to stow their printed reading material was being negligent.

I finally put my iPad away, which made her happy, but then she did the unbelievable—she walked right by my friend, seated in the row ahead of me, and completely ignored the fact that he was reading a book. I asked if he had heard our exchange and he said, "Yup." We shared a laugh.

But seriously—what's with the double standard? This was far from an isolated incident. Airline staff always crack down on electronic devices, transmitting or not, but are fine with printed matter (including the airline's own magazines stuffed into the seat pockets). The conspiracy-minded would say it's because laptops, iPods, and iPads are sucking away revenue from airlines' pay-per-use entertainment systems, but I don't believe it's that simple.

That said, I can't explain it as anything other than electronic discrimination. When will our gadgets finally get equal treatment? Can't we all just get along? ◆

RESPONDING

DISCUSSION QUESTIONS

COMPARING TEXTS
Analyze the message in "My Challenge to You: Only Speak Like a Human" and "Electronic Discrimination in the Skies." Compare the voice, word choice, and sentence fluency in each text. How do those elements affect each writer's message?

ANALYZING ORGANIZATION
For one of these two texts, outline the opinion, main points, supporting facts, and conclusion. Include quotations from the text.

ANALYZING LITERARY DEVICES
Identify the irony in "Electronic Discrimination in the Skies." Explain why it is used.

TASKS

DEVELOPING DIALOGUE
Write dialogue for a scene in which you have been given a rule with a double standard. Try to consider each perspective. Rehearse and present the dialogue.

WRITING A STORY
Imagine a person who could only speak "professionalese." Write a short story that relates an emotional moment in that character's life. Illustrate through effective word choice and sentence fluency the character's struggle to express himself or herself while trapped in a professional personality.

WHAT DO YOU THINK? + AGREE − DISAGREE
Books are dead.

TURNING the Page

Personal Essay by Robert Costanzo, from the *Globe and Mail*

DANTE'S *INFERNO*

Inferno is part of a fourteenth-century epic poem called the *Divine Comedy*. In the poem, Dante Alighieri describes nine circles of Hell. The poem continues to inspire writers and artists to this day. The punishments meted out in Dante's nine circles have been represented in every form of expression, from Lego to great works of art.

While quietly minding my own business in a bathroom stall at school recently, I overheard two of my students who didn't know, or perhaps didn't care, that I was there.

"Yo, dude, did you finish reading the novel for the English test today?"

"Me, naw, skimmed through it."

"Dude, you're screwed."

"Nope, I read summaries and analysis online. I haven't finished a book in two years."

Naturally, I was horrified. My horror turned to shock when, peeking through the crack, I saw that the book skimmer was one of my top students.

I teach English at the Crescent School in Toronto, an independent boys' school. For the past decade, I've joined many of my brother and sister English teachers lamenting the supposed decline of reading among young people.

Using all my creative powers, and motivated by genuine pedagogical paranoia, I've sought clever ways to bring my pupils back to their books. Surely, I thought, the world will descend into the seventh circle of Dante's *Inferno* if they don't.

Yet, despite good intentions and varied approaches by teachers, every year seems to bring greater apathy among students toward spending quiet hours engrossed in a book. Kids don't seem to be reading as much for pleasure; kids don't seem to be reading as much from their required texts; kids don't seem to be reading as much, period.

222 Nelson English Unit 4: Perspective

The cause, frustrated teachers agree, is the growing distraction of electronic media. We could include other modern distractions and compile a sobering list of factors that drive a wedge between children and the kind of close reading we identify as central to the educational experience.

Some people argue that kids are in fact reading more; they are just reading less, more often, and from an increasing spectrum of interest. Aren't they reading blogs, texts, tweets, and Facebook pages, after all?

Though this is certainly true, the concern teachers have is about quality over quantity: kids may be reading, but they are reading crap.

But are we ready for what some regard as a disturbing reality: that deep, prolonged reading is losing its relevance, and may be gone forever?

Students are surviving English class by sampling, scanning, and browsing—precisely the same kind of reading they do on the Internet.

Staggering overstimulation has required young people to become excellent multi-taskers. They're not alone; a glance in the direction of a modern office reveals work stations with two or three monitors, a desktop computer, a laptop, and a mobile device being balanced by employees required not to do more with less, but more with more.

Where does this leave English teachers like me, who desperately want their students to pore over the novels of Conrad, Austen, and Dickens the same way they used to when mustache-beards were in?

Maybe we should be letting them do what they do best: browse and sample.

As soon as I assign my students a piece of reading, they begin searching for Web-based shortcuts. They read biographies on authors, commentaries on style and context, explanations of themes and conflicts. Just the sort of thing I want to be doing with them, but they beat me to it.

They don't know it, but this has enriched in-class discussions and layered their writing. Students may be reading only part of the text, but by nature they are driven to read around it, too.

ANALYZING OPINION PIECES

As you read, remember to distinguish between the facts and the opinions. Is "they are reading crap" an opinion or a fact? How do you distinguish between opinion and fact?

ANALYZING WORD CHOICE

Robert Costanzo first wrote this article with an adult audience in mind. Consider which words and phrases most strongly suggest that audience and how that language might change if he were writing for teens.

Despite all my concern, they don't seem to be suffering; in fact, their writing and speaking is as good as or better than I've seen in previous years.

So, perhaps it is time to meet students where the new reality finds them—reading shorter pieces, more often. Traditionalists may furrow their brows, but steady improvements in provincial testing suggest students haven't reverted to cave-dwelling yet.

English teachers have held on to the nineteenth- and twentieth-century novel with grasping, wrenching fingers. I've been one of them and, truthfully, I'm not sure why.

The novel is a distinctly Western convention, and a new one at that—it arrived two centuries after the printing press. The Industrial Revolution increased leisure time, so longer pieces became more attractive—and writers benefited from being paid by the word.

While a teen's reading material 100 years ago might have been as narrow as a few books on a bedroom shelf, a student in my class today has an endless range of possibilities.

Lately, in my own classroom, we have started sampling text. Instead of reading one novel thoroughly, we may read the first eight pages of several novels and examine the varying styles, content, and perspectives. We then sample from deeper within the works, and compare the styles of endings.

Students are free to read in depth from the works that truly interest them, and they often do. I recently sought out the reading shirker from the washroom incident to compliment him on an outstanding paper.

We chatted about his reading habits for a while before he said: "I read all the time, sir, but I haven't owned a book for years."

Like it or not, the digital natives entering our educational institutions seem to be ready for school.

The question is this: Are schools ready for them? ◆

ANALYZING RHETORICAL DEVICES

Consider why this essay ends with a rhetorical question and the response Costanzo expects readers to have.

RESPONDING

DISCUSSION QUESTIONS

RESPONDING PERSONALLY
How much do you see yourself in Robert Costanzo's description of his students? What goals do you have for your reading skills and habits?

DIGITAL LITERACY
Discuss what the term *digital native* means. How does it apply to Costanzo's argument about the curriculum of English classes?

EVALUATING
Identify the point in the essay at which the writer's thinking turns around. What is Costanzo's opinion at the beginning of the essay? What is it at the end of the essay? How effectively is his opinion expressed or developed?

TASKS

RESEARCH AND INQUIRY
Create a questionnaire to survey at least five fellow students about their reading habits. Give the same questionnaire to at least five adults you know. Prepare a report that compares the reading habits of the different groups.

RESPONDING CREATIVELY
Respond to Costanzo's essay using one of the following options:
- Write a letter to the *Globe and Mail* giving a student's point of view on this issue.
- Develop and deliver a speech suggesting how schools can adapt to digital natives.
- Create a series of tableaux to suggest how readers have changed in their habits over the last few generations.
- Choose another way to respond.

WHO KILLED THE Wooden HOCKEY STICK?

WHAT DO YOU THINK? + AGREE — DISAGREE
Technology cannot make up for a lack of talent.

Opinion Piece by Joe O'Connor, from the *National Post*, November 19, 2012

Heritage Wood Specialties Inc. is one of the last wooden hockey stick makers.

Ted Lindsay, or "Terrible Ted," the craggy-faced old Detroit Red Wings star, worked as a broadcaster on New York Rangers games in the 1960s and 1970s.

Terrible Ted would howl with glee when the players were "laying the lumber." Wielding their wooden sticks like war clubs. Whacking each other on the shins. Playing old-time hockey with their old-time wooden hockey sticks.

The lumber, alas, has largely left the game over the past 15 years, leaving us, the shinny kings and hockey parents, mulling over the purchases of the latest NHL-player-endorsed, composite-carbon-fibre hockey-stick, with Kevlar-wrapped blades and wallet-jarring price tags, and no real connection to the Great North Woods that provided Gordie Howe and Bobby Hull and even the Great One himself with their magic wands.

For me, there has only ever been one stick: the Sher-Wood Feather-Lite 5030 "Paul Coffey" model. Even now, in my 40s, I cling to my Paul Coffey Sher-Wood like a dinosaur clinging to the equator during its end days.

ANALYZING WORD CHOICE

Joe O'Connor uses some jargon in this opinion piece; he also discusses some people and events that not every reader will know about. As you read, identify words or lines that require specialized knowledge. What background knowledge does O'Connor expect readers to have in order to understand this opinion piece?

ANALYZING WORD CHOICE

As you read, consider how O'Connor creates vivid descriptions through careful word choice. For example, what comes to mind when you read the description of Heritage Wood Specialties?

Wooden sticks ruled for more than a century. They are steeped in lore and bygone stories of Mi'kmaw stick makers fashioning sticks out of hornbeam trees; of Ernie "Moose" Johnson playing with a 191-centimetre branch; of Stan Mikita, the Chicago Blackhawks legend, unwittingly inventing the curved blade after catching his straight wooden blade in the players' bench door and bending it like a banana.

Once ubiquitous, wood is in full retreat. Not a single NHL forward or defenceman, save for the Edmonton Oilers' old warhorse Ryan Smyth—who uses a wood blade anchored to a composite shaft—still uses a wooden stick.

What killed the wooden hockey stick? Is the answer as simple as technology? And are the new sticks, with all their bells and whistles and promises of a harder slapshot, truly any better than what we had, or merely a pricey hockey status symbol?

On a recent afternoon, I went looking for answers. I found them in a 112-year-old factory nestled next to the Speed River in Cambridge, Ontario. Heritage Wood Specialties resembles a working museum. The flooring inside the main office is a quilt-work of hockey sticks.

Paul Henderson (left) of Canada and Yevgeny Zimin (right) of the Soviet Union wait for the faceoff during Game 1 of the 1972 Summit Series. Henderson, using a wooden hockey stick, makes history when he scores the series-winning goal in Game 8.

Are composite sticks like these the reason Canada won gold at the 2010 Olympics? Hayley Wickenheiser (centre) celebrates the win with her teammates.

In 2004, Nike Bauer, the then-owner of the facility, announced it was closing the plant. Five employees bought it back to life, thus saving an enterprise that during its heyday in the mid-1990s manufactured 1.4 million wooden sticks a year and employed 150 people. Today, about 40 workers are making a few hundred thousand sticks annually.

Ask around the factory floor and many of the woodworkers offer a similar theory about the demise of their product. They believe the wooden stick has been mortally wounded by mass marketing and profit margins. Kids want to use what Sidney Crosby is using. Companies can charge three, four, five—seven times more for a composite stick than your typical Sher-Wood.

Does that mean they are seven times better?

Alain Haché, an experimental physicist at the University of Moncton and author of the book *The Physics of Hockey*, says no.

"I would say that for some players, the elite players, composite sticks do make a difference, but for most of us they are going to make very little difference," he says.

Mr. Haché argues that the technology of a $200 to $300 stick is simply too much technology for the masses. In other words, it takes a race-car driver to drive a race car and yet, here we are, 75 percent of us, zooming around the rinks with our fancy new sticks.

"We are coming to the end of the life cycle of the wood product," says Heritage Wood Specialties CEO, Curtis Clairmont, a former goalie at Cornell University.

I feel glum, pulling away from the factory. Still, I haven't given up on my Sher-Wood, and I wonder if I'm not alone. I wonder: What does [former NHL star] Paul Coffey think?

"I still use the Paul Coffey 5030 model," Paul Coffey says. "I actually got a bunch of them around the house. We [former NHL stars Chris Chelios, Guy Lafleur, and Ray Bourque] all thought that they were the Ferrari of sticks—and no two were ever the same.

"I remember I would ask Claude Larose, a former NHLer and an equipment representative, why I could get seven of my sticks and each one would be different. Claude would say to me, 'Well, Paul, no two trees are ever the same.'"

Even Mr. Coffey has been caught up in the crush of composites, in the great leap forward in stick technology. Blake, his 14-year-old son, was, up until a few years ago, still wedded to the wood.

"Blake went to a hockey camp and he was the only kid there with a wooden stick, and the other kids were laughing at him," Mr. Coffey says. "I told him he could use a different stick, but it had to be because he wanted to—not because he was being laughed at."

Blake Coffey switched sticks.

"Unfortunately, this is today's world," his father says. "We all want the best for our kids and we all get caught up in it. Are the $200 to $300 composite sticks a better hockey stick? Sure they are. But are they really that much better than a Sher-Wood that costs, what, 30 bucks?" ◆

RESPONDING

DISCUSSION QUESTIONS

MAKING INFERENCES
From the text, what can you infer are the qualities that distinguish composite sticks from wooden sticks? Support your response with specific details.

ANALYZING LITERARY DEVICES
How effective is the rhetorical question at the end of this opinion piece? As a writer, what criteria help you decide when to use rhetorical questions?

ANALYZING SENTENCE FLUENCY
Which paragraph most effectively demonstrates sentence fluency? Why?

TASKS

DEVELOPING DIALOGUE
Create a dialogue that gives voices to two hockey sticks, one wooden and one composite, debating which one is better. In your personification of the hockey sticks, demonstrate how you have researched their technology. Make use of effective word choice, ideas, and sentence fluency to create a distinctive voice for each stick.

WRITING A PERSUASIVE ESSAY
Has technology ruined sports? Research this question for your favourite sport and respond with a persuasive essay. Consider the connection between technology and world records and how sporting organizations have tried to regulate the use of technology. Convince readers that technology has or has not ruined the sport.

ABOUT THE AUTHOR
Joe O'Connor describes himself on his *National Post* profile as a "Hiker, biker, sports junkie, dog lover, new father, yarn-spinner, and story writer on an eclectic array of topics."

> **WHAT DO YOU THINK?**
> Why are people attracted to stories about the end of the world?

Maybe ZOMBIES Can Save Us from Our Comforts

Opinion Piece by Tisha McComb

ANALYZING POINT OF VIEW

Consider the effect that using the second-person perspective has on readers.

You wake up in a sunny hospital room. There are IVs in your arms and you are thirsty, hungry, and disoriented. None of the machines around your bed beeps. It seems, in fact, that the power is out. The door to your room is locked. You call out, peering into the empty hallway. No one answers. Looking down, you find a key that has been thrown under the door. As you leave the building, you see tables overturned, supplies strewn about, and papers scattered everywhere. The cafeteria doors are chained and bolted shut. It is eerily quiet.

Outside, you hear no cars, no electric hum, no footsteps. Again, you call out but no one responds. You walk the streets, which look as if a riot has passed through. There are smashed cars, rolled-over buses, charred pavement, and garbage everywhere. You stop at a newsstand and read headlines: Evacuation. Total Devastation.

Then you notice a body. You stare. It stares back. You cannot look away from the rotting mess. A strange noise comes from the corpse. Its arms raise and it moans as its teeth come for you. You run, noticing other shuffling bodies in the streets, bloody and dismembered. Zombies.

This scenario is similar to the opening of the comic series *The Walking Dead*. It is far-fetched. It is terrifying. It is exactly what we want.

With zombies appearing in movies and TV shows, video games, comics, books, art, music, zombie walks, and Halloween costumes, the zombie-genre economy is worth almost $6 billion.

Ask around: I bet you know someone who has read *The Zombie Survival Guide* or *Pride, Prejudice and Zombies*. And someone who thinks about zombie apocalypse. You might even know someone who has planned for it (it's a good idea to be prepared if you want to survive).

Recently, there has been a shift in the industry toward post-apocalyptic survival. (Check out the movie *I Am Legend* or the TV series *The Walking Dead*.) We have moved beyond the blood and guts. We want to know what happens next.

The majority of searches for zombies on Google are concentrated in North America, Japan, and Europe. Why are the most privileged people in the world searching for adversity? Why are we imagining new problems instead of fixing the ones we have?

People are dissatisfied with their routine, comfortable lives. There are things we dislike or abhor, but changing them would require a lot of effort. If we wait long enough, a catastrophe will occur and we can begin again on our own terms. That is one of our secret desires—an overhaul of the system.

We want to take back control without a revolution. To have the freedom to do as we please and take what we like, to walk away from menial obligations like jobs and homework.

We dream of living. Not just breathing, but existing with purpose and meaning. We want to prove ourselves with each day we survive. We believe our true humanity will be easier to find in a world stripped of frivolities. We will unite against a common enemy.

Robert Kirkman writes in *The Walking Dead*, "In a world ruled by the dead, we are forced to start living." Must we wait until then? ◆

RESPONDING

DISCUSSION QUESTIONS

ANALYZING SENTENCE FLUENCY
How has Tisha McComb used sentence fluency throughout this opinion piece to deliver strong conclusions? Support your analysis with specific examples.

EVALUATING
Respond to the following quotation: "People are dissatisfied with their routine, comfortable lives. There are things we dislike or abhor, but changing them would require a lot of effort."

METACOGNITION
What helps you identify an author's opinion? What critical strategies do you use when reading opinion pieces?

TASKS

DEBATING
With a partner, prepare to debate the proposition: "The world is a mess; we need to start over." Research economic, health, and demographic information to support or oppose the proposition. Be ready to argue effectively for either side.

WRITING A STORY
Imagine that a scientist has created a zombie virus and plans to unleash it on the world. Write a short story in which a young person is the world's last hope. Your hero must talk the scientist out of this evil plan. Demonstrate through the characters in your story the battle between hope and resignation that McComb outlines in her article.

Up for Debate

> People live their lives bound by what they accept as **correct** and **true**. That's how they **define reality**. But what does it mean to be 'correct' or 'true'? Merely vague concepts…. Their reality may all be a **mirage**. Can we consider them to simply be living in their own world, shaped by their **beliefs**?
>
> —Masashi Kishimoto

> 'Fairy Tales always have a happy ending.' That depends … on whether you are Rumpelstiltskin or the Queen.
>
> —Jane Yolen, *Briar Rose*

Our opinions are based on what we think we know …

What we think we know …

What we actually know.

Homeless or Homefree?

Sometimes, the words we use to describe ourselves are really just a matter of perspective. Take Heidemarie Schwermer, who discovered that her empty nest was more burden than benefit. When her children moved out, she decided to sell her apartment and give all her possessions away. For almost two decades, she's been living without money or a permanent home, trading for anything she needs. She says of her decision, "For some people, I'm a provocation. But for others, I'm an answer."

> Often, it isn't the **mountains** ahead that wear you out, it's the little pebble in your shoe.
>
> —Muhammad Ali

FOCUS ON media

As the cost to produce a media text goes up, the influence of the people paying to produce the media text also goes up.

EVALUATING PRODUCTION PERSPECTIVES

Media productions can be very expensive. The average cost of a feature film is over $50 million. The cost of a TV program can range from $200 000 to over $15 million per episode. Even a 30-second national TV commercial might cost over $1 million to produce. So, you can be certain that the people in charge of the money work very closely with the writers, directors, set designers, set decorators, wardrobe people, and casting agents to ensure that every creative decision also involves financial considerations. This is referred to as *production perspectives*.

EVALUATING PRODUCTION PERSPECTIVES

When evaluating the production perspectives of a media text, ask yourself the following questions:

- What is the text's purpose? Who is the intended audience?
- How does this text connect to other texts?
- How might production perspectives have influenced this media text?
- What choices did the creators make that were directly connected to the cost of making the media text? Consider choices in setting, characters, actors, the use of stereotypes, product placement, and so on.

Note that the production perspectives can change as the context of production changes. Consider the remake of an old movie: The new movie may introduce product placement as the director searches for new ways to pay for it. Or consider how a cop show made 20 years ago would never have shown anything remotely gritty; nowadays, if cop shows aren't gritty, they risk losing their audience to other shows.

EXAMPLES OF PRODUCTION PERSPECTIVES

A singer writes a song with language the recording company considers offensive. The recording company has the singer record another version of the song without the offensive language so that the song can be played on the radio.

A producer has an idea for a sitcom set in Winnipeg. The TV network buying the sitcom insists on changing the setting to an anonymous North American city because the network executives believe it will help them sell the program in the United States.

BIAS AND PRODUCTION PERSPECTIVES

Production perspectives are a form of bias. Businesses exist to make money and so are biased toward decisions that will help them earn a profit. Of course, economics are not the only source of bias in media texts. Media creators may also have biases that they bring to the texts.

When analyzing media texts, be aware of biases related to

- gender
- socio-economic status
- faith
- age
- culture or race
- geography
- sexual orientation
- ability

WHAT DO YOU THINK?
Copyright becomes meaningless in a digital age.
👍 STRONGLY AGREE 👎 STRONGLY DISAGREE

Whose ART Is It, Anyway?

Newspaper Article by René Adams

What's the difference between using someone else's ideas to make your own art and stealing someone's ideas and passing them off as your own? Sometimes it's a fine line.

Shepard Fairey was a skateboard kid who started putting up stickers around his neighbourhood. The stickers had a picture of the pro wrestler André the Giant, and they said "André the Giant Has a Posse." What were they supposed to mean? Nothing, really. Nothing more than a funny inside joke aimed at skateboarders and hip-hop kids. The idea was to put as many stickers out there as possible and see how far they would penetrate into pop culture.

Well, they penetrated, all right ... to the point where Titan Sports, the people who owned the trademarked name "André the Giant," came after Fairey, claiming that he was using the name without permission. They threatened a lawsuit. So he stopped using the name, changed the image a little, and created the now infamous logo "OBEY Giant."

//**Analyzing Rhetorical Devices**

René Adams uses rhetorical questions in the title and in the first sentence of the article. As you read, consider your initial response to each question, as well as how your answer changes as you continue to read.

Appropriation artist Barbara Kruger creates works of art that rely heavily on typography. She often uses iconic images from magazines and advertising or takes over public spaces. This is a piece of public art created by Kruger in Manhattan. Her works explore messages of consumerism, feminism, and capitalism.

//Making Connections

The 1988 science-fiction film *They Live* is a cult classic directed by John Carpenter. In the movie, a man finds a pair of special glasses that allow him to see rampant subliminal messages, such as *obey, consume, no independent thought*. Consider how the work of the artists shown in this selection might have been influenced by this movie.

//Visual Literacy

As you examine visual art, ask yourself: What has the artist done to make the piece striking? What gives the work interest? How do colour, line, texture, and textual elements work together?

OBEY Giant (a stylized André the Giant face that often has the word "OBEY" printed beneath it) became Fairey's way of spreading his art. He was trying to make a point about propaganda: If you repeat any message often enough, even a message that's total nonsense, people will begin to think it means something. Fairey encouraged others to spread his "message" wherever they could. OBEY signs started appearing all over the world—on stickers, on posters, stencilled on walls, and on T-shirts. It became an international brand, but it didn't represent a product.

The logo was one step removed from Fairey's original sticker, so nobody could claim that he was stealing someone else's ideas. It's the same argument used by other *appropriation artists*—artists who take other people's work and modify it to create their own art. Once an idea, a piece of art, or any other creative work has been changed enough from its original form and purpose, it becomes a new thing altogether, and the original copyright doesn't apply. In Canada, it's called *fair dealing*. In the United States, it's called *fair use*. The idea is basically the same: Once I change something enough, it's no longer yours—it's mine.

Now Fairey is a famous designer. He's done album covers for the Black Eyed Peas and The Smashing Pumpkins, and worked on campaigns for Pepsi and Levi's. But he still uses other people's work to create his own art. During the 2008 presidential campaign in the United States, Fairey became famous for his stylized image of Barack Obama, which was plastered all over the nation like the OBEY Giant image. Manny Garcia, a photographer who works for the Associated Press, claimed that to design the image, Fairey had started by using his photo. You guessed it—Fairey didn't ask for permission first. The Associated Press threatened to take him to court. So Fairey filed a lawsuit against them, claiming that his art was covered under the fair use law. It was a huge legal mess. What's really fair? It's still anybody's guess.

And here's the funny part—apparently Fairey can't take his own medicine. During the SARS outbreak, a graphic designer from Texas took Fairey's OBEY Giant logo and drew a respiratory mask on it. He got a letter from Fairey's lawyers threatening to sue him because it violated Fairey's trademark. History repeats itself. ◆

An OBEY Giant logo painted on a wall.

Shepard Fairey at work in his studio.

RESPONDING

DISCUSSION QUESTIONS

MAKING INFERENCES
What has the OBEY symbol come to mean? Did Shepard Fairey achieve his original goal for his art? Support your response.

ANALYZING PRODUCTION PERSPECTIVES
Fairey initially published his art for free. Now he is a professional artist who works for corporations. How do you think this change in status influences Fairey's work?

TASKS

PREPARING A PRESENTATION
A *meme* is a concept that spreads rapidly from person to person. Fairey's OBEY Giant image became a meme. Identify another meme, and create an oral presentation that illustrates its life cycle. Explain the meme's origins, describe how it became popular, and evaluate its longevity.

WRITING A SUMMARY
Create a summary for this article that clearly articulates the two sides of the fine line mentioned in the first paragraph. Show your summary to someone who has not read the article and see if he or she is able to understand both sides of the argument.

CREATING A VISUAL TEXT
Respond to the ideas in this article by creating a visual text that owes its inspiration to another work of art. Consider how you can create something that does not infringe on another artist's rights. Share your finished work, as well as your inspiration, with others. Discuss the choices you've made.

WHAT DO YOU THINK? + AGREE — DISAGREE
Songs can be bad for you.

New Tool Provides Food for Thought

Press Release by the Boston Public Health Commission

BOSTON—The next time you're ready to download that song from iTunes, you may want to check out how healthy it is for you. Just as a nutritional label allows you to count the calories in a fast-food hamburger, the Boston Public Health Commission's Start Strong Initiative has made it easier to measure what's in the songs you listen to. Today, the Initiative announced the Sound Relationships Nutritional Label, a new tool to help music lovers evaluate how healthy—or unhealthy—songs are.

"Music, like food, can feed our brains and give us energy," said Casey Corcoran, director of the Commission's Start Strong Initiative. "But songs can affect our health and the health of our relationships."

The tool, patterned after common food nutritional labels, invites consumers to become song-lyric nutritionists by helping them identify relationship ingredients that make up a song. Using printed song lyrics as a guide, users can tally the number of healthy relationship themes, such as respect, equality, and trust, which are present in the song. And, like fattening calories, unhealthy relationship themes—possession, disrespect, and manipulation—are also counted. The number of times these themes are mentioned also factor into the song's total nutritional value. Corcoran recommends consuming lots of "healthy relationship" ingredients for a balanced media diet.

The model was developed by 14 peer leaders in the Commission's Start Strong Initiative. The teens, who range in age from 15 to 19 years old, attended a seven-week "Healthy Relationship Institute," where they were trained in teen dating violence prevention and healthy relationship promotion. They also learned to look at media texts critically, breaking them down to better understand the healthy or unhealthy relationship messages they may contain, such as power, control, equality, and gender roles.

"It's important to have youth involved in this effort because teenagers are the main audience of the music," said peer leader Shaquilla Terry, age 15, of Boston. "It's important to actually listen to and think about the lyrics of a song and not just the beat."

ANALYZING PRODUCTION PERSPECTIVES

In order to avoid legislation forcing them to rate their music, record companies introduced a voluntary "Parental Advisory" label in the 1990s. Critics of the system accused record companies of using the label as a promotional tool to lure young people with promises of adult content.

On average, American youth listen to music from 1.5 to 2.5 hours per day, according to the American Academy of Pediatrics (AAP). The AAP found that listening to explicit music lyrics—with references to drugs, sex, or violence—can affect schoolwork and social interactions, and produce significant changes in mood and behaviour.

"By encouraging young people to employ the Sound Relationships Nutritional Label, parents and educators can begin a dialogue about how romantic relationships are portrayed in songs—and how those portrayals might shape [young people's] ideas about what makes a relationship healthy or unhealthy," said Dr. Michael Rich, director of the Center on Media and Child Health. "I hope that using this tool will help adolescents become more aware of the messages they are receiving, help them begin to make healthier, more self-respecting media choices, and tune in to their music—in more ways than one." ◆

Nutritional Impact

Artist:
Song title:
Serving Size: Min: Sec:

Amount per serving:	Present (X)	Intensity level (1–10)
Unhealthy Relationship Ingredients		
Drama		
Possession/obsession		
Disrespect		
Relationship = sex		
Manipulation		
Total Unhealthy		
Healthy Relationship Ingredients		
Fun/Enjoyable		
Support		
Respect		
Equality		
Trust		
Total Healthy		

RESPONDING

DISCUSSION QUESTIONS

EVALUATING
Based on the nutritional values described in this selection, how balanced are your musical tastes? Is there a particular song you've listened to recently that you consider healthy or unhealthy? Why?

SYNTHESIZING
How effective will labelling the nutritional value of music be? Will it convince people to choose music with positive messages? Refer to specific details in the selection and your experiences to support your answer.

MEDIA LITERACY
Does a music company have a responsibility to distribute and promote songs that only feature respectful and positive relationships? How might a music company executive defend a decision to distribute a song that was disrespectful or featured negative relationships?

TASKS

CREATING A PLAYLIST
Create a playlist with at least five current songs that the Boston Public Health Commission would be willing to post on its website. Share your list with a partner and be prepared to justify your choices.

REWRITING A SONG
Identify a song that might fail the nutritional value standards described in this selection. Rewrite the song with new lyrics that transform its negative messages into positive ones. Ask others for feedback on how successfully you've captured the message of the original song.

> **WHAT DO YOU THINK?** + AGREE − DISAGREE
> Filmmakers have a responsibility to present the truth.

DON'T TRUST HOLLYWOOD to Teach You History

Quality versus Equality: Why It's More Important to Be Ethical Than Entertaining

Opinion Piece by And Palladino, posted on *Tail Slate*

In 1979, the American-backed Shah of Iran was overthrown by a revolution led by Ayatollah Khomeini. When the Shah was allowed into the United States for medical treatment, Iranian militants expressed their anger by taking more than 70 people hostage in the American Embassy in Tehran. Six Americans managed to avoid capture. They found refuge with Kenneth Taylor, the Canadian Ambassador, and John Sheardown, a Canadian immigration official. Taylor, Sheardown, and other Canadian diplomats risked their lives to hide the Americans. The Canadians also worked closely with the CIA, including agent Antonio (Tony) Mendez, to help the Americans escape Iran.

In 2012, the story of the Americans' escape was depicted in the movie *Argo*. Although the movie was highly praised by audience and critics, several people pointed out the historical inaccuracies in its script. The following article also questions the appropriateness of its casting.

Antonio (Tony) Mendez was the CIA agent in charge of rescuing the Americans who were trapped in Iran.

Ben Affleck portrays the character of Tony Mendez in the movie *Argo*.

Most people tend to think of the medium of film as nothing more than entertainment, and once upon a time I probably did, too.

But it isn't true, not in the slightest.

Film is an extremely powerful medium that affects the way our society sees the world. And, as such, it has the power to inflict great hurt on people. A common saying is: "It's all fun and games until someone gets hurt." So when that line is crossed, it needs to be addressed.

Argo has been praised at multiple festivals and is receiving rave reviews from critics. The subject is a true story about how, during the Iran hostage crisis, a CIA agent got the ball rolling on a fake film production that saved the lives of several people trapped in that country. The movie is directed by and stars Ben Affleck.

But there is a huge problem, one that should not be happening in this day and age: Affleck is white. The real-life man he is playing, Tony Mendez, is not.

When I see the true Mendez, I see someone that looks more like Esai Morales or Edward James Olmos than Affleck. There are plenty of talented Latino actors in Hollywood who could easily have played the role. Yet, once again, Hollywood chose to whitewash the part and add yet another example to its long history of racial discrimination (a UCLA study found that of all leading roles, only 1.2 percent go to Latino actors).

Yet, not a single review out there has mentioned this. None of them. Not even Roger Ebert, who has brought up such issues for other films. It boggles my mind that any fellow critic with a brain, heart, spine, or conscience would outright ignore this fact.

But what makes this film especially offensive is that it's based on real events and real people.

I'm reminded of *U-571*, which presented the Americans as the ones who cracked the Enigma code during World War II. This is a complete lie; the code was actually cracked by the British. *Argo* apparently does something similar, as it portrays the involvement of the Canadian government in the operation as having less of a role than it really did. A role that was perhaps even more important than the CIA. So, credit for an incredible, heroic feat by a Latino man and the Canadians is now given to white Americans.

So, how should a critic judge this film? Do these factual distortions taint everything else about the movie?

Yes.

If I were to review *Argo*, it would receive an automatic 1. Racism like this is not tolerable whatsoever, and those who perpetrate it need to be reviled.

Think of it this way: Do we judge books by the grammar or by the actual words? The bad that these racist and dishonest works do far outweigh any redeeming qualities. In fact, it makes those qualities impossible to value. Who's really going to enjoy the descriptive language in a passage that promotes racial genocide?

WHITEWASHING IN MOVIES

Anger over the whitewashing of non-white characters in Hollywood movies isn't necessarily changing casting decisions. Prior to playing Tonto in the 2013 movie, *The Lone Ranger*, Johnny Depp arranged to become an honorary member of the Cherokee nation. But as one Native American writer said, "Johnny is still wearing face paint that looks like it should be in Kiss, and he has a dead bird on his head."

Argo wins the Academy Award for Best Picture.

BASED ON A TRUE STORY?

No one ever claimed *Argo* was a documentary. However, the movie's credits include a montage of photos of the lead actors with images of the real people they were portraying. The scene that angers many Canadians depicts two CIA agents agreeing to let the Canadian Embassy staff get credit for the rescue in order to not further inflame anti-American feelings in Iran.

So, now let's transfer this over to film. The heyday of obvious propaganda may be behind us, but films that serve as propaganda still get made, and that is precisely what *Argo* has become. By stripping away the true identities of those involved, the movie only fosters racist attitudes, undermines Canadian valour, and could go so far as to goad Americans into supporting yet another war with a Middle Eastern country.

People will see this film and believe it, and, in many cases, remain ignorant of its distortions and lies.

Think about it: What sticks with an audience the most after they leave the theatre? Do they discuss the acting and camera tricks? Probably only if the acting and tricks are very incompetent. What sticks is the overall message. And what you think about that message is what you take away from the whole thing.

Social justice is of a much higher importance than amusement. No matter how large the amount of the latter there may be, it means nothing if it's in something that contributes to this world's evil. When themes of morality and decency are present, then the factors that provide the entertainment can truly be appreciated. ◆

RESPONDING

DISCUSSION QUESTIONS

MEDIA LITERACY
How might Ben Affleck (who produced, directed, and starred in *Argo*) respond to And Palladino's charge that choosing a non-Latino actor to play Tony Mendez was racist?

ANALYZING VOICE
Describe the voice Palladino uses in this opinion piece. Support your analysis with specific examples.

ANALYZING PERSPECTIVES
Evaluate the last four paragraphs and the word choices in this opinion piece. How do you respond to Palladino's argument? Does he go too far, or is his opinion justified? Support your evaluation.

TASKS

WRITING A BLOG ENTRY
Research to find evidence to either support or refute Palladino's argument about the whitewashing of characters in Hollywood movies. Write a blog entry presenting your perspective on the argument.

RESEARCH AND INQUIRY
Select and view a movie based on a historical event. Research commentary about the movie's accuracy. Create an oral or digital presentation that answers the following questions:
- How accurately does the movie portray the historical figures?
- What might moviegoers misunderstand about the actual events if their knowledge was based only on the movie?
- What reasons might the filmmakers have had for straying from historical accuracy?

FOCUS ON Writing

Fluency is the quality in writing that you do not appreciate unless it's missing. Fluent writing flows.

CREATING FLUENCY

Sentence fluency dramatically improves the readability and coherence of any text.

TIPS TO IMPROVE YOUR WRITING FLUENCY

1. Reading your text aloud can help you identify problems with fluency. Check that:
   - your sentences flow and do not run on
   - transitions lead readers from idea to idea
   - quotations or dialogue are seamlessly woven into the body of the text
2. As you are writing or revising your work, check for ambiguity in your use of pronouns. Be sure it is clear who or what is being referred to by each *he*, *she*, *they*, or *it*.
3. When editing, be aware of sentence length and type. Make an effort to include sentences of varying lengths and in a variety of patterns. Especially in formal essays, using formulaic sentence structures can be a bad habit. Include the occasional short, declarative sentence (e.g., "This author is a genius.") to provide variety.
4. It is easy to fall into a repeating pattern of subject followed by predicate, particularly in narrative writing (e.g., "Jane runs. Jack runs. Spot runs fast."). When revising your work, consider breaking up or reordering your sentences to change the rhythm of your text (e.g., "Run, Jane, run! Jack may run as fast as Spot, but not as far as Jane."). Punctuation and sentence structures can be used inventively to create dramatic pauses and emphasize a point.

POETIC FLUENCY

Poets need to pay particular attention to the fluency of their writing. Another word for fluency in a poem would be rhythm—good poems have rhythm.

Using Quotations Fluently

Incorporating quotations into your work requires strong sentence-fluency skills. Use punctuation to ensure that there is no confusion about which words and ideas are yours.

SAMPLE: I really love author John Green's motto, "Be awesome."

Always connect the quotation you are including in the text to your own words. Use ellipses to indicate if any text from the original quotation was left out.

SAMPLE: There are many funny lines in the story "World of Warcraft versus My Girlfriend." One of the funniest passages, "I'm sorry I was so late picking you up from the library … and I'm sorry you had to stand outside alone for two hours," made me laugh out loud.

In academic essays, it is important to properly reference the sources of your quotations. Different academic disciplines have developed different standards for citations. Ask your teacher which one you are expected to use.

USING TRANSITIONS

To improve fluency, use transitions, such as the following:

Also …	Another reason …
As well as …	In addition to …
Since …	In spite of …
This means that …	However …
Due to …	Although …

WHAT DO YOU THINK?
How is knowledge different from wisdom?

Who Are the Elders?

Personal Essay by Daniel Crowfeather

It seems there are many people these days who are trying to find a spirituality that they can believe in. For whatever reason, we are beginning to pay more attention to our spirit and to our direction in life. Many of us have found ourselves drawn to the First Nations beliefs, perhaps because they are seen as clean and pure, and based on the simpler times that we all seem to miss. As we make our way along the Red Road (spiritual path), with luck we are led to a person who has been given the wisdom and knowledge to be a teacher. We call these people Elders, and from them we begin to learn the ways and traditions that form the heart of First Nations beliefs. While these Elders generally do not think of themselves as anything special, they are usually highly regarded and treated with great respect.

For some of us, however, these early times can be dangerous. Being human, most of us have a desire to be respected by the people around us. When we see the respect being given to our Elders, we may begin to hope that, someday, we may earn that respect for ourselves. We try to learn as much as we can as quickly as we can, hoping to impress people with our wisdom. We forget that knowledge of facts is not the same as wisdom, which only comes from a lifetime of reflecting on these facts.

//**Analyzing Sentence Fluency**

Read the second paragraph aloud and consider how Daniel Crowfeather has structured his sentences to give them a very specific pacing. How does this pacing help readers comprehend and reflect on ideas?

At best, these people learn from real Seers, and then pass on the visions as their own. At worst, they will invent any vision that will impress their audience.

The danger is greatest at the time when we realize there are people who share our road that know even less than we do. These people may be easily impressed by the tiny amount of knowledge that we carry. Such people might even mistake that knowledge for wisdom, and we may find ourselves receiving some of that respect that we crave. We may find we enjoy the taste of that respect, and our egos may even lead us to think of ourselves as Elders ... and the trap is sprung!

It is important to understand what an Elder is. Aboriginal traditions hold the elderly in high regard because a long life full of experience leads to wisdom. But an Elder in the spiritual sense is not just old; today an elderly person may have no knowledge whatsoever of spirituality. While such a person may have valuable wisdom in other areas of life, he or she obviously cannot be a spiritual Elder. A real Elder carries facts about their traditions *and* the wisdom that comes from long study and practice of those traditions. However, when you are just starting out on the path, it can be hard to tell the difference. Those who are impressionable can be fooled by an older person with a small amount of knowledge claiming to be an Elder.

Another very popular claim is to be a Healer. True Healers are those who are given the ability to heal others using only their own energies and resources. Such people are extremely rare—perhaps a handful walk the earth today. My wife and I do not know of any, and probably neither do you. If you know someone who is claiming to be a Healer, rest assured they are either lying or deluded ... true Healers never advertise because they know that the people who need them will be brought to them, quietly and without fuss. They do not seek recognition because they are only too aware of the heavy burden of responsibility that they carry, and they do not wish to add to it.

//Juxtaposition

Throughout this essay, Crowfeather juxtaposes several concepts: knowledge and wisdom; Elders and the elderly; true Healers and those that claim they can heal; and self-proclaimed Visionaries and real Seers. Consider how he defines each concept and how all of these concepts connect to one another to support his point.

Finally, there are all the self-proclaimed Visionaries. At best, these people learn from real Seers, and then pass on the visions as their own. At worst, they will invent any vision that will impress their audience. Once again, if the person brags of it, then it is not so. True Seers do not advertise because they do not need to. Again, those who need their help will be brought to them, and they know it. They never seek the spotlight.

Each of us has a best possible path to walk, and each of us is here for some specific purpose.

The lure of prestige and notoriety can be hard to resist. I am saddened that there are people within our own circle of friends who have started to call themselves Elders, and pretend to carry far more knowledge than they actually have. There is one who has appointed himself a spiritual leader, and he has created a following of people who have virtually no knowledge of tradition. He tells them they are Elders as well. There is another who claims to be a Healer, and performs smudging and purification ceremonies for others. Because she has not learned the proper use and purposes of sacred medicines, she has no understanding of the danger this poses for both herself and the people she tries to help. There are still others who ask questions of Elders, and then pass on the answers to other people, claiming to have received them direct from the spirits. We call this "riding someone else's tobacco"; it is a simple attempt to gain notoriety at the expense of others. In each case, these people have brought a great deal of trouble into their own lives by doing these things. However, despite these warnings, their egos lead them to continue to misguide others, and they cause much suffering as a result.

Each of us has a best possible path to walk, and each of us is here for some specific purpose. For most of us, our walk is all about learning. While we may not see this as significant, the Creator does not make mistakes: Each life interacts with many others, so each one is as important as any other. Ignoring our path and trying to do something more spectacular simply wastes a lifetime, and possibly endangers ourselves and others. While a person's life is his or her own to waste if they so choose, causing others to waste or misuse their lives is perhaps the vilest and most disgusting thing one human can do to another.

It is time for all the pedestals to be torn down, and for each of us to walk the paths we were intended to walk. We must push aside our egos, and listen to the spirits and the quiet voice of our own hearts. To do any less is to break faith with ourselves, and with the spirits who agreed to help and guide us. Let the true Elders do the teaching. Let the Healers do the healing. Let the Seers do the seeing. Be content that your life, lived as it is supposed to be lived, is as important and necessary as that of any other person. Learn, love, and be humble. ◆

RESPONDING

DISCUSSION QUESTIONS

ANALYZING PURPOSE AND AUDIENCE
Who do you believe Daniel Crowfeather had in mind as his audience while he was writing this personal essay? What was his purpose? Support your analysis.

ANALYZING SENTENCE FLUENCY
Reread the final paragraph of the text. How does Crowfeather use sentence fluency to build toward his conclusion? Support your analysis.

TASKS

CREATING A FOUND POEM
Choose a short passage from this personal essay to create a *found poem* (a poem created by taking someone else's words and rearranging them on the page in the form of a poem). You may want to add an image. When you present your found poem, remember that the original author needs to be properly credited. Share your poem and explain how this exercise helped you evaluate Crowfeather's message.

WRITING A STORY
Choose an idea from this personal essay to use as the inspiration for a short story. Use effective voice and sentence fluency to create distinctive characters that bring the idea to life.

ABOUT THE AUTHOR
Daniel Crowfeather was born with Cree blood, but was adopted through marriage into the Mi'kmaq First Nation in Nova Scotia. He has benefited from being mentored in traditional beliefs by very knowledgeable Elders, including his wife, Muin'iskw. They share these teachings in the hopes of reducing the misconceptions that many have about the Mi'kmaq and about First Nations in general.

WHAT DO YOU THINK?

Poetry is all about perspective.

On Unmaking Contact

Poem by Deena Kara Shaffer

ANALYZING SENTENCE FLUENCY

When a poet uses no punctuation, readers have to make inferences about how the lines flow together, when to pause, and when to read fluidly from line to line. Reading a poem aloud can help make it clear where punctuation could have been included.

I deleted
From Facebook
Your friendship
No more
Picture stalks
Update scans
A non-continuation
Half retaliation
You're off
My Skype

No more
Late night
Calls, scripts
Part self-protection
Contact obliteration
But if
You requested
Online reacquaintance
I'd accept
Delete, accept
Like always

Sifter

Poem by Naomi Shihab Nye

When our English teacher gave
our first writing invitation of the year,
*Become a kitchen implement
in 2 descriptive paragraphs,* I did not think
butcher knife or frying pan,
I thought immediately
of soft flour showering through the little holes
of the sifter and the sifter's pleasing circular
swishing sound, and wrote it down.
Rhoda became a teaspoon,
Roberto a funnel,
Jim a muffin tin
and Forrest a soup pot.
We read our paragraphs out loud.
Abby was a blender. Everyone laughed
and acted giddy but the more we thought about it,
we were all everything in the whole kitchen,
drawers and drainers
singing teapot and grapefruit spoon
with serrated edges, we were all the
empty cup, the tray.
This, said our teacher, *is the beauty of metaphor.
It opens doors.*
What I could not know then
was how being a sifter
would help me all year long.
When bad days came
I would close my eyes and feel them passing
through the tiny holes.
When good days came
I would try to contain them gently
the way flour remains
in the sifter until you turn the handle.
Time, Time. I was a sweet sifter in time
and no one ever knew.

Life

Poem by Charlotte Brontë

Life, believe, is not a dream
So dark as sages say;
Oft a little morning rain
Foretells a pleasant day.
Sometimes there are clouds of gloom,
But these are transient all;
If the shower will make the roses bloom,
O why lament its fall?
Rapidly, merrily,
Life's sunny hours flit by,
Gratefully, cheerily,
Enjoy them as they fly!
What though Death at times steps in
And calls our Best away?
What though sorrow seems to win,
O'er hope, a heavy sway?
Yet Hope again elastic springs,
Unconquered, though she fell;
Still buoyant are her golden wings
Still strong to bear us well.
Manfully, fearlessly,
The day of trial bear,
For gloriously, victoriously,
Can courage quell despair!

ANALYZING SENTENCE FLUENCY

Poets use a technique called *enjambment* that flows ideas across the ends of lines. Notice when you study a poem how the poet uses line breaks to highlight words and ideas. Use the punctuation and your comprehension of the ideas to read the lines fluently.

Regeneration

Poem by Glynnis Ritchie

It is difficult to say
how many people you've been,
even at seventeen.

Every seven years
you are new—
no piece of your body
the same,
no cell left
unchanged.

There have been two and a
   half of you
bending the space around
   your body,
pushing through the air.
Which of you has pressed
   the most
on your surroundings,
created the most tension,
filled the greatest space?

Which, in the next few years,
will seem the stronger half?
One day soon
you will look in the mirror
and not see
yourself,
but instead
some other person
whom you've never met.

When you die, you'll have
   been twelve people.

When are you most
   yourself?
On that last day
of the sixth year
when your face is the sum
of the last twenty-five
   hundred yous?

Or today
and every day
that you wake up
and meet a stranger?

RESPONDING

DISCUSSION QUESTIONS

COMPARING TEXTS
Choose two of these poems. What theme unites the two poems? Support your response with specific details.

ANALYZING VOICE
Describe the voice in one of these poems. Support your analysis with specific details.

EVALUATING
Choose one poem. Which image in it is most effective? Identify what creates the image (e.g., word choice or literary devices), and explain why the image is effective.

TASKS

WRITING FLASH FICTION
Select one idea from one of the poems as an inspiration for a piece of flash fiction. Demonstrate your appreciation of the poem through your adoption of the author's imagery, language, or ideas.

RESPONDING CREATIVELY
Create a visual accompaniment for an oral reading of one of these poems. Use graphics, images, music, and/or video to add to your interpretation of the meaning of the poem.

ABOUT THE AUTHORS

Canadian poet Deena Kara Shaffer says she is compelled to write by a love of language, a need to make sense of experience, and the fulfilling challenge of poetry's brevity and rhythms.

Naomi Shihab Nye's poetry gives readers a fresh perspective on ordinary objects and events. She says of her poetry, "The primary source ... has always been local life, random characters met on the streets, our own ancestry sifting down to us through small, essential daily tasks."

Charlotte Brontë (1816–1855) was a British poet and novelist. She is best known for her novel *Jane Eyre*. She wrote under the pen name Currer Bell.

Glynnis Ritchie started her own media production business in 2012, working on short films, photography, and web development. Ritchie explains that she writes to examine her own experiences, particularly those involving her relationships with others, growing up, and trying to make sense of even the smallest events in life.

CHARITY OR SCAM?

Report by Norah Muldoon

> **WHAT DO YOU THINK?**
> What makes an online scam successful?

WHO TO TRUST

There are so many ways for charities to approach you today that it is hard to know whom to trust. You may have been asked for contributions by text, tweet, or email. You've probably also seen sites on the Web that claim to donate money to charity when you play their games or even click a button. Are these charities legitimate, or are they trying to scam you? The short answer is that many of these charities are real. But there are also a lot of scams and misinformation going around.

The scams are usually easy to spot. Charities, even online ones, commonly have high-profile campaigns—how are you going to raise money if you don't get your message out, right? This means you should be able to find information about these charities in more than one place. If you can't find anything about a charity on the Web or through other research, you might not want to trust the campaign. In fact, if it asks for too much personal information, watch out—this is a common feature of scam or phishing websites and emails.

Misinformation is often believed because it comes through the most trusted medium—word of mouth. People unwittingly spread misinformation about charities and charity campaigns all the time. Often the bad information is based on truth, which makes it that much easier to believe.

The misinformation based on truth is harder to sort out. One trick scammers use is to send you an email or text using a name that is very close to the name of an organization you can trust. For example, they might use the name "Free Children," which could be mistaken for the legitimate charity "Free *The* Children." You've probably also seen campaigns to text a word to a certain number in order to donate to a legitimate cause. The donated amount will show up on your next phone bill. Scammers set up similar numbers, and then keep most, if not all, of the proceeds for themselves.

The scams seem to get even worse after natural disasters such as Hurricane Sandy, which hit the Eastern Seaboard in 2012. Social media users reported receiving Twitter or Facebook posts requesting money from victims they didn't know. They couldn't confirm who the people were, or even if they were in the United States during the hurricane. In such cases, it is much safer to make donations through well-known organizations, such as the Red Cross.

WIN-WIN

All this e-confusion shouldn't turn you off of online charities. They're one of the fastest-growing ways of making money for good causes. In one win-win situation, people use a website in some way and are exposed to the sponsor's advertising. The sponsors pay for the charitable donations instead of paying for other forms of advertising.

The website FreeRice is a good example of a win-win situation. On this site, you can play a word definition game or other educational games, and every time you click on the correct answer, 10 grains of rice are donated to hungry people worldwide. The site was created by computer programmer John Breen in 2007, and less than two years later, he donated the site to the United Nations World Food Programme. Since it started, FreeRice has donated about 98 billion grains of rice! The rice is paid for by advertisers whose banner ads appear on the screen every time you click an answer.

One advantage of online charities is that their messages can spread at an amazing speed. On its first day, FreeRice donated just over 800 grains of rice. Only a month later, they donated over 100 million grains in one day. The site went viral as a result of word of mouth and social networking. FreeRice has generated as much as a billion grains of rice every month.

So the next time you're asked to click a button, play a silly game, or watch a video to donate to a good cause, don't just assume that it's a scam. Yes, it's always a good idea to look into the charity to make sure you're not wasting your time—especially before you forward it to all your friends on Facebook! But these new online charities are changing the way we think about donating, and they need your support. ◆

ANALYZING SENTENCE STRUCTURE

Writers use parallel structure to make their sentences more fluent. Ideas or items in a series (e.g., "So the next time you're asked to click a button, play a silly game, or watch a video …") are presented in a similar, or parallel, way so that they are easier to understand and follow.

You have now donated 10 grains of rice.

Learn more ways to fight hunger.

RESPONDING

DISCUSSION QUESTIONS

MAKING INFERENCES
Consider some of the charity appeals you've seen online or on TV. Based on the information charities include and the way the requests are presented, what can you infer about the criteria that motivates people to donate money?

ANALYZING PERSPECTIVES
Identify Norah Muldoon's opinion about online charities. Describe the different perspectives people might have on this topic.

TASKS

PREPARING A PRESENTATION
Develop an oral presentation that highlights the work of a successful online charity. Identify the elements that contribute to making the charity successful.

DIGITAL LITERACY
Research what *phishing* means and how the term was developed. Create a digital presentation to define this term and explain how phishing is used to steal from people.

CREATING A BROCHURE
Imagine you work for the police as a fraud investigator. Create a brochure that explains some common Internet-based scams and how they can be avoided. Your purpose is to educate members of the general public so they can feel safe when using the Internet.

World of Warcraft versus My Girlfriend

WHAT DO YOU THINK?
Offline relationships are more important than online relationships.
+ AGREE
− DISAGREE

Short Story by Tyler Curry

ANALYZING POINT OF VIEW

As you read, keep in mind that Tyler Curry is presenting only how the narrator perceives the argument and events. Consider how the girlfriend may have perceived them.

Dear Ashley,

I've had a lot of time to think about our last conversation, particularly since you ended it by ramming a keyboard through my monitor. I understand that we were both upset at the time and perhaps we said some things we didn't mean. Well, maybe you more than me, considering I mostly just listened to you shriek and cowered in the corner.

I do not think I am, as you so eloquently screamed, "addicted to World of Warcraft." I have, however, made a number of unfortunate mistakes, for which I would like to apologize.

I'm sorry I was so late picking you up from the library. I didn't know they locked the doors at 8, and I'm sorry you had to stand outside alone for two hours. If it makes you feel better, despite its reputation to the contrary, that portion of the city does not have a violent crime rate significantly above the national average.

You have to consider the position I was in. I was heading a party with five players in it, all of whom were counting on me to help them defeat Mekgineer Thermaplugg and liberate the Gnomish city of Gnomeregan. Those are the needs of five people, in contrast to just yours, alone. (Note that I'm not even counting the needs of the Gnomish people here, Ashley.) As Spock once famously said, "The needs of the many outweigh the needs of the few. Or the one." You were that one.

Had I looked outside and noticed the freezing rain, I might have made a different decision. Probably not, though.

I also have some things to say that I think you should hear and, since you forgot to pause long enough for me to speak before your charming little bout of property damage and subsequent stormy departure, I would like to say them now.

Ashley, you have never been willing to accommodate my World of Warcraft needs or even to compromise the slightest bit.

Last month, when your mother was in a car accident, you called and not only demanded I drive you to the hospital but insisted I stay there to provide "emotional support"—despite knowing full well that I had booked that evening off to fight forest trolls in Zul'Aman. When I suggested you take a cab and that I join you in three to four hours, you unleashed a string of expletives that even my therapist found disturbing. You also refused to wait until we finished off the Eagle Boss, the one who drops the helm piece I have been trying to get for months.

For the record, she turned out fine anyway.

However, in the midst of your raging diatribe, sandwiched between the curses and the flailing limbs, you made some very good points. In fact, the words you spoke about commitment, loyalty, and "being there when someone needs you" have sort of inspired me.

Ashley, when I gave you that ring and pledged to spend my life with you, what I didn't mention was that, eight months prior, in the Level 10 quest "For the Horde," I had already pledged eternal fealty and service to Warchief Thrall.

Now, with the gates of Ahn'Qiraj opening and the threat of the Silithid invasion looming over Azeroth, the call has gone out for all able-bodied members of the horde to band together in the great war effort. An event like this only happens once in a server's life, and I cannot honourably abandon my online brethren in this hour of need. I understand that you need me to be there for you but, Ashley, the truth is, right now, the horde just needs me more. ◆

RESPONDING

DISCUSSION QUESTIONS

ANALYZING POINT OF VIEW
Consider how this short story would have changed if it had been written in the third person as a dialogue between the gamer and his girlfriend. Why did Tyler Curry choose to use the first person for this story?

CRITICAL LITERACY
For comic effect, Curry uses stereotypical characters. Do his intentions play a part in determining whether or not the stereotypes are offensive? Support your response.

TASKS

DEVELOPING A MONOLOGUE
Analyze how Curry uses sentence fluency to create the voice of his narrator. Use this selection as a model to write and perform a monologue where this narrator does one of the following:
- calls to make an insurance claim to replace his broken monitor
- speaks to a friend about why his girlfriend broke up with him
- creates a video for an online dating service describing his perfect match

WRITING A STORY
Imagine that the girlfriend and other friends of the narrator decide to work together and confront this gamer about his behaviour. Write a short story describing what happens when they intervene.

DIGITAL LITERACY
Research online addiction. Create a blog, infographic, or other representation that explains the origins of the term, perspectives on the seriousness of the issue, and your recommendations to other teenagers for appropriately using the Internet.

> **WHAT DO YOU THINK?** + AGREE − DISAGREE
> It's cheating to work with others on homework.

Facebook Controversy

Newspaper Reports by Louise Brown, from the *Toronto Star*

The following two news reports are about the same topic: one from before and one from after the trial of a student accused of cheating. If found guilty, he faced expulsion.

Student faces Facebook consequences
Student hit with 147 academic charges for online study network
March 6, 2008

ANALYZING LITERARY DEVICES

In the first paragraph of this article, Louise Brown plays with the different meanings of the word *virtual* to draw the reader into the article. *The ivory tower* is a metaphor for universities that suggests they are not part of the real world.

Study groups may be a virtual trademark of the ivory tower—but a virtual study group has been slammed as cheating at Toronto's Ryerson University.

First-year student Chris Avenir is fighting charges of academic misconduct for helping run an online chemistry study group via Facebook last term, where 146 classmates swapped tips on homework questions that counted for 10 percent of their mark.

The computer engineering student has been charged with one count of academic misconduct for helping run the group—called Dungeons/Mastering Chemistry Solutions after the popular Ryerson basement study room that engineering students call The Dungeon—and another 146 counts, one for each classmate who used the site.

Avenir, 18, faces an expulsion hearing before the engineering faculty appeals committee. If he loses that appeal, he can take his case to the university's senate.

The incident has sent shock waves through student ranks, said Kim Neale, 26, the student union's advocacy coordinator, who will represent Avenir at the hearing.

"All these students are scared now about using Facebook to talk about schoolwork, when actually it's no different than any study group working together on homework in a library," said Neale.

"That's the worst part; it's creating this culture of fear, where if I post a question about physics homework on my friend's wall [a Facebook bulletin board] and ask if anyone has any ideas how to approach this—and my prof sees this, am I cheating?" said Neale, who has used Facebook study groups herself.

Chris Avenir faces charges of academic misconduct.

Ryerson officials have declined to comment while the case continues. Ryerson's academic misconduct policy, which is being updated, defines it as "any deliberate activity to gain academic advantage, including actions that have a negative effect on the integrity of the learning environment."

Yet students argue Facebook groups are simply the new study hall for the wired generation. Avenir said he joined the Facebook group last fall to get help with some of the questions the professor would give students to do online. As the network grew, he took over as its administrator, which is why he believes he alone has been charged.

"So we each would be given chemistry questions and if we were having trouble, we'd post the question and say, 'Does anyone get how to do this one? I didn't get it right and I don't know what I'm doing wrong.' Exactly what we would say to each other if we were sitting in the Dungeon," said Avenir yesterday.

He's still attending classes pending his hearing, but admits the stress of the accusations is affecting his midterm exam results.

"But if this kind of help is cheating, then so is tutoring and all the mentoring programs the university runs and the discussions we do in tutorials," he said.

Neale said the Facebook account appeared to have been pulled offline yesterday, although Avenir said it has not been in use since the course ended in December.

He had earned a B in the class, but after the professor discovered the Facebook group over the holidays, the mark was changed to an F. The professor reported the incident to the school's student conduct officer and recommended expulsion.

Neale said that Avenir had missed two meetings to discuss the matter because of a miscommunication. Tuesday's hearing was arranged to give him a chance to make his case against expulsion. Ryerson is not obliged to make a case for expulsion.

CREATING FLUENCY

When used correctly, quotations can create fluency, provide credibility, and add to the voice of a text. Examine how Brown sets up, supports, and transitions between quotations.

While Neale admitted the professor specified the online homework questions were to be done independently, she said it has long been a tradition for students to brainstorm homework in groups, particularly in heavy programs such as law, engineering, and medicine.

Each student in the course received slightly different questions to prevent cheating, she said, and she did not see evidence of students doing complete solutions for each other. Instead, she said, they would brainstorm about techniques.

"They'd say to each other stuff like, 'Remember what to do when you have positive cations [a type of positively charged ion]' and that sort of thing," she said.

But Neale admitted the invitation to the Facebook group may have been what landed them in trouble. It read: "If you request to join, please use the forms to discuss/post solutions to the chemistry assignments. Please input your solutions if they are not already posted."

Still, said Neale, "No one did post a full final solution. It was more the back and forth that you get in any study group."

Many Canadian students complete their homework by studying together—often online.

Facebook user can stay at Ryerson

Engineering student ducks expulsion for running shared-homework site

March 19, 2008

Facebook advocate Chris Avenir says he'll be "a little more attentive to school policies" on matters like cheating from now on, even though the Ryerson student has no regrets about running an online homework group that nearly got him expelled.

In a landmark ruling on Internet use, a disciplinary panel at Ryerson has ruled the first-year engineering student should not be drummed out for helping run a Facebook study group in chemistry last fall, and ordered his passing mark in the course restored.

In a seven-page ruling, the engineering faculty appeals committee found no proof the Facebook site actually led to cheating by any of its 147 users, even though it invited them to "post solutions" to homework that was worth 10 percent of the final mark.

But the committee ruled that because the site provided "the potential for large-scale cheating," Avenir should get zero on that 10 percent portion—which won't change his passing grade—and that he attend a workshop on academic integrity.

"I'm really relieved—it's good news, and I guess I'll be more attentive to [misconduct] policies when my name is on the line—even though I don't really have any regrets about the Facebook group," said Avenir last night. "Maybe every student should have to go to this kind of workshop."

The committee also ruled Avenir should receive a disciplinary notation in his student record, which he can appeal. The course's professor had said the homework was to be done independently, so upon discovering the homework site after the course ended, he dropped Avenir's mark from B to F and recommended the 18-year-old's expulsion be considered—both steps the three-person panel overruled.

"We're very excited Avenir won't be expelled, and this is very good news for students who want to use Facebook to study," said Nora Loreto, head of the Ryerson Students' Union.

Technology Dean James Norrie said the ruling showed "due process works" and hoped the case "will spark a broader debate on these deep issues."

"Are we Luddites here at Ryerson?" he asks. "No, but our academic misconduct code says if work is to be done individually and students collaborate, that's cheating, whether it's by Facebook, fax, or mimeograph." ◆

Avenir smiles victoriously after his day in court.

RESPONDING

DISCUSSION QUESTIONS

EVALUATING
Review both articles and evaluate Louise Brown's opinion, as well as any bias the articles have. How balanced is her account of these events? Identify evidence in her word choice, organization, or ideas.

DIGITAL LITERACY
Online services for students range from sites that provide tutoring and information to sites that sell pre-written essays. What is your school's academic integrity policy? At what point does seeking help with your schoolwork become cheating? Explain.

TASKS

DELIVERING A CLOSING ARGUMENT
Imagine you are making the case either for or against Chris Avenir in the disciplinary hearing. Prepare a closing argument that could be delivered to the disciplinary panel (your fellow classmates). Your argument needs to convince the panel of either Avenir's innocence or his guilt.

WRITING AN ESSAY
Write an expository essay that explains how Facebook or another social network could be used by students and teachers in educationally appropriate ways. Alternatively, create a persuasive essay to argue that cheating is a serious issue in schools. Identify resources cheaters use and resources schools use to catch cheaters. Assess your sentence fluency and your use of quotations.

WHAT DO YOU THINK NOW?

Think back to your original response to this statement:

"It is impossible to be completely objective."

How has your thinking about this statement changed since you began this unit?

Creating a Reader's Blog

Reflect on your experience reading the texts in this unit. Create a reading journal blog that relates your emotional and intellectual responses to two or more of the texts from the unit. Through your blog, communicate the context for your reading and the role that your life experiences have had on your responses to the texts. Remember to

- create a clear context for each of your blog entries;
- organize your ideas to support your responses to the texts;
- choose quotations to support your ideas; and
- develop an appropriate voice using effective word choice and sentence fluency.

Developing a Presentation

Create an oral presentation that explains the thematic connections between two or more of the texts in this unit. Through your presentation, demonstrate your understanding of the unit theme. Remember to

- organize your ideas effectively;
- choose quotations to support your ideas;
- use supporting visuals; and
- use a formal voice, sentence fluency, and effective word choice to persuade your audience.

Selecting or Creating a New Text

Imagine that you have been asked by the publisher of this book to find or create another selection that might fit in this unit. Research to find a story, poem, essay, visual, or other type of text. Alternatively, create a selection that would fit in any form you choose. Submit your selection to others, with a short written summary explaining why it belongs in this unit. Include a note about which other texts in the unit your selection connects with most strongly. Review the feedback you receive. Use it to make any improvements to the piece, including more research if necessary.

Index

Art, Music, and Movies
Artists Respond to Conflict, 48
Design That Fits to a Tee, 93
The Pocket Camera Moment, 100
The Mobile Photo Explosion, 102
Giving Garments a Second Chance, 130
My Mom Is an English Teacher, 176
How *Willy Wonka & the Chocolate Factory* Should Have Ended, 186
No Word for …, 206
Whose Art Is It, Anyway?, 233
New Tool Provides Food for Thought, 236
Don't Trust Hollywood to Teach You History, 238

Authors
Abbott, Ryan, 55
Adams, René, 233
Aker, Don, 23
Bascaramurty, Dakshana, 12
Berrell, Celia, 78
Boston Public Health Commission, 236
Brontë, Charlotte, 248
Brown, Louise, 254
Clark, Liat, 199
CNN, 126
Cooper, Tim, 160, 162
Costanzo, Robert, 222
Crowfeather, Daniel, 243
Curry, Tyler, 252
Davies, Alex, 121
D'Cunha, Patricia, 130
Dillabough, Danny, 186
Doctorow, Cory, 202
Dolny, Tamie, 64
Eggers, Dave, 36
Evon, Dan, 208
Feschuk, Scott, 128, 188
Finn Garner, James, 137
Gilbert, Cheryl, 96
Globe and Mail, 12
Green, John, 144
Greenman, Ben, 164
Gregoire, Lisa, 84
Harris, Joanne, 210
Haque, Sabina Zeba, 50
Heysen, Nora, 52
Hoppe, Neil, 151
House, Laura, 93
Hughes, Langston, 79
Jalees, Sabrina, 142
Jetelina, Margaret, 88
Johnson, Pauline, 63
Jutzi, Alison, 176
Keats, Jonathon, 100
Kelly, Cathal, 116
Kelly, Maura, 80
King, Thomas, 190
Lawrence, Katherine, 35
McComb, Tisha, 228
Mabunda, Gonçalo, 48
McGonigal, Jane, 110
McNulty, Johnny, 169
Muldoon, Nora, 250
Nowak, Peter, 220
Nye, Naomi Shahib, 38, 247
O'Connor, Joe, 225
Ott, Haley Joelle, 174
Over, 102
Owen, Wilfred, 62
Palladino, And, 238
Pearce, Jacqueline, 5
Pfeffer, Susan Beth, 30
Pink, Daniel H., 217
Porter, Jody, 66
Potter, Andrew, 58
Rabinowitz, Aharon, 151
Ritchie, Glynnis, 249
Shaffer, Deena Kara, 246
Tan, Amy, 16
The Onion, 178, 183
Thompson, Clive, 114
Visual Capitalist, 107
Wagamese, Richard, 18
Weber, Karin, 140
Westhead, Rick, 45
Wilson, Shelia North, 206
Worley, Seth, 151
Yu, Charles, 73

Blog Entries
Gay Kids Need It to "Get Better" Now, Rick Mercer Rants, 12
Saving the World through Game Design, 110
Really?!?, 142
No Word for …, 206

Discussion Questions
Analyzing Audience Responses, 177
Analyzing Bias/Point of View/Perspectives
   Analyzing Point of View and Bias, 52
   Analyzing Perspective(s), 61, 185, 240, 251
   Analyzing Point of View, 148, 214, 253
Analyzing Character(s), 41, 148, 193
Analyzing Conflict, 29, 35, 57
Analyzing Context, 65
Analyzing Fluency, 207
Analyzing Form, 180, 189
Analyzing Genre, 159
Analyzing Humour, 148, 163, 193
Analyzing Ideas, 61
Analyzing Language Conventions, 37
Analyzing Literary Devices, 11, 29, 37, 57, 67, 113, 141, 221, 227
Analyzing Organization, 87, 99, 125, 129, 131, 221
Analyzing Production Perspectives, 235, 240
Analyzing Purpose and Audience, 57, 65, 245
Analyzing Sentence Fluency, 201, 209, 227, 229, 245
Analyzing Short Stories, 37
Analyzing Techniques, 125
Analyzing Theme, 180
Analyzing Thesis, 103
Analyzing Voice, 35, 63, 77, 113, 165, 173, 177, 205, 240, 249
Analyzing Writing, 95
Analyzing Word Choice, 103, 141, 187
Comparing Texts, 15, 20, 35, 63, 79, 143, 177, 214, 221, 249
Constructing/Extending Meaning
Constructing Meaning, 139, 141, 185
Extending Meaning, 143, 185
Critical Literacy, 17, 47, 52, 61, 87, 90, 99, 109, 115, 118, 127, 139, 159, 163, 173, 180, 193, 205, 253
Critical Thinking, 20, 83, 87
Digital Literacy, 15, 224, 257
Drawing Conclusions, 83, 201, 205, 207
Evaluating, 11, 17, 67, 95, 99, 115, 118, 163, 201, 207, 209, 214, 224, 229, 237, 249, 257
Making Connections, 127
Making Inferences, 11, 20, 65, 67, 90, 109, 113, 118, 127, 159, 173, 187, 227, 235, 251
Media Literacy, 47, 109, 237, 240
Metacognition, 15, 17, 29, 52, 63, 77, 90, 115, 187, 189, 229
Responding Critically, 103, 125, 129
Responding Personally, 41, 77, 79, 224
Synthesizing, 131, 139, 165, 189, 237
Visual Literacy, 79

Essays
Worldwide We, 96
The Pocket Camera Moment, 100
Airbus: Plane of the Future, 121
The Kitchen at the End of the Universe, 128
Turning the Page, 222
Who Are the Elders?, 243

Fiction
The Trickster, 5
Scars, 23
Ashes, 30
Accident, 36
Tomorrow, Summer, 38
My Emergency Contact Information, 55
Earth (A Gift Shop), 73
Little Red Riding Hood, 137
Invasion of the Snotty Badgers, 140
The Fault in Our Stars, 144
Form 17, 151
Yeti, 160
The World Ends on Wednesday, 162
I Am the Invisible Thing That Holds Together the Two Halves of a Compound Word, 164
Campaign Emails from the Donahue Family Pet Debate, 169
A Teenage Philosopher Defends Missing Her Curfew, 174
My Mom Is an English Teacher, 176
iPhone Left in Hot Car, 178
Sunken Oil Tanker Will Be Habitat for Marine Life, 183
How *Willy Wonka & the Chocolate Factory* Should Have Ended, 186
Not Enough Horses, 190
Winston, 202
Heartbeat, 208
Would You Like to Reconnect?, 210
World of Warcraft versus My Girlfriend, 252

Focus Pages
Making Connections to Infer, 3
Analyzing Narrative Writing and the Short Story, 21
Identifying Point of View and Bias, 43
Developing Ideas and Voice, 53
Responding Personally, Critically, and Creatively, 71
Analyzing Expository Writing and the Essay, 91
Analyzing Codes, Conventions, and Techniques, 105
Organizing Ideas, 119
Constructing and Extending Meaning, 135
Analyzing Narrative and Expository Writing in Scripts, 150
Analyzing Audience Responses, 167
Improving Word Choice, 181
Evaluating to Form Opinions, 197
Analyzing Persuasive Writing and the Opinion Piece, 215
Evaluating Production Perspectives, 231
Creating Fluency, 241

Letters
My Emergency Contact Information, 55
Remembering Joyce Atcheson, 66
Really?!?, 142
I See You Think I'm Not Very Interesting, 188
World of Warcraft versus My Girlfriend, 252

Media and Visual Texts
Gay Kids Need It to "Get Better" Now, Rick Mercer Rants, 12
No, Rick Mercer, Not All Gay Public Figures Need to Step Forward, 14
You Will Not Stop Me from Learning, 45
Artists Respond to Conflict, 48
Why People Can't Help Themselves, 58
Teen on Strike, 64
Preserving Knowledge, Empowering Communities, 84
Design That Fits to a Tee, 93
The Pocket Camera Moment, 100
The Mobile Photo Explosion, 102
Canadian Oil Boom, 107
Saving the World through Game Design, 110
In Defense of Pinterest, 114
Jeremy Gutsche: Mister Chaos, 116
Airbus: Plane of the Future, 121
The Kitchen at the End of the Universe, 128
Giving Garments a Second Chance, 130
Really?!?, 142
Form 17, 151
Yeti, 160
The World Ends on Wednesday, 162
I Am the Invisible Thing That Holds Together the Two Halves of a Compound Word, 164
Campaign Emails from the Donahue Family Pet Debate, 169
A Teenage Philosopher Defends Missing Her Curfew, 174
My Mom Is an English Teacher, 176
Anonymous Targets School for Suspending Student Who Refused a Tracking Chip, 199
No Word for …, 206
New Tool Provides Food for Thought, 236

Nonfiction
Gay Kids Need It to "Get Better" Now, Rick Mercer Rants, 12
No, Rick Mercer, Not All Gay Public Figures Need to Step Forward, 14
Fish Cheeks, 16
What We Share, 18
You Will Not Stop Me from Learning, 45
Why People Can't Help Themselves, 58
Teen on Strike, 64
Remembering Joyce Atcheson, 66
Samantha Nutt: A Letter from 12 War Zones, 80
Preserving Knowledge, Empowering Communities, 84
Top of the World, 88
Design That Fits to a Tee, 93
Worldwide We, 96
The Pocket Camera Moment, 100
The Mobile Photo Explosion, 102
Canadian Oil Boom, 107
Saving the World through Game Design, 110
In Defense of Pinterest, 114
Jeremy Gutsche: Mister Chaos, 116
Top 25 Innovations, 126
Giving Garments a Second Chance, 130
Anonymous Targets School for Suspending Student Who Refused a Tracking Chip, 199
No Word for …, 206
My Challenge to You: Only Speak Like a Human, 217
Electronic Discrimination in the Skies, 220
Turning the Page, 222
Who Killed the Wooden Hockey Stick?, 225
Whose Art Is It, Anyway?, 233
New Tool Provides Food for Thought, 236
Don't Trust Hollywood to Teach You History, 238
Who Are the Elders?, 243
Charity or Scam?, 250
Facebook Controversy, 254

Opinion Pieces
Why People Can't Help Themselves, 58
My Challenge to You: Only Speak Like a Human, 217
Electronic Discrimination in the Skies, 220
Who Killed the Wooden Hockey Stick?, 225
Maybe Zombies Can Save Us from Our Comforts, 228
Don't Trust Hollywood to Teach You History, 238
Charity or Scam?, 250

Poetry
Beyond Pastel, 35
Dulce et Decorum Est, 62
And He Said, Fight On, 63
Mother of Invention, 78
Dreamer, 79
On Unmaking Contact, 246
Sifter, 247
Life, 248
Regeneration, 249

Scripts
Form 17, 151
Yeti, 160
The World Ends on Wednesday, 162
I Am the Invisible Thing That Holds Together the Two Halves of a Compound Word, 164
How Willy Wonka & the Chocolate Factory Should Have Ended, 186

Short Stories
The Trickster, 5
Scars, 23
Ashes, 30
Accident, 36
Tomorrow, Summer, 38
Earth (A Gift Shop), 73
Invasion of the Snotty Badgers, 140
Not Enough Horses, 190
Heartbeat, 208
Would You Like to Reconnect?, 210
World of Warcraft versus My Girlfriend, 252

Tasks
Representing/ Creating Media Texts
Creating a Brochure, 251
Creating a Digital Presentation, 99
Creating a Found Poem, 245
Creating an Ad, 131
Creating an Annotated Map, 87
Creating a Media Text, 127, 205
Creating a News Report, 11
Creating a Playlist, 237
Creating a Visual Essay, 115
Creating a Visual Representation, 180
Creating a Visual Text, 235
Designing a T-Shirt, 95
Developing a Blog Entry, 143
Developing an Ad Campaign, 125
Developing Tweets, 63
Digital Literacy, 37, 47, 83, 118, 141, 148, 187, 209, 251, 253
Evaluating Podcasts, 201
Making Comparisons, 95
Research and Inquiry, 20, 65, 131, 240
Responding Creatively, 29, 41, 79, 90, 103, 207, 214, 224, 249

Speaking and Listening/ Oral Communication
Brainstorming Ideas, 125
Communicating Ideas, 20
Conducting a Survey, 65, 131
Creating a Digital Presentation, 99
Creating a Monologue, 159
Creating and Delivering a Rant, 15
Creating a Radio Ad, 209
Debating, 90, 109, 180, 229
Delivering a Closing Argument. 257
Delivering a Monologue, 52, 83
Developing a Monologue, 253
Developing a Scene, 189
Developing a Speech, 139
Developing Dialogue, 17, 35, 37, 113, 221, 227
Developing Oral Readings, 141
Digital Literacy, 115, 187, 205, 251
Performing a Scene, 143, 163, 165, 185, 187
Performing a Script, 173
Performing the Story, 77
Preparing an Oral Presentation, 61
Preparing a Presentation, 11, 207, 251
Presenting a Script, 118
Presenting a Speech, 129
Presenting the Poem, 63
Research and Inquiry, 20, 63, 87, 129, 163, 177, 214, 240
Responding Creatively, 224, 249
Role-Playing, 99, 148
Role-Playing an Interview, 47
Sharing Stories, 67

Writing
Categorizing Information, 127
Creating a News Report, 11
Designing a T-Shirt, 95
Developing a Blog Entry, 143
Developing a Comparison, 61
Digital Literacy, 57, 187
Research and Inquiry, 79, 109, 224
Responding Creatively, 224
Responding Personally, 67
Rewriting a Song, 237
Writing a Blog Entry, 103, 240
Writing a Conclusion, 41
Writing a Fractured Fairy Tale, 139
Writing a Letter, 47
Writing an Art Review, 52
Writing an Epistolary Story, 173
Writing an Essay, 257
Writing a News Parody, 185
Writing an Open Letter, 189
Writing a Note, 41
Writing a Persuasive Essay, 227
Writing a Review, 177
Writing a Script, 165
Writing a Speech, 201
Writing a Story, 57, 143, 193, 221, 229, 245, 253
Writing a Summary, 235
Writing Expository Paragraphs, 83
Writing Flash Fiction, 209, 249
Writing in Character, 35
Writing in Role, 159
Writing Text Messages, 129
Writing to Persuade, 163
Writing to Respond, 15, 17, 29, 77, 113

Credits

Text

5: "The Trickster" by Jacqueline Pearce from *Opening Tricks* (Thistledown Press, 1998). Reprinted with permission. 12: © The *Globe and Mail* Inc. All Rights Reserved. All rights reserved. Licensed by Nelson Education Ltd for 10,000 estimated copies in circulation on May 9, 2013. 13: Excerpted from *A Nation Worth Ranting About* by Rick Mercer. Copyright © 2012 Rick Mercer. Reprinted by permission of Doubleday Canada. 14: © The *Globe and Mail* Inc. All Rights Reserved. Licensed by Nelson Education Ltd for 10,000 estimated copies in circulation on May 9, 2013. 16: © 1987 by Amy Tan. First appeared in *Seventeen Magazine*. Reprinted by permission of the author and the Sandra Dijkstra Literary Agency. 18: "What We Share" by Richard Wagamese, found in the book *One Story, One Song*, published in 2011 by Douglas and McIntyre: a division of Harbour Publishing Ltd. Reprinted with permission from the publisher. 23: Reprinted by permission of the author. 30: Reprinted by permission of the author. 35: Reprinted by permission of the author. 36: Reprinted by permission of the author. 38: Text copyright © 2011 Naomi Shihab Nye. 45: "'You will not stop me from learning': Teen activist awes us with her courage" by Rick Westhead, *Toronto Star*, October 9, 2012. Reprinted with permission - Torstar Syndication Services. 55: By Ryan Abbott. Originally appeared on McSweeney's Internet Tendency. 58: Reprinted by permission of the author. 64: Reprinted by permission of the author. 66: Courtesy *Wawatay News*. 70: (Hadfield/Shatner tweets) © Canadian Space Agency. 73: Reprinted by permission of the author. 78: Celia Berrell's Science Rhymes. 79: "Dreamer" from THE COLLECTED POEMS OF LANGSTON HUGHES by Langston Hughes, edited by Arnold Rampersad with David Roessel, Associate Editor, copyright © 1994 by the Estate of Langston Hughes. Used by permission of Alfred A. Knopf, a division of Random House, Inc. Any third party use of this material, outside of this publication, is prohibited. Interested parties must apply directly Random House, Inc. for permission. 80: Courtesy War Child Canada. 81: Originally appeared on More.com. Reprinted with permission. 84: By Lisa Gregoire. Courtesy The Canada Foundation for Innovation. 88: Reprinted with permission from Canadian Immigrant magazine. 93: "Design that fits to a Tee" by Laura House. Originally published by AIGA (May 16, 2008), www.aiga.org/content.cfm/design-that-fits-to-a-tee. 100: Wired.com © 2012. "The Pocket Camera Moment" by Jonathan Keats. Condé Nast Publications. All rights reserved. 110: Reprinted by permission of Jane McGonigal. 114: Wired.com. © 2012 "In Defense of Pinterest" by Clive Thompson. Condé Nast Publications. All rights reserved. 116: Cathal Kelly, "Jeremy Gutsche: Mr. Chaos," *Toronto Star*, September 13, 2009. Reprinted with permission - Torstar Syndication Services. From an article originally appearing in the *Toronto Star*, September 2009. 121: "Take a Virtual Tour of Airbus' crazily futuristic concept plane" by Alex Davies, From *Business Insider*, November 21, 2012. Reprinted with permission. 126: From CNN.com, 2005 © 2005 Cable News Network, Inc. All rights reserved. Used by permission and protected by the Copyright Laws of the United States. The printing, copying, and redistribution, or retransmission of this Content without express permission is prohibited. 128: Reprinted by permission of the author. 130: Courtesy of *Metro Canada*. 137: James Finn Garner is the author of the *Politically Correct Bedtime Stories* trilogy and Honk Honk, My Darling: A rex Koko, private Clown Mystery, among others. 140: Reprinted by permission of Karin Macphail Weber. 142: Reprinted by permission of Sabrina Jalees: YTV's *In Real Life*, Much's *Video on Trial*, NBC's *Last Comic Standing*. 144: From THE FAULT IN OUR STARS by John Green, copyright © 2012 by John Green. Used by permission of Dutton Children's Books, a division of Penguin Group (USA) Inc. 151–159: "Tempo" script written by Seth Worley, Aharon Rabinowitz, Neil Hoppe. 160, 162: Reprinted by permission of the author. 164: Reprinted by permission of SLL/Sterling Lord Literistic, Inc. Copyright by Ben Greenman. 169: Reprinted by permission of the author. 174: Reprinted by permission of the author. 176: Reprinted by permission of the author. 178: Reprinted with the permission of *The Onion*. Copyright © 2009, by ONION, INC. www.theonion.com. 180: Source: Protect Your Bubble. 183: Reprinted with permission of *The Onion*. Copyright © 2013, by ONION, INC. www.theonion.com. 186: Reprinted by permission of the author. 188: Reprinted by permission of the author. 191: "Not Enough Horses" by Thomas King *From A Short History of Indians in Canada* by Thomas King. Published by HarperCollins Publishers Ltd. Copyright © 2005 Dead Dog Café Productions Inc. With Permission of the author. All rights reserved. 199: Liat Clark/Wired © The Condé Nast Publications Ltd. 202: Copyright 2008 CorDoc-Co, Ltd. Some rights reserved under a Creative Commons BY-NC-SA-3.0 License. Audio rights: From LITTLE BROTHER by Cory Doctorow. Used by permission of Random House Audio Publishing Group, a division of Random House, Inc. Any third party use of this material, outside of this publication, is prohibited. Interested parties must apply directly to Random House, Inc. for permission. 206: © CBC. Reprinted with permission. 208: Reprinted by permission of the author. 210: "Would you Like to Reconnect?" taken from *A Cat, A Hat and a Piece of String* by Joanne Harris. Published by Doubleday. Reprinted by permission of The Random House Group Limited. 217: © Telegraph Media Group Limited 2013. 220: Peter Nowak. Reprinted with permission. 222: Reprinted by permission of the author. 225: From "Who Killed the Wooden Hockey Stick" by Joe O'Connor, in the *National Post*, November 18, 2012. Material reprinted with the express permission of: *National Post*, a division of Postmedia Network Inc. 228: First printed in *Geez* magazine, Spring 2012. Reprinted by permission of the author. 236: (text and table) Start Strong Program of the Boston Public Health Commission. 238: Reprinted by permission of the author. 243: Reprinted by permission of the author. 246: Reprinted by permission of the author. 247: Text copyright © 2005 Naomi Shihab Nye. 249: "Regeneration" by Glynnis Ritchie. Reprinted with permission 252: Reprinted by permission of Tyler Curry.

254: Louise Brown, "Student faces Facebook consequences," *Toronto Star*, March 6, 2008. Reprinted with permission - Torstar Syndication Services. From an article originally appearing in the *Toronto Star*, March 2008. Reprinted with permission - Torstar Syndication Services. 260: Louise Brown, "Facebook user can stay at Ryerson," *Toronto Star*, March 19 2008. Reprinted with permission - Torstar Syndication Services. From an article originally appearing in the *Toronto Star*, March 2008. Reprinted with permission - Torstar Syndication Services.

Photos

2: THE CANADIAN PRESS/Adrian Wyld. 5: (coyote) Geoffrey Kuchera/Shutterstock; (jacket) Jeffrey Moore/Shutterstock. 8: (boy) Sascha Burkard/Shutterstock. 9: (bus) photos.com. 10–11: cynoclub/Shutterstock. 13: Photo: Asylum Artists. 14: CBC/Rick Mercer Report. 16: KristinaShu/Shutterstock. 17: © Eddie Gerald/Alamy. 18: Debra Powell. 24: © Ian Jeffrey/iStockphoto.com. 25: Neil Webster/Shutterstock. 26: Courtney Hellam. 27: Knud Nielsen/Shutterstock. 28: Courtney Hellam. 30: 123RF. 32: Jason Todd/Getty Images. 34: Karin Smeds/Getty Images. 36: Stuart McCall/Getty Images. 39: © ZUMA Press, Inc./Alamy. 40–41: (empty school hallway) Neil Shapiro/Shutterstock; (busy school hallway) Matty Symons/Shutterstock. 42: (dove) © FORRAY Didier/SAGAPHOTO.COM/Alamy. 45: (Malala Yousafzai) © epa european pressphoto agency b.v./Alamy; (inside of a bus) Suzanne Tucker/Shutterstock. 46: (two protestors holding signs) © Jenny Matthews/In Pictures/Corbis; (protestor holding sign) © Bimal Nepal/Demotix/Corbis. 46–47: (vigil) © T. MUGHAL/epa/Corbis. 48: AFP/Getty Images. 52: Australian War Memorial, image ID 085073. Reproduced with permission. 55: Lukas Radavicius/Shutterstock. 56: maigi/Shutterstock. 59: © National Post/Tyler Anderson. 60: arindambanerjee/Shutterstock. 62: (trench) Inc./Shutterstock; (soldiers carrying coffin) © Stefano Rellandini/Reuters/Corbis; (sandbags) stephen mulcahey/Shutterstock. 63: (cannons) Panoramic Images/Getty Images; (drummer) Ron Watts/Getty Images; (stone fortress) Ruslan Kudrin/Shutterstock. 64: Richard Lautens/GetStock.com. 70: Michal Modzelewski/Shutterstock. 73: (crystal ball) Andresr/Shutterstock; (motel sign) © Dave Park/iStockphoto; (woman holding child) Aletia/Shutterstock; (boy) AJP/Shutterstock; (skateboarder) Monkey Business Images/Shutterstock; (father and daughter) bikeriderlondon/Shutterstock; (Earth graphic) Vadim Georgiev/Shutterstock. 74: (two girls) Vlue/Shutterstock; (Statue of Liberty) UbjsP / Shutterstock; (couple shopping) Odua Images/Shutterstock; (footbridge) lafoto/Shutterstock; (shopping bags) Borislav Bajkic/Shutterstock; (sign) Natalia Bratslavsky/Shutterstock; (pillar) Kamira /Shutterstock; (caveman) ladyphoto/Shutterstock; (ruins) Edyta Pawlowska/Shutterstock; (dinosaur) DM7/Shutterstock; (Chinatown arch) DM7/Shutterstock. 75: (boardwalk) pio3/Shutterstock; (family) oliveromg/Shutterstock; (wood) ermess/Shutterstock; (barrier) Wong Hock weng/Shutterstock; (ferris wheel) Stephane Bidouze/Shutterstock; (fence) Wuttichok Painichiwarapun/Shutterstock; (wooden surface) swoon/Shutterstock; (roller coaster) GOLFX/Shutterstock; (pointing finger) Tribalium/Shutterstock; (overflowing shopping bags) Vectomart/Shutterstock; (kids running) iofoto/Shutterstock; (fries sign) Arvind Balaraman/Shutterstock; (Coney Island) Andrew F. Kazmierski/Shutterstock. 77: (prosthesis) Jamie Roach/Shutterstock; (hand) lendy16/Shutterstock; (button) ladyfortune/Shutterstock; (vintage car) efiplus/Shutterstock; (rocket) gkuna/Shutterstock; (gas station) cdrin/Shutterstock; (solar panel) ALMAGAMI/Shutterstock; (icons) justone/Shutterstock; (speech bubbles) Lena Pantiukh/Shutterstock; (T-shirts) Stanisv/Shutterstock; (shopping cart icon) Zudy and Kysa/Shutterstock; (red rocket) James Steidl/Shutterstock; (truck) Frontpage/Shutterstock; (woman) Dan Kosmayer/Shutterstock; (UFO) qcontrol/Shutterstock; (rocket launching) Nikonaft/Shutterstock; (bus) John Panella/Shutterstock; (space craft) Algol/Shutterstock; (rocket on launcher) Igor Plotnikov/Shutterstock. 78: Francois Loubser/Shutterstock. 80: REUTERS/Chris Wattie. 81: Alyson Rowe © War Child Canada. 82: (photo) ASSOCIATED PRESS; (War Child Canada logo) © War Child Canada. 84–85: © Ryerson Clark/iStockphoto. 86: Inuit Siku (sea ice) Atlas, Geomatics and Cartographic Research Centre, Carleton University. 88: CP PHOTO/*Toronto Star*-Rick Madonik. 88: Getty Images. 90: © Uncornered Market http://www.uncorneredmarket.com/photos/picture/5515887735/. 93: Ben Baker/Redux. 95: Copyrighted 2013. Chicago. 98288:413JM. 96: Photo courtesy of Guy Labissonière. 97: Photo courtesy of Free The Children. 98: (concert) Colin Mcconnell/GetStock.com; (Spencer West) © Splash News/Corbis. 99: Photo of Jordyn Harrison reproduced with permission. 100: © (Brownie camera) Al Parrish/iStockphoto; (old photo) © Ekely/iStockphoto. 101: MCT via Getty Images. 102: (infographic) Courtesy of madewithover.com, Designed by NowSourcing.com; (KODAK logo) Courtesy KODAK; (Facebook logo) © Facebook; (Instagram logo) © Instagram. 104: (bottom) © Copyright Touch Bionics Inc. and Touch EMAS Ltd. All rights reserved; (top) © Paul Foreman/mindmapinspiration.com. 107–109: "Canadian Oil Boom" by VisualCapitalist.com CC BY-ND 3.0. 110: (Jane McGonigal) © Matthew Stylianou/Corbis Outline; (climbing man graphic) alphaspirit/Shutterstock; (woman jumping graphic) YanLev/Shutterstock; (hikers graphic) Warren Goldswain/Shutterstock; (football player graphic) Pete Saloutos/Shutterstock. 111: (person in gas mask) Stokkete/Shutterstock; (tech graphic) Yes - Royalty Free/Shutterstock; (empty playground) Marijus Auruskevicius/Shutterstock; (empty park) Marijus Auruskevicius/Shutterstock; (businessman jumping graphic) Luis Louro/Shutterstock; 112: (handshake) charles whitefield/Shutterstock; (heart icon) iconspro/Shutterstock; (mountain) Angelo Ferraris/Shutterstock; (organs) Anastasiia Kucherenko/Shutterstock; (contour map) Robert Adrian Hillman/Shutterstock. 113: (man on mountain) ollyy/Shutterstock. 114: (all photos) ollyy/Shutterstock. 116, 117: Courtesy Jeremy Gutsche. 121–125: Courtesy Airbus. 126: kropic1/Shutterstock.com. 127: Olga Miltsova/Shutterstock.com. 130: (modelling

Orphanage Clothing) Photo: Brent McCombs; (modelling Preloved clothing) Courtesy Preloved Clothing. 131: Courtesy Preloved Clothing. 134: (newspaper pieces) © macida/iStockphoto, © Trevor Hunt/iStockphoto ; (Jolly Green Giant comic) Joe Dator/www.cartoonbank.com. 137: (girl) karla08/Shutterstock; (cabin) Samuel Acosta/Shutterstock; (forest) kwest/Shutterstock; (leaves) javarman/Shutterstock; (solar panel) Liz Van Steenburgh/Shutterstock; (basket) Olena Pivnenko/Shutterstock; (fruit) Serg64/Shutterstock; (water bottle) sevenke/Shutterstock. 138: (girl) karla08/Shutterstock. 139: (wooden panels) Zibedik /Shutterstock; (organic label) LHF Graphics/Shutterstock; (blank poster) Lagui/Shutterstock; (recycle sign) Stephan Bonk/Shutterstock; (fruits and vegetables) Le Do/Shutterstock; (table) Simon Krzic/Shutterstock; (laptop) Chris Baynham/Shutterstock; (wolf) Cynthia Kidwell/Shutterstock; (fur) Arsgera/Shutterstock; (woman with axe) © Андрей Снегирев/iStockphoto; (business woman) © Jacob Wackerhausen/iStockphoto. 140: (cityscape vector) Emir Simsek/Shutterstock; (tree) cla78/Shutterstock. 142: (switchboard operator) Everett Collection/Shutterstock; (ripped paper) STILLFX/Shutterstock; (Sabrina Jalees) Courtesy Sabrina Jalees. 152–159: Images courtesy Red Giant. 161: © Aspix/Alamy. 162 (sign) Thinkstock; (people crossing street) Mlenny Photography/Getty Images; (arm) (businessman jumping graphic) Luis Louro/Shutterstock. 166: (clown) Natalie Dee; (Rejected Canadian Flags) Excerpt from Picnicface's Canada © 2011 by Picnicface Productions Ltd. Published by HarperCollins Publishers Ltd. All rights reserved. (newspaper pieces) © Robyn Mackenzie/iStockphoto. 169: (sky) Bplanet/Shutterstock; (dog) Sarah Fields Photography/Shutterstock; (suit) Nejron Photo/Shutterstock; (circle element) Garsya/Shutterstock; (dog vector) NLshop/Shutterstock. 170: (cats) ingret/Shutterstock; (dog) Jeroen van den Broek/Shutterstock. 171: (room) DOPhoto/Shutterstock; (dog) Toloubaev Stanislav/Shutterstock; (top hat model) Kiselev Andrey Valerevich/Shutterstock; (top hat) flowerstock/Shutterstock. 172: (puppy) Luis Carlos Torres/Shutterstock. 173: (running dog) JPagetRFPhotos/Shutterstock;(confetti) Alhovik/Shutterstock; (dog paw)Susan Schmitz/Shutterstock. 174: Nicku/Shutterstock. 175: (Descartes) Gunnar Pippel/Shutterstock; (statue of Socrates) Nick Pavlakis/Shutterstock. 176: rubberball/Getty Images. 178: © Tom Carter/PhotoEdit. 179: (car in parking lot) © JoeFox/Alamy; (iPhone) Getty Images. 183–184: © Emre YILDIZ/iStockphoto. 183: © Radius Images/Alamy. 184: © Darryl Peroni/iStockphoto. 186: (chocolate swirl) Thinkstock; (Johnny Depp as Willy Wonka) WARNER BROS./THE KOBAL COLLECTION. 188: Dragon Images/Shutterstock. 190: Christina Handley/Masterfile. 193: © seraficus/iStockphoto. 196: (buildings bursting from Earth) © Mikhail Tolstoy/Alamy; (comic) NON SEQUITUR © 2011 Wiley Ink, Inc. Dist. By UNIVERSAL UCLICK. Reprinted with permission. All rights reserved. 199: Michelangelus/Shutterstock. 200: Pedro Rufo/Shutterstock. 201: © ZUMA Press, Inc./Alamy. 202: © George Paul/iStockphoto. 203: kwest/Shutterstock. 204 (sketch of surveillance camera) © Александр Мельник/iStockphoto; (blue background) © Daniel Halvorson/iStockphoto. 206: We Were Children © 2012 National Film Board of Canada. All rights reserved. 208: Thinkstock. 211: Thinkstock. 212, 214: Thinkstock. 218: Nuno Andre/Shutterstock. 220–221 © Marek Mnich /iStockphoto. 220: Emmanuel Aguirre /Getty Images. 221: IM_photo/Shutterstock. 222: Sashkin/Shutterstock. 223: © CJG - Technology/Alamy. 225: National Post/Peter J. Thompson. 226 (Paul Henderson) Melchior DiGiacomo/Contributor/Getty Images; (Canada Women's Olympic hockey team) Bob Thomas/Popperfoto/Contributor/Getty Images. 228–229: Prezoom.nl/iStockphoto. 230: © Photocase Addicts GmbH/Alamy. 233: George Koroneos/Shutterstock. 234: © Washington Imaging/Alamy. 235: (office) MICKE Sebastien/Contributor/Getty Images; (OBEY) © ArtAngel/Alamy. 236: ollyy/Shutterstock. 238: (Tony Mendez) © Scott McDermott/Corbis Outline; (Ben Affleck as Tony Mendez) WARNER BROS. PICTURES/THE KOBAL COLLECTION. 239: Photo by Chris Pizzello/Invision/AP. 243: Katrina Brown/Shutterstock. 244 (abstract painting background) Happy person/Shutterstock; (path) andreiuc88/Shutterstock; (sun through clouds) Ritu Manoj Jethani/Shutterstock; (power lines) Jason Poston/Shutterstock; (sun rise) andreiuc88/Shutterstock; (coyote) Rob McKay/Shutterstock. 246: © MHJ/iStockphoto. 247: (open door) © MHJ/iStockphoto. 248: © Giorgio Fochesato/iStockphoto. 249: © MHJ/iStockphoto. 250: © Chris Lamphear/iStockphoto. 251: © World Food Programme http://freerice.com/. 255: Andrew Wallace/GetStock.com. 256: Monkey Business Images/Shutterstock. 257: The Canadian Press/Colin Perkel.

Art

2: (painting of Harriet Tubman) © National Geographic Society/Corbis. 42: "your days are numbered" by Nidal El-Khairy. Courtesy the artist. 49: Artworks by Gonçalo Mabunda courtesy of Jack Bell Gallery. 50–51: Photo and Artworks Copyright 2013 Sabina Haque, www.sabinahaque.com. 52: Australian War Memorial, image ID ART24393. Reproduced with permission. 70: Infographic courtesy of GE. 79: Reproduced by permission of Natasha Capstick. 118: Ian Berry/www.denimu.com 196: Marcia Dietz, "I Draw!" 12x14 Acrylic on panel, 2011. www.Dietzign.com; (Venn diagram) Illustration by Chank Diesel; Perspective Box of a Dutch Interior, 1663 (oil paint, glass mirror & walnut), Hoogstraten, Samuel van (1627–78)/Detroit Institute of Arts, USA/The Bridgeman Art Library. 252: Illustarted by Bob Kayganich.

3 2950 71378 702 4